BARRON'S

HOW TO PREPARE FOR THE

TAKS*

TEXAS ASSESSMENT OF KNOWLEDGE AND SKILLS

ENGLISH LANGUAGE ARTS

Peggy Kennedy, M. Ed.
Everman JCB High School
Everman, Texas

Linda Powley, M. Ed.
Everman JCB High School
Everman, Texas

BARRON'S

*TAKS is a registered trademark of the Texas Education Association. This publication has been neither reviewed nor endorsed by the Texas Education Association.

Permission
Happenings. Text copyright © 2002 Linda Powley. Used with permission from HarperCollins Publishers.

© Copyright 2004 by Barron's Educational Series, Inc.

All rights reserved.
No part of this book may be reproduced in any form, by photostat, microfilm, xerography, or any other means, or incorporated into any information retrieval system, electronic or mechanical, without the written permission of the copyright owner.

All inquiries should be addressed to:
Barron's Educational Series, Inc.
250 Wireless Boulevard
Hauppauge, New York 11788
http://www.barronseduc.com

International Standard Book No. 0-7641-2614-8

Library of Congress Catalog Card No. 2003060507

PRINTED IN THE UNITED STATES OF AMERICA
9 8 7 6 5 4 3 2 1

Contents

Preface / v

Part One: Understanding the Test

    Chapter 1: Examining the Structure of the Test / 3
    Chapter 2: Surveying the ELA TAKS Objectives / 8

Part Two: Exploring Strategies for Success

    Chapter 3: Answering Objective Questions / 15
    Chapter 4: Responding to Open-Ended Questions / 25
    Chapter 5: Writing the Composition / 42

Part Three: Mastering Objectives 1, 2, and 3

    Chapter 6: Identifying Literary Elements / 63
    Chapter 7: Utilizing Reading Strategies / 74
    Chapter 8: Detecting Historical Impact on Literary Texts / 90
    Chapter 9: Determining an Author's Purpose / 96
    Chapter 10: Comprehending Visual Representatives / 106

Part Four: Mastering Objectives 4, 5, and 6

    Chapter 11: Distinguishing Voice and Style / 113
    Chapter 12: Investigating Organizational Patterns in Writing / 119
    Chapter 13: Studying the Development of Ideas / 124
    Chapter 14: Reviewing Mechanics and Usage / 128
    Chapter 15: Analyzing Proofreading Skills / 140

Part Five: Practice Tests for the ELA TAKS

    Chapter 16: Practice Test A / 149
    Chapter 17: Practice Test B / 178
    Chapter 18: Final Review / 206

Glossary / 209
Index / 215

Preface

Since the early '80s, the statutes of the state of Texas have required assessment testing. Initially this consisted of measuring minimum skills, but changes in state law ten years later shifted the emphasis to the measurement of academic skills, specifically reading, writing, and math. In the mid-'90s, additional data was compiled through the administration of English, math, science, and social studies end-of-course exams. Finally, in 1999, the 76th Session of the Texas Legislature mandated and expanded a more comprehensive testing program, and the Texas Assessment of Knowledge and Skills, or TAKS test, was born.

It has always been the goal of the state, through these assessments, to measure student progress. The development of the test was extensive. Materials were carefully aligned to what students were being taught daily in the classroom. Field testing fell under tough scrutiny. Teachers, parents, professional organizations, and collegiate staff were among the many groups asked for input. It was a slow, meticulous process, but once objectives were finalized and student expectations defined, the TAKS test became a part of academic life for students in the public schools of Texas.

At the eleventh grade level, much rides on a student's success. When the 76th Texas Legislature mandated that the TAKS be administered beginning in the 2002–2003 school year, it also made passing the exit level test a prerequisite for a high school diploma. In layman's terms, if a student is unsuccessful with the TAKS exam, graduation is denied.

Because the test is based on what is being taught daily in the classroom, most students who have worked hard and made academic progress as they have advanced through the years of school are educationally ready. But testing environments are stressful, especially when so much is at stake. The more that is known about the test, the better prepared the test taker will be to excel.

And that is where this book can help, because it will connect the pieces of the English Language Arts, or ELA, TAKS puzzle. Within the book's covers, the reader will find in-depth discussions of this assessment. *How to Prepare for the TAKS: ELA TEXAS ASSESSMENT OF KNOWLEDGE AND SKILLS* is designed to build on, not replace, what students have learned in the classroom so that they can approach test day with confidence.

Think of the exam as you would a job assessment, because in many ways, it is just that: a performance review of academic work since kindergarten. To do a job well, the worker has to understand the instrument of measurement. To perform well on a test, the student has to understand how it will be administered. What kind of questions will be on the test? What is the best way to prepare? What is the best approach to writing the composition? Each test taker needs to know these answers and to understand the correct way to deliver information in order to receive the maximum score.

The purpose of this book is to do just that, to raise the level of understanding about the exit level ELA TAKS by breaking the test into smaller, doable pieces. Through detailed explanations of the objectives, practice exercises similar to those found on the exam, and specific test-taking tips, the reader will gain the confidence needed to prevail.

It will take time. Learning to understand something that has taken almost a decade to design isn't easy. But when the pieces all connect, when the picture of the ELA TAKS is complete, the image seen will be success.

 Students: The more you know about the ELA TAKS, the better your chances for success.

 Parents: Build your child's test taking confidence.

 Teachers: Activities directly relate to the Texas Essential Knowledge and Skills, or TEKS, requirements.

Part One
Understanding the Test

Chapter 1

Examining the Structure of the Test

"You're going to be taking a test today."
Don't you just hate those words?
"And if you don't pass this test, you will not graduate."
Talk about pressure!

But dealing with pressure is all about growing up. In the future you will have to deal with a boss who says, "Do this, or else." No, you say? You are going to run your own business so will you have your freedom? Oh, but you will still have to please customers, the ones who say, "Do this, or else." And, do you think your Drill Sergeant will back off, just because something asked makes you feel uncomfortable?

Welcome to the real world, the one with requirements and demands and expectations. Welcome to the world of ELA TAKS.

The good news is, as far as assessments go, ELA TAKS is a very doable test. Although it is designed to evaluate what you have learned over the last eleven or so years of school, it allows you the freedom to express yourself. Still, the more prepared you are, the more you understand the nature of the test, the more relaxed you will feel on testing day. So, let's take a closer look at this thing called the English Language Arts Texas Assessment of Knowledge and Skills, or ELA TAKS, and see how it's put together.

The Structure of the Test

First, the purpose of this test is twofold. On the one hand it is designed to make sure schools, administrators, and teachers are doing a good job preparing students academically. On the other hand, it is specially intended to measure an individual student's ability to read and write effectively, skills that enhance success in the real world. Thus, on testing day, several opportunities are presented to do both.

Essentially the test is divided into two sections: Part I, titled "Reading and Written Composition," and Part II, designated "Revising and Editing." Part I measures your reading ability, as well as how well you write a two-page composition. Part II checks your ability to see and correct errors within given texts.

Part I of the Test

The Triplet

The first section of Part I will be based on a thematically linked set of three pieces, called a triplet, consisting of a literary selection (fiction), an expository selection (informational and non-fiction), and a one-page viewing and representing piece (such as a chart, advertisement, or illustration). Combined, the literary and expository pieces will be somewhere between 3,000–3,500 words. Also, the paragraphs are numbered. This helps you make quick reference to the text when answering the questions, which can be either multiple-choice (where one answer will be correct) or open-ended (where you will have to write your own answer).

 The reading section is based on two reading passages and a visual.

The visual for the viewing and representing piece will be a one-page presentation with minimal text tied to the theme of the reading passages. It will be something you are used to seeing—an advertisement, a cartoon, a web site, a photograph, or maybe even a chart. What you will need to do is to think about the message, and then respond to three multiple-choice-type questions.

There are specific strategies you can learn and apply to each area, and these will be discussed later in the book. For now, though, we are looking only at the structure of the test itself.

The Written Composition

The second section of Part I offers a written prompt and asks you to produce a polished draft essay. The question will be loosely tied to the theme suggested by the triplet, so you will already have formed some reaction to the general topic. But unlike the open-ended questions where you *must* reference the literary pieces, the composition is based on your own ideas and reflections. The triplet serves merely as a springboard to inspire you and does not have to be directly referenced in your essay.

In the writing section, you will have to produce a polished draft.

Thematic Connection

Because there is a strong connection between parts of the triplet, such as a common question, problem, idea, or theme, test makers like to think of the test as focused and unified. For instance, you might read a story about a person who has just immigrated into this country and then a journal written by a soldier serving our country overseas, and then you might see an advertisement for a new restaurant with home-style cooking.

The Questions

A series of multiple-choice questions following the triplet includes inquiries about each passage individually as well as two crossover questions requiring you to think about both selections to find the correct answer. These are followed by three open-ended questions, at least one of which is a crossover item. To get credit for answering these open-ended queries, you must build into your response a specific reference to the triplet. There is room in the test booklet to plan, so you can work out your answer, revise it as needed, then neatly copy it onto the answer document.

Responses to open-ended questions must be clearly and specifically linked to the triplet.

A composition prompt continuing the theme of the triplet follows the open-ended questions. The readings help provide stimulation for your writing, but your own reflections and thoughtful insights form the core of your words.

Again, there is plenty of space in the test booklet to plan the essay, and plan you must. Because you have access to a dictionary and thesaurus, you are expected to have a clean product with no errors in spelling, usage, capitalization, word choice, and so on. This composition will be graded as a finished draft. What you write onto the answer document should have previously been carefully drafted, edited, and revised in your test booklet before being transferred.

Part II of the Test

Part II of the ELA TAKS, the revising and editing section, is also in multiple-choice format. Before beginning this section, you must turn in your dictionary and thesaurus. You will then read two passages resembling a student-produced essay and select strategies for improvement. Questions might center on grammar, spelling, sentence structure, paragraphing, or even organization. The sentences are numbered, and the questions refer to a specific portion of text, so you can easily review the passage as need be. Keep in mind that you don't have to come up with the solutions; you just have to recognize the correct one.

Granted, it is quite an intense day to have to read passages, write a composition, and edit two selections. You definitely have to work. However, with access to a dictionary and thesaurus for the reading and writing portions of the test, a common theme, numbered paragraphs and sentences, and time and space to prewrite your answers, ELA TAKS is a doable test.

Scoring

So, with all of this in mind, how is the ELA TAKS test scored? What, in this exit level test, determines if you meet the requirements for graduation?

First of all, different sections of the test have different grading standards. For the objective questions on the reading pieces and on the revising and editing questions, only one answer is correct.

On the other hand, the open-ended questions are judged on a scale from 0–3, with the lowest being 0 for which no credit is given. A score of 2 is said to be *sufficient,* whereas a score of 3 is considered *exemplary. All answers must reference the triplet to receive credit.*

The composition will also be graded holistically on a four-point scale. A 1 is *ineffective,* a 2 *somewhat effective,* a 3 *generally effective*, and a 4 *highly effective*. Essays are judged on focus and coherence, organization, development of ideas, voice, and conventions, all things evident in a polished draft.

It may sound intimidating, but knowledge is a powerful tool. As you progress through this book, each aspect of the test will be covered, and your confidence will build. So be patient, and read on. However, while you are learning how to succeed on the test, you can also do basic things to strengthen your language arts skills.

Academic Strategies

 First, practice sustained reading, working with several passages at one sitting so the length of the triplet won't throw you off. Read short stories like the ones in your literature book as well as editorials, articles, essays, and news magazines. Then think of questions like those you might see on the test.

 Next, be on the lookout for passages with similar themes, and make up questions that cover both pieces.

 Then, think of some general issues that might apply to two pieces you are reading or have read in your English classes. Again, imagine an essay prompt that might be based on the same theme.

 Remember the value of editing. Always practice reading your own writing—or that of your friends—with the goal of finding ways to improve it through word choice, organization, sentence construction, usage, grammar, or a combination of these.

Strategies for Test Day

Other tactics can help ensure a positive testing experience, too.

Get plenty of rest, not just the night before, but develop a good practice of productive hours and restful hours so you are alert and energized. The ELS TAKS test is a long test; you will need to build stamina to last through it.

Then, on the day of the test, eat a good breakfast, but nothing too heavy or too different from what you are used to. You don't want your body to be confused.

In general, you aren't allowed to have food or drinks in the testing site, so keep chewing gum or hard candies handy to help you stay awake and alert. If you have a cold, cough, or sore throat, bring tissues or throat lozenges to make yourself more comfortable. You will need to clear this with your test administrator, though, to be sure it's okay.

Also, you will be doing lots of writing, so be sure to have two pencils with clean erasers. If you decide you need to change an answer, you must completely erase your previous choice so the machine won't mistake your choice.

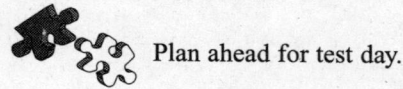 Plan ahead for test day.

Once you arrive at the test site, look around. Find the dictionary and thesaurus assigned to you for the first part of the test. Make sure you have room for your legs and arms. Then, during the test, pace yourself. It is important to take your time and do a good job, but if you linger too long on one section, you may become tired and end up performing poorly. So keep on task, but in a calm, steady manner.

Use small motor skills to relieve tension. Roll your head around to relax neck muscles, rotate your ankles to make sure your legs and feet stay awake, and tense and release your shoulders to stay alert. Find a place in the room where you can look to relax your eyes—the ceiling, a spot on your desk, the board. Be sure this area is away from where other students will be working on their tests so it won't appear that you are cheating. Just keep in mind that occasionally changing the distance of your eyes' focus can ease fatigue.

If you start to feel drowsy, take a restroom pass. Splash water on your face, walk around a bit, and perhaps get a drink. Remember that this test is not timed. You will want to stay on task and not let your thoughts wander, but you can take your time.

So now that you know the structure of the test, the grading standards, and some general strategies, you are headed toward success. When you walk into the room on testing day, you won't be surprised. You will know what to do and how to do it.

And when you walk out, for you, the ELA TAKS will be yesterday's news.

Review Box
→ The ELA TAKS test is approximately thirty pages long.
→ The test will include objective questions, open-ended questions, and a composition.
→ You may write in the test document.
→ ELA TAKS is an untimed test.
→ Part I consists of Reading and Written Composition questions.
→ You will have access to a dictionary for Part I of the test
→ Part II covers Revising and Editing.
→ With work and preparation, passing the ELA TAKS test is an achievable task.

Chapter 2

Surveying the ELA TAKS Objectives

Now that you know the structure of the test, let's go to the specifics: the objectives. The ELA TAKS test has only six, and they are broken into two groups: Reading Objectives and Writing Objectives. Together these cover the scope of all you should have learned in English class up through the eleventh grade.

Objective 1—Reading

The first objective covers reading. It states that you must be able to show a basic understanding of what you read using various culturally diverse texts. As you will recall, the ELA TAKS test will include a triplet that is based on a fictional work, a nonfictional piece, and a visual of some kind. The way you respond to questions after your reading will be used to determine a reading score. You will find queries on vocabulary and comprehension, as well as the identification of main idea and appropriate summaries.

Vocabulary

With vocabulary, for instance, you will have to show your ability to use various strategies to determine the meaning of unfamiliar words. You might need to rely on context clues; prefixes, roots and suffixes; reference materials; or relationships to other words such as analogies, homonyms, synonyms, and antonyms. The question might cite a word in the text and ask you to choose its best synonym, or it might give a dictionary definition and ask you how it applies to a word in the reading.

For example, an excerpt from Thoreau's "The Maine Woods" might be used as the expository piece. In the fourth paragraph, the essay reads, "[The tracks] were particularly numerous where there was a small bay, or pokelogan, as it is called, bordered by a strip of meadow, or separated from the river by a low peninsula covered with coarse grass, wool-grass, etc., wherein they [the moose] had waded back and forth and eaten the pads." A question covering this objective might ask:

> **Example 1** In paragraph 4 of "The Maine Woods," the word *pokelogan* means—
>   **A** meadow
>   **B** peninsula
>   **C** bay
>   **D** moose

The correct answer would be **C**, *bay*, because it is the definition associated with the synonym context clue ("a small bay, or pokelogan, as it is called").

Or, Edgar Allan Poe's "The Tell-Tale Heart" might be used for the fictional passage. His opening line is, "True!—nervous—very, very dreadfully nervous I had been and am; but why *will* you say that I am mad? The disease had sharpened my senses—not destroyed—not dulled them." A question like the following might appear:

> **Example 2** Read the following dictionary entry.
> **mad** \mad*adjective* **1.** suffering from mental confusion; insane **2.** feeling or showing an intense enthusiasm **3.** angry, bitter **4.** lacking control; unrestrained
> Which definition would be best for the word *mad* in the paragraph above?
>   **A** Definition 1
>   **B** Definition 2
>   **C** Definition 3
>   **D** Definition 4

The correct choice, of course, would be **A**, because the narrator talks about being nervous (confused) and having a disease (insanity), not about being uncontrolled or angry. All vocabulary questions require you to apply the knowledge you've gained through reading to the ways words are used in texts, but you still may consult the dictionary if need be.

 Take advantage of the reference materials available for your use on the test.

Main Idea and Details

A second area tested under Objective 1 involves identifying the main ideas, supporting ideas, and summaries. Although in the multiple-choice section you will be picking only the correct response, having your own answer in mind before you look at the possible choices is an excellent test-taking strategy. It will keep you from being fooled by the use of distracters—answers that sound right, but aren't.

 Always think of your own answer before looking at the choices.

For main-idea questions, be sure you read and understand exactly what the question means. Which main idea is being requested? Is it one for a section, a paragraph, or the whole selection? Also, remember that all supporting details must be in the passage. If you can't find an answer choice, then don't pick that response.

Finding details is a skill practiced in class on a regular basis. When you are given an assignment to read with questions to answer, you are typically being asked for details. Many chapters and stories in your textbooks are followed by such questions. Pay attention to these, even if your teacher does not make doing so a requirement. It will not only help you in the classroom but also serve as great practice for the ELA TAKS.

Objective 1 is also tested in the open-ended section, where you have to supply your own answers. For example, a question regarding Thoreau's "The Maine Woods" might be as follows:

> **How was Thoreau affected by his experience in nature?**
> **Support your answer with evidence from the text.**

Rather than choosing from possible answer choices, you would have to write your own response, using two or three complete sentences. To get full credit, you would have to include in your answer a summary, a synopsis, or a direct quote supporting your ideas with information found in the triplet. Again, in school you practice this all the time, particularly in English class, but in class your justification is often oral, through discussion. On the test you will have to make sure that the support for your answer is written into your response, but there are more ideas for how to do this in chapter 3.

Remember that main ideas and supporting details are found in all kinds of literature—letters, speeches, maps, newspapers, and so on. So practice creating summaries in your mind and finding supporting details in everything you read. (More on reading skills can be found in chapter 7.)

 Practice finding the main idea, summarizing, and looking for supporting details in everything you read.

Objective 2—Reading

The second reading objective of the ELA TAKS test is based on understanding the effects of literary elements and techniques on writing. These questions actually go a step beyond merely asking you to identify various aspects of the text. Rather, they ask you to analyze how the use of a particular literary skill increases your understanding or appreciation. What this means is you must be able to apply all those literary terms you discuss in your English classes. If you forget a definition, you will be able to use your dictionary to refresh your memory, but you will have to be able to relate the term to the text. What is the flashback? What is foreshadowed? How is the character developed? What does the metaphor accomplish? How is the historical setting important? How is the passage ironic? What does the tone suggest? What is the author using a simile to describe? How is the conflict resolved? These are questions that require you to prove that you understand what the author is saying.

Pay attention in English class when literary terms are being presented.

Objective 3—Reading

The third objective in the reading section involves critical evaluation. This might at first sound intimidating, but chapters 6, 7, 8, and 11 will offer ideas to help you prepare. For instance, you might be asked to determine the effects of a certain word on the reader (the denotative and connotative meanings). Or, you might be asked how a certain text is organized. (Does the writer portray a cause and effect relationship? Are the events chronological? Is a comparison being made?) You will also need to be able to make inferences, conclusions, generalizations, and predictions—things you do every day. Deciding what to read, which movies to watch, which car to buy, where to work, which college to attend, or which classes you want to take with which teacher, all involve critical thinking. Be aware of when you process information, and then think about what influenced your final answer.

Objective 3 is also tested through questions about the viewing and representing piece. You must determine if the visual is informative, entertaining, or persuasive, but strategies for this can be found in chapter 10.

Analyze everything you read.
Think. Think. Think.

Objectives 4 and 5—Writing

Objectives 4 and 5 require you to produce an effective composition, something written as an academic polished draft. Your writing should show organization and support for your ideas as well as correct sentence structure and development. These are the types of essays you would present to your English teacher for a test grade or submit with a college application. The graders will also use this composition to measure your correct use of spelling, capitalization, punctuation, grammar, usage, and sentence structure, so this essay should reflect your best writing. You will still have access to a dictionary on this phase of the test, so your piece should have few, if any, errors. (See chapters 5 and 14.)

Each time you write a composition, try to learn something new about how to write.

Objective 6—Writing

The sixth objective requires you to show your ability to proofread and revise a piece of writing for the purpose of clarifying understanding. Although all questions are multiple-choice, when you get to this section of the test, you will no longer be permitted to use reference materials. You might be asked something about organization, content, style, sentence structure, word choice, spelling, capitalization, punctuation, grammar, and usage. So listen closely in English class, and practice revision. It does help. (Chapter 15 centers on proofreading strategies.)

Just going to school and staying engaged in the instruction provides the best foundation for succeeding on the ELA TAKS test. And whether a question is based on Objective 2 or Objective 5 isn't particularly relevant—if you get it right. But awareness goes a long way toward building a comfort zone that will make testing day more relaxed.

If you feel overwhelmed, don't worry. You will find plenty of support and help in the following chapters. Although the ELA TAKS probably isn't the worst test you will ever take in your life, for now it is the most significant. It definitely is a test, though, that can be conquered. If you learn everything you can about the test beforehand and carefully take your preparatory steps, your efforts will pay off.

And the victory will be yours.

Review Box
→ Objective 1 gauges your understanding of vocabulary, main idea, summary, and details.
→ Objective 2 examines your understanding of literary elements and their influence on text.
→ Objective 3 measures analytical and critical-thinking skills.
→ Objective 4 requires you to write a polished compositional draft.
→ Objective 5 judges your ability to produce error-free writing.
→ Objective 6 determines how well you can revise and proofread to correct and clarify written text.

Part Two
Exploring Strategies for Success

Chapter 3

Answering Objective Questions

For most students, the objective part of the ELA TAKS test feels the most comfortable. Why? Because answering multiple-choice questions has been a part of academic life since kindergarten. At first teachers may have offered a simple two-choice possibility, and the response may have been oral. Perhaps a crayon was presented and then the question, "What color do you see? Blue or Red?" To answer you had to make a choice.

And that is exactly what you will have to do on the ELA TAKS—evaluate possible responses to a question or complete a partial sentence by picking the correct conclusion. So let's review some strategies to help you do your best.

Preparatory Work

On any untimed test with multiple-choice questions, preparatory work is always worthwhile. Before you actually start reading, take a few minutes to look at the questions. These will consist of a stem, or the actual question itself, and several possible answer choices. Don't look at the possible answers, though, because you will want to draw your own conclusions. Instead, do a quick analysis of the stem, before reading the triplet or looking at the editing and revising selection, and your work will be more effective.

 Read and highlight questions before reading text.

First, ask yourself where you will find the answer. Will it be directly stated in the text? If a specific line or paragraph is noted, find it. Then put a number in the margin that corresponds to the question. Jot a brief note of reminder, such as *summary* or *find link to metaphor* or *author's intent*. These markings do not have to be neat. Use whatever shorthand you find comfortable, and do it quickly. The purpose of this strategy is not to labor over the questions, but to establish a purpose for reading.

If the answer is one that must be derived from connecting several parts of the passage, or one that is not specifically drawn from hints given throughout the passage, record this at the top of the page. Then as you read, highlight and make notes that will help you form the right conclusion.

For example, if a question asked, "How did the main character grow by the incident that occurred during the course of the story?" To answer this type of question, you would have to compare the main character's traits at the beginning of the story with those at the end. You would have to think about and analyze the information as you read, reminding yourself to be on the lookout for change. So at the top of the second or third page of the text, you might write "change in main character" to keep yourself focused.

Let's say the following questions appeared on an ELA TAKS exam.

1 What is the meaning of the word *posterity* as used in paragraph 2?
2 What is paragraph 1 mainly about?
3 According to the author, what is the source of American patriotism?

Remember that initially you do not read the answer choices, because you want to come to your own conclusions without influence. You are looking for the core of what is being asked. The first question is asking for a definition, the second for a main idea, and the third for an interpretation of theme.

Now, say these questions were relating to the passage below. This is how your highlighting might look.

excerpt from *Letters from an American Farmer*
St. Jean de Crèvecoeur, 1782

Source of Patriotism

1   What then is the American, this new man? He is either an European, or the descendant of an European, hence that strange mixture of blood, which you will find in no other country. I could point out to you a family whose grandfather was an Englishman, whose wife was Dutch, whose son married a French woman, and whose present four sons have now four wives of different nations. *He* is an American, who leaving behind him all his ancient prejudices and manners, receives new ones from the new mode of life he has embraced, the new government he obeys, and the new rank he holds. He becomes an American by being received in the broad lap of our great *Alma Mater*.

2   Here individuals of all nations are melted into a new race of men, whose labours and posterity will one day cause great change in the world. Americans are the western pilgrims, who are carrying along with them that great mass of arts, sciences, vigour, and industry which began long since in the east; they will finish the great circle. The Americans were once scattered all over Europe; here they are incorporated into one of the finest systems of population which has ever appeared, and which will hereafter become distinct by the power of the different climates they inhabit. The American ought therefore to love this country much better than that wherein either he or his forefathers were born. Here the rewards of his industry follow with equal steps the progress of his labour; his labour is founded on the basis of nature, *self-interest*; can it want a stronger allurement? Wives and children, who before in vain demanded of him a morsel of bread, now, fat and frolicsome, gladly help their father to clear those fields whence exuberant crops are to arise to feed and to clothe them all; without any part being claimed, either by a despotic prince, a rich abbot, or a mighty lord. Here religion demands but little of him; a small voluntary salary to the minister, and gratitude to God; can he refuse these? The American is a new man, who acts upon new principles; he must therefore entertain new ideas, and form new opinions. From involuntary idleness, servile dependence, penury, and useless labour, he has passed to toils of a very different nature, rewarded by ample subsistence.—This is an American.

Main Idea

definition

After you've read the questions and initially highlighted specific reminders, you would then carefully read the passage. When doing so you would highlight or make notes about anything significant to the reminders. For example, you might have highlighted "Here the rewards of his industry follow with equal steps the progress of his labour" because this clause seems to address the issue of patriotism.

Again, you want to put your mental energy into actually reading the passage, not analyzing the questions. But if you get some idea beforehand of what you will be looking for, your brain will recognize the information more readily, thus making the actual reading process more successful.

Your intent is to encourage yourself to pay particular attention when you come to a part noted by marginal markings. Your preparatory work needs to be done efficiently, but quickly, so you can move on at a reasonable pace to reading the triplet or the revising and editing selection.

Reading the Passage

As you read, be sure to concentrate on the words. Form a mental image of what the author is saying. Then, when you have finished one part of the triplet, find the questions that address that section. Answer them carefully, before you return to the reading.

Answer each set of questions immediately after reading the passage to which they refer.

Answering the Questions

Overall there will be approximately 30 objective questions addressing the triplet, with at least one being a crossover item that will require you to address two or more parts of the triplet and draw a reasonable conclusion.

And there is that word again: *reasonable*.

You must be able to support whatever answer you choose with direct evidence from the text. Although this may initially sound intimidating, the questions will typically contain a reference to a specific paragraph or section of the triplet. So the process of discovering the correct answer becomes one of rereading and rethinking an exact portion of text, not a hit-and-miss hope of finding the right response.

Always be sure you can support your answer with evidence from the text.

For example, a question may say, "In paragraph 11, the author uses a simile to—" You would first go back to the text, find paragraph 11, look for the simile and find the comparison. Then, after asking yourself what impact the simile made on the text, you would look at the possible answers and pick the one that most closely resembles your own conclusion.

Or, perhaps the following appeared on a test: "How does the author develop the idea that spending time in nature brings inner serenity and peace?" Although this is a direct question, the answer would be drawn from several sections of the text. Essentially, you are being asked to make a mental connection between two or more parts of the passage.

First, skim the text quickly, check your highlighting and marginal notes, and draw a reasonable conclusion based on the reading. Then check the possible responses, and find the best match for your answer.

Practice, Practice, Practice

Okay, time to practice. Read the story below, just as you would if it appeared on an ELA TAKS test. First, read the questions and make marginal notes to help you identify information you will need to know. Then thoughtfully read the story, highlighting sections of information you feel will help you answer the questions. Finally, read each question, determine your own answer, and pick the choice that best matches what you've concluded.

Punch, Brothers, Punch
by Mark Twain

1 Will the reader please to cast his eye over the following verses, and see if he can discover anything harmful in them?

"Conductor, when you receive a fare,
Punch in the presence of the passenjare!
A blue trip slip for an eight-cent fare,
A buff trip slip for a six-cent fare,
A pink trip slip for a three-cent fare,
Punch in the presence of the passenjare!
   CHORUS.
Punch, brothers! punch with care!
Punch in the presence of the passenjare!"

2 I came across these jingling rhymes in a newspaper, a little while ago, and read them a couple of times. They took instant and entire possession of me. All through breakfast they went waltzing through my brain; and when, at last, I rolled up my napkin, I could not tell whether I had eaten anything or not. I had carefully laid out my day's work the day before,—a thrilling tragedy in the novel which I am writing. I went to my den to begin my deed of blood. I took up my pen, but all I could get it to say was, "Punch in the presence of the passenjare." I fought hard for an hour, but it was useless. My head kept humming, "A blue trip slip for an eight-cent fare, a buff trip slip for a six-cent fare," and so on and so on, without peace or respite. The day's work was ruined—I could see that plainly enough. I gave up and drifted down town, and presently discovered that my feet were keeping time to that relentless jingle. When I could stand it no longer I altered my step. But it did no good; those rhymes accommodated themselves to the new step and went on harassing me just as before. I returned home, and suffered all the afternoon; suffered all through an unconscious and unrefreshing dinner; suffered, and cried, and jingled all through the evening; went to bed and rolled, tossed, and jingled right along, the same as ever; got up at midnight frantic, and tried to read; but there was nothing visible upon the whirling page except "Punch! punch in the presence of the passenjare." By sunrise I was out of my mind, and everybody marveled and was distressed at the idiotic burden of my ravings,—"Punch! oh, punch! punch in the presence of the passenjare!"

3 Two days later, on Saturday morning, I arose, a tottering wreck, and went forth to fulfill an engagement with a valued friend, the Rev. Mr. -------- , to walk to the Talcott Tower, ten miles distant. He stared at me, but asked no questions. We started. Mr. -------- talked, talked, talked — as is his wont. I said nothing; I heard nothing. At the end of a mile, Mr. -------- said,—

4 "Mark, are you sick? I never saw a man look so haggard and worn and absent-minded. Say something; do!"

5 Drearily, without enthusiasm, I said: "Punch, brothers, punch with care! Punch in the presence of the passenjare!"

6 My friend eyed me blankly, looked perplexed, then said,—

7 "I do not think I get your drift, Mark. There does not seem to be any relevancy in what you have said, certainly nothing sad; and yet—maybe it was the way you said the words—I never heard anything that sounded so pathetic. What is—"

8 But I heard no more. I was already far away with my pitiless, heart-breaking "blue trip slip for an eight-cent fare, buff trip slip for a six-cent fare, pink trip slip for a three-cent fare; punch in the presence of the passenjare." I do not know what

occurred during the other nine miles. However, all of a sudden Mr. -------- laid his hand on my shoulder and shouted,—

9 "Oh, wake up! wake up! wake up! Don't sleep all day! Here we are at the Tower, man! I have talked myself deaf and dumb and blind, and never got a response. Just look at this magnificent autumn landscape! Look at it! look at it! Feast your eyes on it! You have traveled; you have seen boasted landscapes elsewhere. Come, now, deliver an honest opinion. What do you say to this?"

10 I sighed wearily, and murmured,—

11 "A buff trip slip for a six-cent fare, a pink trip slip for a three-cent fare, punch in the presence of the passenjare."

12 Rev. Mr. -------- stood there, very grave, full of concern, apparently, and looked long at me; then he said,—

13 "Mark, there is something about this that I cannot understand. Those are about the same words you said before; there does not seem to be anything in them, and yet they nearly break my heart when you say them. Punch in the—how is it they go?"

14 I began at the beginning and repeated all the lines. My friend's face lighted with interest. He said,—

15 "Why, what a captivating jingle it is! It is almost music. It flows along so nicely. I have nearly caught the rhymes myself. Say them over just once more, and then I'll have them, sure."

16 I said them over. Then Mr. -------- said them. He made one little mistake, which I corrected. The next time and the next he got them right. Now a great burden seemed to tumble from my shoulders. That torturing jingle departed out of my brain, and a grateful sense of rest and peace descended upon me. I was lighthearted enough to sing; and I did sing for half an hour, straight along, as we went jogging homeward. Then my freed tongue found blessed speech again, and the pent talk of many a weary hour began to gush and flow. It flowed on and on, joyously, jubilantly, until the fountain was empty and dry. As I wrung my friend's hand at parting, I said,—

17 "Haven't we had a royal good time! But now I remember, you haven't said a word for two hours. Come, come, out with something!"

18 The Rev. Mr. -------- turned a lacklustre eye upon me, drew a deep sigh, and said, without animation, without apparent consciousness,—

19 "Punch, brothers, punch with care! Punch in the presence of the passenjare!"

20 A pang shot through me as I said to myself, "Poor fellow, poor fellow! he has got it, now."

21 I did not see Mr. -------- for two or three days after that. Then, on Tuesday evening, he staggered into my presence and sank dejectedly into a seat. He was pale, worn; he was a wreck. He lifted his faded eyes to my face and said,—

22 "Ah, Mark, it was a ruinous investment that I made in those heartless rhymes. They have ridden me like a nightmare, day and night, hour after hour, to this very moment. Since I saw you I have suffered the torments of the lost. Saturday evening I had a sudden call, by telegraph, and took the night train for Boston. The occasion was the death of a valued old friend who had requested that I should preach his funeral sermon. I took my seat in the cars and set myself to framing the discourse. But I never got beyond the opening paragraph; for then the train started and the car-wheels began their 'clack, clack—clack-clack-clack! clack, clack—clack-clack-clack!' and right away those odious rhymes fitted themselves to that accompaniment. For an hour I sat there and set a syllable of those rhymes to every separate and distinct clack the carwheels made. Why, I was as fagged out, then, as if I had been chopping wood all day. My skull was splitting with headache. It seemed to me that I must go mad if I sat there any longer; so I undressed and went to bed. I stretched myself out in my berth, and—well, you know what the result was. The thing went right along, just the same. 'Clack-clack-clack, a blue trip slip, clack-clack-clack, for an eight-cent fare; clack-clack-clack, a buff trip slip, clack-clack-clack, for a six-cent fare, and so on, and so on, and so on—punch, in the presence of the passenjare!' Sleep? Not a single wink! I was almost a lunatic when I got to Boston. Don't ask me about the funeral. I did the best I could, but every solemn individual sentence was meshed and tangled and

woven in and out with 'Punch, brothers, punch with care, punch in the presence of the passenjare.' And the most distressing thing was that my delivery dropped into the undulating rhythm of those pulsing rhymes, and I could actually catch absent-minded people nodding time to the swing of it with their stupid heads. And, Mark, you may believe it or not, but before I got through, the entire assemblage were placidly bobbing their heads in solemn unison, mourners, undertaker, and all. The moment I had finished, I fled to the anteroom in a state bordering on frenzy. Of course it would be my luck to find a sorrowing and aged maiden aunt of the deceased there, who had arrived from Springfield too late to get into the church. She began to sob, and said,—

23 "'Oh, oh, he is gone, he is gone, and I didn't see him before he died!'

24 "'Yes!' I said, 'he is gone, he is gone, he is gone——oh, will this suffering never cease!'

25 "'You loved him, then! Oh, you too loved him!'

26 "'Loved him! Loved who?'

27 "'Why, my poor George! my poor nephew!'

28 "'Oh—him! Yes—oh, yes, yes. Certainly—certainly. Punch—punch—oh, this misery will kill me!'

29 "'Bless you! bless you, sir, for these sweet words! I, too, suffer in this dear loss. Were you present during his last moments?'

30 "'Yes! I—whose last moments?'

31 "'His. The dear departed's.'

32 "'Yes! Oh, yes—yes—yes! I suppose so, I think so, I don't know! Oh, certainly—I was there—I was there!'

33 "'Oh, what a privilege! what a precious privilege! And his last words—oh, tell me, tell me his last words! What did he say?'

34 "'He said—he said—oh, my head, my head, my head! He said—he said—he never said anything but Punch, punch, punch in the presence of the passenjare! Oh, leave me, madam! In the name of all that is generous, leave me to my madness, my misery, my despair!—a buff trip slip for a six-cent fare, a pink trip slip for a three-cent fare—endurance can no further go!—PUNCH in the presence of the passenjare!'"

35 My friend's hopeless eyes rested upon mine a pregnant minute, and then he said impressively,—

36 "Mark, you do not say anything. You do not offer me any hope. But, ah me, it is just as well—it is just as well. You could not do me any good. The time has long gone by when words could comfort me. Something tells me that my tongue is doomed to wag forever to the jigger of that remorseless jingle. There—there it is coming on me again: a blue trip slip for an eight-cent fare, a buff trip slip for a—"

37 Thus murmuring faint and fainter, my friend sank into a peaceful trance and forgot his sufferings in a blessed respite.

38 How did I finally save him from the asylum? I took him to a neighboring university and made him discharge the burden of his persecuting rhymes into the eager ears of the poor, unthinking students. How is it with them, now? The result is too sad to tell. Why did I write this article? It was for a worthy, even a noble, purpose. It was to warn you, reader, if you should come across those merciless rhymes, to avoid them—avoid them as you would a pestilence!

Use "Punch, Brothers, Punch" to answer questions 1–10

Multiple-Choice Questions

1 What is the effect of the author's constant use of rhythm in this piece?
   A It distracts the reader from Twain's real message.
   B It establishes a humorous tone.
   C It moves the piece along at a rapid pace.
   D It slows the piece down, keeping the reader involved.

2   In paragraph 2 the word *respite* means—
    F   melody
    G   coordination
    H   relief
    J   silence

3   Paragraph 2 is mainly about—
    A   Twain's thrilling tragedy
    B   how the jingle overtook Twain's sanity
    C   how Twain suffered with insomnia
    D   Twain's daily habits

4   Which of the following contributes to the overall humorous tone of the article?
    F   Opening with a short verse
    G   The Rev. Mr. -------- account of the funeral
    H   Exaggeration
    J   The details about Twain's life

5   Twain's friends are initially concerned because—
    A   he tells them he is sick
    B   his behavior is atypical of Twain
    C   he hasn't finished his writing
    D   he doesn't eat his dinner

6   Read the following dictionary entries.
    pang\pang\ *noun,* **1.** a brief, sharp pain **2.** a strong attack of conscience **3.** a physical spasm
    pang, verb **1.** torment

    Which definition best matches the meaning of the word *pang* as it is used in paragraph 20 of this essay?
    F   Noun 1
    G   Noun 2
    H   Noun 3
    J   Verb 1

7   The author includes a description of the "magnificent autumn landscape" in paragraph 9 because—
    A   it offers the reader a break from the jingle
    B   it serves as a contrast to Twain's bleak mental stupor
    C   it slows down the pace of the writing
    D   it defines the time of year

8   The reason the author includes the account of Mr. -------- funeral oration is because—
    F   it illustrates the absorbing effect of the jingle
    G   it explains why Mr. -------- went on the train trip
    H   it shows Mr. -------- to be a heartless, uncaring individual
    J   it illustrates that Mr. -------- is a gifted speaker

9   Which line best describes Twain's overall message about his experience with the words of the jingle?
    A   *They took instant and entire possession of me.*
    B   *. . . avoid them as you would a pestilence.*
    C   *That torturing jingle departed out of my brain, and a grateful sense of rest and peace descended upon me.*
    D   *Why, what a captivating jingle it is! It is almost music.*

10 Why is Twain's answer to his question—"Why did I write this article?"—ironic?
  F The question is never really answered.
  G It explains why he told the story about Mr. --------.
  H It explains, but doesn't actually talk about, his experience with mental illness.
  J By the time you've reached the end of the article, you realize you have already encountered the rhyme.

Answer Explanations

Now let's talk about strategy. At this point, knowing how to select the correct answer is important.

Question 1: When you were scanning and highlighting the questions before the test, you should have marked the words *effect* and *rhythm*. Then, somewhere around the middle of the essay, to the side or at the top, you should have written "effect of rhythm?" In selecting the correct answer, you needed to ask yourself, "Why did Twain use such a strong beat? What was his purpose?" The answer to that question should evolve into something like, "His purpose was to entertain and be funny, and the constant use of the jingle makes the reader laugh." Reasoning like this, the only answer that matches your own rationale is **B**.

Question 2: Here is where reading the question before the test really helps. There are two uses of *respite* in the passage, one in paragraph 2 and another in paragraph 37. When you scanned the questions you should have found and marked *respite* in paragraph 2, which would avoid any confusion. The context clue, *peace*, indicates that Twain was seeking some kind of release from the constant mental intrusion of the jingle. So the best answer is **H**.

Question 3: Before the test you should have somehow separated paragraph 2, either by boxing it in or putting a line down the side. Beside the paragraph you should have written something like "main idea" or "mostly about." As you read you should have been thinking about the overall meaning. When you are answering the question it is a good idea to go back to the paragraph and reread it alone, without the influence of all that is around it. Remember that you are trying to come up with your own answers *before* you read the choices. Although Twain's habits and insomnia are mentioned, they are not the core of the paragraph. The fact that he can think about nothing but the jingle is all-inclusive. So your best answer is **B**.

Question 4: If you read this question before taking the test, you would have one advantage because you would know that the test makers classify the essay as humorous. So you would think to yourself, "Okay. *How* is this funny?" As you read, Twain's repetition of the jingle and understated exaggeration should have been obvious. The best answer is **H**.

Question 5: Reading this question beforehand doesn't tell you much except at some point Twain's friends are concerned. The word *initially*, though, tells you this will be somewhere near the beginning of either the essay or, if there is a flashback, the experience. So as you read you would look for this sense of concern. The best answer is **B**, but you might not catch this if you do not immediately know the meaning of the word *atypical*. Remember not to leave anything to chance. Look up any word you do not know.

Question 6: The best way to approach this question is to find the word *pang* in paragraph 20 and highlight it before the test. Then, after the test, after you understand the tone and the gist of the article, go back and plug each possible definition into paragraph 20 in place of *pang*. When Twain says, "A pang shot through me," it doesn't seem to be a physical thing, but rather a twinge of conscience. The best answer is **G**.

Question 7: During your highlighting, before reading the passage, you should have gone to paragraph 9 and noted the words *magnificent autumn landscape*, and in the margin written the word *why*. As you read, the contrast between the magnificent site and Twain's mental bleakness should have been somewhat apparent. When you then look at the possible answers, although **A**, **C**, and **D** do apply in a loose way, the *best* answer is **C**. If you'd come to this conclusion before reading, the incorrect choices wouldn't fool you.

Question 8: The word *funeral* is a pretty memorable word. Highlighting it would help it stick in your mind, as would jotting it down, along with the word *why*, in the margin of the page. Then, as you read you would pay particular notice to why Twain included this account. Yes, it does explain why Mr. -------- went on a train trip, but that isn't the best answer. Choice **H**, is simply incorrect and can be immediately crossed off, and there is not enough information on Mr. --------'s speaking ability to select **J**. The purpose of the account of the funeral, though, seems to be to show that Mr. -------- had difficulty functioning. Why? Because the jingle was stuck in his mind. Therefore, the best answer would be **F**.

Question 9: You would not want to take the time to find each possible answer beforehand, but being aware that you need to understand Twain's overall message, or theme, is what is important. Before you begin, you should write *theme* either in the margin or at the top of the page, and then read. When you finish, ask yourself, "What was Twain's message?" After you answer this question in your mind, look at the choices. You know the words of the jingle had a negative effect on the author, and you know that he wanted to be rid of them. If you took the time to look up the word *pestilence*, you would know that it means a serious, contagious disease like a plague. If you didn't look it up, and you were not aware of this meaning, **C** might appear to be the correct choice. But Twain wanted to be rid of the jingle, and his advice to the reader is to avoid it at all cost. So the best answer is **B**.

Question 10: During the preparation process you should have gone to the end of the piece, quickly found the question "Why did I write this article?" and highlighted it, and then written the word *irony* in the margin. If you didn't know what this word meant, you should have taken the time to quickly look it up in the dictionary so that as you read you would be thinking about the concept. Then when you were finished and were answering question 10, you should have asked yourself, "How is the ending ironic?" Understanding that the word *ironic* means to use words to say something other that what is meant, a contrast between what is actually said and what is true, you recognize that by the time the reader gets to the end of the article, the words of the jingle have been repeated so many times, they are imbedded in the reader's mind, which is exactly what Twain intended. So the best answer is **J**.

Final Thoughts

Hopefully by now you are beginning to see the value of highlighting, how it gives your thinking a "heads up" about what information will be needed.

The process is the same for all multiple-choice questions, including those on Part II of the test: revising and editing. In this section, about twenty questions ask you to correct or improve specific sentences or paragraphs, or maybe to strengthen the organizational pattern of the composition. Again, the sentences are numbered. Your task is to quickly review the composition or analyze the specific section in question, draw a reasonable conclusion, and then find the answer that best matches your response.

In either case, all multiple-choice questions are presented in the same way. They start with a stem that either asks a question or offers a partial statement to be completed. Then four possible answers or conclusions are provided. Your task is to pick the best one.

And there is another confusing word: *best*.

No answer will appear on ELA TAKS that does not have at least the sound of reasonability. But often you can rule out one or more responses as wrong. If so, cross them off right in the test booklet. Then look at the remaining choices. If you have formulated your own conclusion before actually looking at the possible answers, one will usually match your own findings better than the others. If so, pick that answer.

If you are stumped, go back to the triplet or the revising and editing piece. Ask yourself, "Have I missed anything?" Reread the question again. Use the dictionary to look up any word you may not know. And then, if you are still unsure, guess.

Never, ever leave a question unanswered.

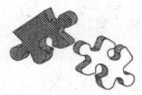 Be sure to answer all questions.

For the most part, though, guesses aren't necessary. You have to work—that is, think, reason, and use your dictionary. You have to approach the test with careful thought and consideration, and you have to take your time. But the answers are there. Like locating the correct pieces of a puzzle, all you have to do is find them.

And the objective sections of ELA TAKS are just a part of your high school history.

Review Box
→ Quickly read the stems of each question, asking yourself where the information is located: in the text or in your head.
→ If the stem makes reference to a certain portion of the triplet, find it and make note of the information that is required.
→ Carefully read each part of the triplet.
→ Answer questions dealing with a specific section of the triplet after reading that section.
→ Mentally construct your own answer before looking at the possible choices. Then select the choice that best matches your conclusion.
→ If you cannot find a direct match, reread, rethink, and if necessary, guess.
→ Do not leave any answers blank.

Chapter 4

Responding to Open-Ended Questions

Now for the good news: open-ended questions. Answering open-ended questions is one part of the test over which you have control. Why? In these questions you aren't guessing about an answer, you are supplying it. You are completely in charge of what you write, and for the most part, as long as your answer is *reasonable* and *relevant* you will be given credit. These are key words, and it is important to keep them in mind.

 All open-ended responses must be reasonable and relevant.

Focus on the Text

Unlike some tests or classroom exercises where you are given credit for expressing an opinion, on the ELA TAKS whatever you write must evolve reasonably from the text. You do not want to leave any doubt in the grader's mind that you have read and understand the triplet. So your answer must be clear and exact, backed by a specific reference. Don't say, "as can be seen in paragraph 3" or "the second sentence." Cite the words themselves. To get the best score for your open-ended answers, your wording must convey a depth of understanding that says to the grader, "I know what I'm talking about because [add a specific connection found in your reading]."

Remember that the triplet on the ELA TAKS consists of three sections: a literary piece, an expository work, and a visual. Only the fictional and nonfictional passages are covered with open-ended questions, and each should be approached in a slightly different way to receive the best score.

The Fictional Selection

First, in answering open-ended questions on the fiction piece, you must indicate that you understand more than the simple plot of the story. Anyone can tell what happens, but to score well you need to go deeper. You need to interpret and support written evidence from the text. Ask yourself questions like these:

 What does the story mean?

 How is the main character unique or different than characters in other stories I've read?

 What is the basic conflict in the story?

 Did something happen that changed the direction of the action or the main character's attitude?

 Is there some literary technique, like a simile or figure of speech, I could mention?

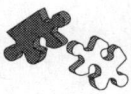 What is the message or theme of this story?

When you are answering questions about the literary piece, you might be asked to talk about a theme, character trait, conflict, change, literary technique, or figurative expression. You should have studied all of these in English class, but if you panic and forget the definition of a specific term, use the dictionary to jog your memory.

Because you control this part of the test, your answer will be unique. Even if you feel uncertain about a specific term, pick your best idea and support it with relevant information from the text. This will earn you some points for your effort, even if what you say isn't completely right.

 All answers must be connected to the text and supported with a quotation, a paraphrase, or a summary.

Literary Themes

For example, here is a list of general themes that commonly appear in literature. Think of how you might apply these to what you're currently reading, a movie you've seen, or a TV show you've watched. Familiarizing yourself with this list would probably help you avoid test anxiety, because it would give you some idea of what to say.

 The individual in nature (e.g., Tom Hanks in the movie *Castaway*, the character Timothy in Theodore Taylor's *The Cay*, or Kate Chopin's "The Storm")

 The individual in society (e.g., Shakespeare's *Julius Caesar*, Mildred Taylor's *Roll of Thunder Hear My Cry*, or Kurt Vonnegut's "Harrison Bergeron")

 An individual's relations to the gods (e.g., Faulkner's *As I Lay Dying* or Sir Thomas Malory's *Morte d'Arthur*)

 Human relations (e.g., Shakespeare's *Romeo and Juliet*, Mark Twain's *Huckleberry Finn*, or Ring Lardner's "Haircut")

 Growth and initiation (e.g., Steinbeck's "The Bear," Stephen Crane's *Red Badge of Courage*, or James Hurst's "The Scarlet Ibis")

 Time (e.g., the movie *Groundhog Day*, Robert Cormier's *After the First Death*, or Ray Bradbury's "A Sound of Thunder")

 Death (e.g., the movie, *The Sixth Sense* or Katherine Anne Porter's "The Jilting of Granny Weatherall")

 Alienation (e.g., Steinbeck's *Of Men and Mice*)

Character Traits

Likewise, here is a list of traditional character traits you could weave into an answer:

 how a character reacts to a situation, the environment, the present, the past, or other characters

 how other characters react toward the main character

 the way a character talks and dresses

Common Conflicts

Standard conflicts commonly include:

 man against man

 man against nature

 man against himself

 man against a higher power

 man against technology

Literary Terms

And of course there are all of those wonderful literary terms you've been discussing in English class for as long as you can remember: plot, characterization, mood, setting, tone, point of view, and theme. The list is endless. Look at all these possibilities: alliteration, allusion, connotation/denotation, dialect, figurative language (simile, metaphor, hyperbole, personification), flashback, foreshadowing, imagery, inference, irony, protagonist/antagonist, satire, sound devices (such as repetition, alliteration, assonance, consonance, onomatopoeia), style, and voice.

If somehow you find yourself unsure of exactly how to answer an open-ended literary question, go back to these old faithfuls and weave them into your response. Any time you can authentically add specific literary references to your answer, the better it will be.

The Nonfiction Selection

For the nonfiction or expository piece, it is important that your ideas show a reasonable, logical conclusion based on the text. It is acceptable to say what you think, but remember, you must give the graders the understanding that you have actually read the piece. So your answer has to reflect the text.

For example, you might be asked to draw a conclusion, offer an interpretation, make a prediction, or analyze or evaluate a characteristic of the text. Or, you might be asked to make a judgment about the author's craft/style, use of repetition, word choice, syntax, punctuation, imagery, genre. These questions go beyond the text. Your answers should reflect your own thinking. Again, if you get stumped, use your dictionary, then trust your instincts to bring together an answer.

The Crossover Questions

As with the objective questions, there will also be queries that are based on both the fiction and nonfiction parts of the triplet. In this crossover section you will be asked the same type of questions as in the expository piece (conclusion, interpretation, prediction, analysis, evaluation), but your response must show that you can make a meaningful connection across both selections. Remember this is called "crossover." To get the highest score, you must write about both pieces, and the key word is *both*. You could draw a conclusion based on both, make an interpretation based on both, or make a prediction based on both, but you must talk about both pieces. You must analyze or evaluate them together, making clear and specific connections.

 When answering the crossover question, you must reference both pieces.

Connecting to the Triplet

Whether you are responding to the fictional passage, the expository piece, or both, it is important that you write in your own style and pattern, using words that you would normally choose, because this is something the graders will notice. Also, you must relate everything to the text. This is what is meant by relevant: How does your idea, your response to the question, connect to the triplet?

 You must connect your answer to the triplet.

At least one of the three things below is required to earn credit for an open-ended response. Graders will be looking for these specifically.

 A direct quote from the piece

A paraphrase of something in the piece

A synopsis

If one of these three strategies is not present in your answer, you will not receive credit.

 Answers must include a direct quote, a paraphrase, or a synopsis to receive credit.

When you incorporate a direct quote, of course, you must be careful to use correct punctuation. Quotes do not have to be referenced as in telling which paragraph or article they are from, but they must be set off in quotations. Never, ever, take something word for word from the triplet without doing so.

On the other hand, a paraphrase is where you do not use the exact words the author uses but instead restate what is said in your own words. When you use this strategy, you must refer exactly to the section of the triplet you are paraphrasing by saying something like, "When the author mentions thus and so on the second page."

A synopsis, which is a brief, general reference condensing the text into a smaller portion, can also be a good tactic. It is usually both focused and specific, like a list or a summary of many different events, and it is a good way to succinctly support your ideas.

An Example

Let's see what these kinds of support look like. Read the following excerpt from Nathaniel Hawthorne's "Young Goodman Brown" and the sample open-ended responses.

Notes

1   Young Goodman Brown came forth at sunset, into the street of Salem village, but put his head back, after crossing the threshold, to exchange a parting kiss with his young wife. And Faith, as the wife was aptly named, thrust her own pretty head into the street, letting the wind play with the pink ribbons of her cap, while she called to Goodman Brown.

2   "Dearest heart," whispered she, softly and rather sadly, when her lips were close to his ear, "pr'ythee, put off your journey until sunrise, and sleep in your own bed tonight. A lone woman is troubled with such dreams and such thoughts, that she's afeard of herself, sometimes. Pray, tarry with me this night, dear husband, of all nights in the year!"

3   "My love and my Faith," replied young Goodman Brown, "of all nights in the year, this one night must I tarry away from thee. My journey, as thou callest it, forth and back again, must needs be done 'twixt now and sunrise. What, my sweet, pretty wife, dost thou doubt me already, and we but three months married!"

4   "Then God bless you!" said Faith, with the pink ribbons, "and may you find all well, when you come back."

5   "Amen!" cried Goodman Brown. "Say thy prayers, dear Faith, and go to bed at dusk, and no harm will come to thee."

6   So they parted; and the young man pursued his way, until, being about to turn the corner by the meeting-house, he looked back and saw the head of Faith still peeping after him, with a melancholy air, in spite of her pink ribbons.

7   "Poor little Faith!" thought he, for his heart smote him. "What a wretch am I, to leave her on such an errand! She talks of dreams, too. Methought, as she spoke, there was trouble in her face, as if a dream had warned her what work is to be done tonight. But, no, no! 'twould kill her to think it. Well; she's a blessed angel on earth; and after this one night, I'll cling to her skirts and follow her to Heaven." . . .

8   The hoofs clattered again, and the voices, talking so strangely in the empty air, passed on through the forest, where no church had ever been gathered, nor solitary Christian prayed. Whither, then, could these holy men be journeying, so deep into the heathen wilderness? Young

Goodman Brown caught hold of a tree, for support, being ready to sink down on the ground, faint and overburthened with the heavy sickness of his heart. He looked up to the sky, doubting whether there really was a Heaven above him. Yet, there was the blue arch, and the stars brightening in it.

9   "With Heaven above, and Faith below, I will yet stand firm against the devil!" cried Goodman Brown.

10   While he still gazed upward, into the deep arch of the firmament, and had lifted his hands to pray, a cloud, though no wind was stirring, hurried across the zenith and hid the brightening stars. The blue sky was still visible, except directly overhead, where this black mass of cloud was sweeping swiftly northward. Aloft in the air, as if from the depths of the cloud, came a confused and doubtful sound of voices. Once, the listener fancied that he could distinguish the accent of townspeople of his own, men and women, both pious and ungodly, many of whom he had met at the communion-table, and had seen others rioting at the tavern. The next moment, so indistinct were the sounds, he doubted whether he had heard aught but the murmur of the old forest, whispering without a wind. Then came a stronger swell of those familiar tones, heard daily in the sunshine at Salem village, but never, until now, from a cloud of night. There was one voice, of a young woman, uttering lamentations, yet with an uncertain sorrow, and entreating for some favor, which, perhaps, it would grieve her to obtain. And all the unseen multitude, both saints and sinners, seemed to encourage her onward.

11   "Faith!" shouted Goodman Brown, in a voice of agony and desperation; and the echoes of the forest mocked him, crying "Faith! Faith!" as if bewildered wretches were seeking her, all through the wilderness.

12   The cry of grief, rage, and terror, was yet piercing the night, when the unhappy husband held his breath for a response. There was a scream, drowned immediately in a louder murmur of voices, fading into far-off laughter, as the dark cloud swept away, leaving the clear and silent sky above Goodman Brown. But something fluttered lightly down through the air, and caught on the branch of a tree. The young man seized it, and beheld a pink ribbon.

13   "My Faith is gone!" cried he, after one stupefied moment. "There is no good on earth; and sin is but a name. Come, devil! for to thee is this world given."

Answering with a Summary

How does the naming of the characters affect the allegorical nature of "Young Goodman Brown"?

By using an abstract quality for the name of his character, Hawthorne helps clarify the theme of the faith journey we travel as we mature. Goodman Brown, trying to be a good man on a journey, is disillusioned when he hears the voice of his wife, Faith, in the forest, and her pink ribbon floats down. Disillusion and loss of faith is part of the journey.

The above answer summarizes or gives a synopsis of the excerpt to support the answer that Hawthorne's characters' names made the meaning or message very clear.

Answering with a Paraphrase

Now look at a response to the same question using the support of the paraphrase:

> By carefully choosing the names for his characters, Hawthorne makes the theme of the faith journey easier to grasp. When the pink ribbon that Faith wore floats down from the sky, Goodman Brown cries that his Faith is gone, that there is nothing good on earth, and that sin is only a name.

The above is a paraphrase because it took the words and ideas expressed and restated them with different words. Again, the response left no doubt that the student thought the names made it easier to grasp the meaning of the story.

Answering with a Direct Quote

Another way of supporting your reasonable and relevant answer to the open-ended question is through the use of direct quotations. Look at the following answer to the same question using a direct quote:

> Carefully chosen characters' names help to clarify the theme of the steps on the faith journey. In the first paragraph Hawthorne says, "And Faith, as the wife was aptly named . . . ." At the end Goodman Brown calls out, "My Faith is gone! ...There is no good on earth; and sin is but a name."

Length of Answer

Not only must one of these strategies be present in your open-ended response, it also has to be evident within a specific space. Although there will be room in your test booklet to carefully work out your ideas, when you transfer your response to the answer document, it will have to fit within a designated boxed area as follows:

 five-line box for fiction piece

 five-line box for the nonfiction piece

 eight-line box for the two pieces together

You must plan carefully to make the best use of this space.

Practice with a Fictional Passage

Now let's practice. Below is a fictional piece for you to read, to think about, and then to try your hand at answering an open-ended question. Plan your answer as you would in the test booklet, copy it neatly into the box provided, and then compare what you've written with sample responses.

[In his novel THE DEERSLAYER, Cooper tells of a day in June when Hurry Harry, a frontiersman, is talking to his friend Deerslayer. They have traveled to an area around the Hudson River, to the foot of a lake which Deerslayer is seeing for the first time.]

excerpt from *The Deerslayer*
by James Fenimore Cooper

Notes

1   An exclamation of surprise broke from the lips of Deerslayer, an exclamation that was low and guardedly made, however, for his habits were much more thoughtful and regulated than those of the reckless Hurry, when, on reaching the margin of the lake, he beheld the view that unexpectedly met his gaze. It was, in truth, sufficiently striking to merit a brief description. On a level with the point lay a broad sheet of water, so placid and limpid, that it resembled a bed of the pure mountain atmosphere, compressed into a setting of hills and woods. Its length was about three leagues, while its breadth was irregular, expanding to half a league, or even more, opposite to the point, and contracting to less than half that distance, more to the southward. Of course, its margin was irregular, being indented by bays and broken by many projecting, low points. At its northern, or nearest end, it was bounded by an isolated mountain, lower land falling off, east and west, gracefully relieving the sweep of the outline. Still the character of the country was mountainous; high hills, or low mountains, rising abruptly from the water, on quite nine-tenths of its circuit. The exceptions, indeed, only served a little to vary the scene; and even beyond the parts of the shore that were comparatively low, the background was high, though more distant.

2   But the most striking peculiarities of this scene were its solemn solitude, and sweet repose. On all sides, wherever the eye turned, nothing met it but the mirror-like surface of the lake, the placid view of heaven,

and the dense setting of woods. So rich and fleecy were the outlines of the forest, that scarce an opening could be seen, the whole visible earth, from the rounded mountaintop to the water's edge, presenting one unvaried hue of unbroken verdure. As if vegetation were not satisfied with a triumph so complete, the trees overhung the lake itself, shooting out towards the light; and there were miles along its eastern shore, where a boat might have pulled beneath the branches of dark Rembrandt-looking hemlocks, "quivering aspens," and melancholy pines. In a word, the hand of man had never yet defaced or deformed any part of this native scene, which lay bathed in the sunlight, a glorious picture of affluent forest-grandeur, softened by the balminess of June, and relieved by the beautiful variety afforded by the presence of so broad an expanse of water.

3   "This is grand!—'t is solemn! —'t is an edication of itself, to look upon!" exclaimed Deerslayer, as he stood leaning on his rifle, and gazing to the right and left, north and south, above and beneath, in whichever direction his eye could wander; "not a tree disturbed even by redskin hand, as I can discover, but every thing left in the ordering of the Lord, to live and die according to his own designs and laws. . . !"

4   "T is your first acquaintance with a lake; [Hurry said] and these idees come over us all, at such times. Lakes have a general character, as I say, being pretty much water and land, and points and bays."

5   As this definition by no means met the feelings that were uppermost in the mind of the young hunter, he made no immediate answer, but stood gazing at the dark hills, and the glassy water, in silent enjoyment.

6   "Have the Governor's, or the King's people given this lake a name?" he suddenly asked, as if struck with a new idea. "If they've not begun to blaze their trees, and set up their compasses, and line off their maps, it's likely they've not bethought them to disturb natur' with a name."

7   "They've not got to that, yet; and the last time I went in with skins, one of the King's surveyors was questioning me consarning all the region hereabouts. He had heard that there was a lake in this quarter, and had got some general notions about it, such as that there was water and hills; but how much of either, he know'd no more than you know of the Mohawk tongue. . . ."

8   "I'm glad it has no name," resumed Deerslayer, "or, at least, no paleface name; for their christenings always foretell waste and destruction. No doubt, however, the redskins have their modes of knowing it, and the hunters and trappers, too; they are likely to call the place by something reasonable and resembling."

9   "As for the tribes, [Hurry said] each has its own tongue, and its own way of calling things; and they treat this part of the world just as they treat all others. Among ourselves, we've got to calling the place 'Glimmerglass,' seeing that its whole basin is often fringed with pines, cast upward from its face; as if it would throw back the hills that hang over it. . . ."

10 Deerslayer made no answer; but he stood leaning on his rifle, gazing at the view which so much delighted him. The reader is not to suppose, however, that it was the picturesque alone which so strongly attracted his attention. The spot was very lovely, of a truth, and it was then seen in one of its most favorable moments, the surface of the lake being as smooth as glass, and as limpid as pure air, throwing back the mountains, clothed in dark pines, along the whole of its eastern boundary, the

Notes

points thrusting forward their trees even to nearly horizontal lines, while the bays were seen glittering through an occasional arch beneath, left by a vault fretted with branches and leaves. It was the air of deep repose—the solitudes, that spoke of scenes and forests untouched by the hands of man—the reign of nature, in a word, that gave so much pure delight to one of his habits and turn of mind. Still, he felt, though it was unconsciously, like a poet also. If he found a pleasure in studying this large, and, to him, unusual opening into the mysteries and forms of the woods, as one is gratified in getting broader views of any subject that has long occupied his thoughts, he was not insensible to the innate loveliness of such a landscape neither, but felt a portion of that soothing of the spirit which is a common attendant of a scene so thoroughly pervaded by the holy calm of nature.

Use *The Deerslayer* to answer the following question.

Why does the name of the lake suggested by Hurry please Deerslayer? Support your answer with evidence from the selection.

 Use the space provided in the test booklet to plan your answer.

Planning Space

_____
_____
_____
_____
_____

Sample Answers

Responses on the open-ended section will vary, of course, based on an individual's expression of what is relevant and reasonable. It is important, though, that you understand what represents a good response, so let's look at a couple of possibilities.

> The lake, "placid and limpid" with a "mirror-like surface" reflecting heaven, overwhelms Deerslayer, who realizes that it is untouched by man, paralleling "the holy calm of nature." The name Glimmerglass metaphorically suggests peace and the glimmer of hope nature has given Deerslayer, thus pleasing him.

This answer would definitely rate a 3, or exemplary, which, if you remember, is the best. The writer not only provides insight into one aspect of the lake (how the name befits the character) but also proceeds to explore and support this trait by revealing how that name correctly describes the lake. Relevant quotes of accurate text are used to support the information. In addition, the student shows insight by suggesting the connotations of *glimmer*.

Another response might be as follows:

> Deerslayer is pleased with Glimmerglass as a name for the lake because it reflects the "mirror-like surface of the lake" and the "holy calm of nature." In addition, the name suggests that nature is untouched by humans and only reveals nature.

This answer would most likely rate a 2, or sufficient, which is still good. It uses both relevant quotes of accurate text and synopsis to answer the question, but it lacks the depth of thought expressed in the first answer.

Use the rubric at the end of the chapter (page 41) to evaluate your response. Did you include a summary, a quote, or a paraphrase? Was your answer thoughtful and insightful? Did your analysis include literary terms or figurative language? If not, how could you have raised your score to a higher level?

Practice with a Nonfiction Piece

Read the nonfiction piece below, and answer the open-ended question that follows. Again, plan your answer as you would in the test booklet, copy it neatly into the box provided, and then compare what you've written with sample responses.

[In his autobiography Up From Slavery, Booker T. Washington, the founder of Tuskegee Normal and Industrial Institute, is trying to tell a simple, straightforward story about his life in response to many requests for this information.]

excerpted from Up From Slavery
by Booker T. Washington

1   After the coming of freedom there were two points upon which practically all the people on our place were agreed, and I found that this was generally true throughout the South: that they must change their names, and that they must leave the old plantation for at least a few days or weeks in order that they might really feel sure that they were free.

2   In some way a feeling got among the coloured people that it was far from proper for them to bear the surname of their former owners, and a great many of them took other surnames. This was one of the first signs of freedom. When they were slaves, a coloured person was simply called "John" or "Susan." There was seldom occasion for more than the use of the one name. If "John" or "Susan" belonged to a white man by the name of "Hatcher," sometimes he was called "John Hatcher," or as often "Hatcher's John." But there was a feeling that "John Hatcher" or "Hatcher's John" was not the proper title by which to denote a freeman; and so in many cases "John Hatcher" was changed to "John S. Lincoln" or "John S. Sherman," the initial "S" standing for no name, it being simply a part of what the coloured man proudly called his "entitles" . . . .

3   [Upon entering school] my second difficulty was with regard to my name, or rather a name. From the time when I could remember anything, I had been called simply "Booker." Before going to school it had never occurred to me that it was needful or appropriate to have an additional name. When I heard the school roll called, I noticed that all of the children had at least two names, and some of them indulged in what seemed to me the extravagance of having three. I was in deep perplexity, because I knew that the teacher would demand of me at least two names, and I had only one. By the time the occasion came for the enrolling of my name, an idea occurred to me which I thought would make me equal to the situation; and so, when the teacher asked me what my full name was, I calmly told him "Booker Washington," as if I had been called by that name all my life; and by that name I have since been known. Later in my life I found that my mother had given me the name of "Booker Taliaferro" soon after I was born, but in some way that part of my name seemed to disappear and for a long while was forgotten, but as soon as I found out about it I revived it, and made my full name "Booker Taliaferro Washington." I think there are not many men in our country who have had the privilege of naming themselves in the way that I have.

4   More than once I have tried to picture myself in the position of a boy or man with an honoured and distinguished ancestry which I could trace back through a period of hundreds of years, and who had not only inherited a name, but fortune and a proud family homestead; and yet I have sometimes had the feeling that if I had inherited these, and had been a member of a more popular race, I should have been inclined to yield to the temptation of depending upon my ancestry and my colour to do that for me which I should do for myself. Years ago I resolved that because I had no ancestry myself I would leave a record of which my children would be proud, and which might encourage them to still higher effort.

Use *Up from Slavery* to answer the following question.

According to Washington, why was it important for slaves to change their names? Use evidence from the selection to support your answer.

Planning Space

Sample Answer

Now let's look at a possible response for this open-ended question on the expository piece:

> *Sharing his reflections on how he acquired his name, Washington emphasizes how the selection of names exhibited the idea of the freedom of all slaves and gave him personal control of his own identity. "I think there are not many men in the country who have the privilege of naming themselves in the way that I have."*

Again, your answer would vary, but hopefully you can see why the above response would merit a 3, or exemplary. This student correctly identified the purpose of writing and supported it with synopsis and direct quotes. It is insightful because the student was able to focus on the importance of names. The student goes the step beyond and suggests that naming is a privilege.

To score a 2, the student would have stopped with the synopsis (summary) and direct quote. The extra depth in thinking regarding the importance of assigning names would not have been present.

Be sure to check your own answer with the rubric on page (41).

A Crossover Question

Now let's look at a question that covers both pieces.

> **How does the idea of the importance of names apply to both *Deerslayer* and the excerpt from *Up From Slavery*?**

Planning Space

Sample Answer

Here is a possible response.

> Both pieces stress the importance placed on names. Whereas Deerslayer shows respect for native names when he says that "they are likely to call the place by something reasonable and resembling," Washington values the freedom of choosing one's own name, even reviving the name given him by his mother. In both pieces, though, it is through names that distinction and individuality are bestowed.

This answer would definitely merit a 3, or exemplary. The writer shows a thoughtful understanding of the attitude toward names in both selections. These ideas are supported by providing a mixture of synopsis, analysis, and direct quotes taken from both pieces. If the introductory statement tying the two together were left out, the answer would only earn a 2, or sufficient.

Of course your answer will be different, but if you study the rubric at the end of the chapter and highlight the differences, you will soon become familiar with what is needed to obtain a score of 3, or exlemplary. Do you see how the expectations move up from *missing* or *lacking clarity* to *thoughtful* and *insightful* with reference to the text? The exemplary ratings all show depth of understanding and direct evidence from the selection, and with practice you will be able to do this with ease.

 Answering open-ended questions is one part of the test that you control.

Final Thoughts

At first, answering open-ended questions can feel uncomfortable, but the more you practice thinking about what you read the more confidence you will gain. While reading, always ask yourself questions. Why did the author use this word? What did the main character mean when he or she said this or did that? How does this reading make me feel? Then, when answering the questions, remember the two Rs: reasonable and relevant. You must not simply restate the plot but rather show that you understand the depth and substance of the piece. Trust your instinct. Support your ideas. Tell why you think you are right. This is your chance to shine.

And you will.

Review Box
→ Both the literary selection and the expository piece will be addressed by open-ended questions.
→ There will be at least one crossover question covering both pieces.
→ You will have access to reference materials during the open-ended section of the test.
→ Your answer must include a direct quote, a paraphrase or a synopsis.
→ A key point to remember when composing your response is that all answers must reasonably and relevantly connect to the triplet.
→ Study the rubric to learn how to earn a 3, or exemplary.

Open-Ended Response Rubric

	0 (insufficient)	1 (partially sufficient)	2 (sufficient)	3 (exemplary)
Objective 2 Literary Selection	• theme, character trait, or change missing or too general to determine if reasonable • inaccurate analysis • presents only a plot summary • does not address the question • incomplete or lacking textual evidence	• theme, character trait, or change reasonable, but support too general or inaccurate • analysis of literary devices accurate, but inadequately supported • weak textual evidence • textual evidence with no connection to analysis	• reasonable theme, character trait, or change noted and supported with reference to the text • analysis of literary technique or figurative language supported with textual evidence	• thoughtful and insightful theme, character or change noted and supported with reference to text • analysis of literary technique of figurative language strongly supported by textual evidence
Objective 3 Expository Selection	• response lacks clarity • conclusion, prediction, or interpretation drawn is not based on selection • conclusion, prediction, or interpretation drawn does not address the question • conclusion, prediction, or interpretation drawn is illogical, and/or unreasonable • incorrect analysis of text • textual evidence with no connection to analysis	• vague or unclear response • conclusion, prediction, or interpretation generally drawn or only partially based on selection • textual evidence inaccurate • textual evidence too general • textual evidence either not connected or weakly connected to conclusion, prediction, or interpretation	• reasonable conclusion, prediction, or interpretation drawn and accurately supported with textual evidence • relevant textual support offered to support an accurate analysis of text • response directly addresses the question in a clear and precise manner	• analysis of conclusion, prediction or interpretation particularly insightful, and strongly supported by textual evidence • a particularly thoughtful analysis of the text is supported by direct evidence from the selection • response directly addresses the question with depth of understanding
Objective 3 Crossover Item	• conclusion, prediction, or interpretation drawn is not based on selection • conclusion, prediction, or interpretation drawn does not address the question • conclusion, prediction, or interpretation drawn is illogical, and/or unreasonable • information given too general to judge relevance • incomplete or nonexistent textual evidence from one or both selections • response lacks clarity • presents ideas, but no development • presents ideas, but development is too vague to understand • presents a plot summary of another published work • omits information, which hinders understanding	• vague or unclear response • conclusion, prediction, or interpretation generally drawn or only partially based on selection • textual evidence inaccurate or offered from only one selection • textual evidence too general or offered from only one selection • textual evidence either not connected or weakly connected to conclusion, prediction, or interpretation or only addresses one selection • textual evidence from both selections presented without offering a conclusion, prediction, or interpretation • connection between texts is unclear	• reasonable conclusion, prediction, or interpretation drawn and accurately supported with textual evidence from both selections • relevant textual support offered to support an accurate analysis of text of both selections • response directly addresses the question in a clear and precise manner • connection between texts is clear and distinct	• analysis of conclusion, prediction or interpretation particularly insightful, and strongly supported by textual evidence from both selections • a particularly thoughtful analysis of the text is supported by direct evidence from the both selections • response directly addresses the question with depth of understanding • connection between texts is clear, distinct, and meaningful, showing a depth of understanding

Chapter 5

Writing the Composition

Ever since you first traced a line through the sandbox with your finger, drawing a symbol that perhaps had meaning only to you, you've been writing.

Writing, and writing, and writing.

In kindergarten, your symbols took on a pattern of consistency as your letters began to form words and a shared sense of meaning emerged. You penned your way on through elementary school, junior high, and now you're still at it, writing in journals, on essay tests, and sometimes even in notes to friends.

Why? Because as humans, we seem to have a basic need to communicate, to tell others our dreams, fears, and hopes. And whether it is a note left by your mom on the refrigerator door or an epic poem about a hero living in a faraway land, the purpose of words is the same: communication. We all want to share our lives with others.

The ELA TAKS Essay

So there is no doubt that you can move a pencil across the page with your hand or let your fingers fly across a keyboard to put words on a screen. Only now it feels different, because now you have to write one of the best essays of your life so that you can pass the ELA TAKS test and graduate.

To make matters worse, your teachers have probably been stressing that the writing must be focused, coherent, and organized. Words such as *original* and *authentic* (and maybe even the word *voice*) may have been used in lessons. It probably sounds so confusing, maybe even bureaucratic, that if you don't write a certain way you won't get credit.

And this is true. You must write a good essay to be successful on the test. However, even though you may be hearing different terms and expressions, how to write that essay isn't something that is new to you.

Admittedly, good writing isn't the easiest thing to do, but composing the essay for ELA TAKS isn't an impossible task. You do need to understand what the test makers want. You do need to think, to learn how to give your essay structure, and to write from the heart, but this is something that all good writing requires. If it isn't focused and coherent, it isn't clear. The same is true if it isn't organized. What about *original*, *authentic* and *insightful*—words that are often cited by the graders as being desirable? Well, if you write with a sense of honest sincerity, if you say what you think in the way only you can, you should have that covered. There is no set number of paragraphs or a formula you must follow. This essay just requires good thinking reflected in good writing.

Good Writing

So don't be afraid of testing terms. Good writing is good writing. It is as simple as that. It is organized and developed. It is interesting to read, and it has a unique sound, a sound only you can give to it. With a little practice and thought, you can learn what you must do to make your ELA TAKS composition measure up to the high standards expected of students in Texas schools.

One thing is important to clearly understand from the start, though. Good writing *is* hard work. If it were easy we'd all have novels on the best-seller list. We don't, and the reason we don't is because good writing takes energy, time, and effort. Published authors write, rewrite, and then rewrite again. And still only a fraction make it to the big time.

So don't, for a moment, think that you can simply dash off a quick ELA TAKS essay and get out early for lunch. Ideas must be nurtured, cherished, and then, when properly germinated, put onto paper. If hurried, they can ramble and bump into each other, failing to bloom.

The writing section of the test is expected to take a good deal of time, and if you prewrite, draft, revise and edit, proofread, and then rewrite, it will. Accept this, and life will be easier. On the day of the test you will work hard—really, really hard—because that's what good writing is all about. The reward will be a passing score, and the sense of pride that comes with doing a job well.

 Good writing is hard work!

Topics

On the plus side, even though you will have to go through the process of writing a good essay, the topic shouldn't be a problem. Remember, you will already have read two literary pieces and examined one visual on a common theme that links to the prompt. As you read, your mind will be reacting and nurturing the information, and you are welcome to use information from the triplet if you want, though this isn't a necessity.

Also, the topic will be broad, one that can easily be adapted to the common experiences of adolescent life. It could pertain to changing plans, meeting someone new, encountering conflict, or maybe even being defeated. Although the possibilities are endless, they will come from the world around you and your everyday world.

For example, imagine that you have just read a story about a teenager who is new to this country, struggling to embrace it as home. And say you have also read an excerpt from Christopher Columbus's diary, where he recorded his first impressions of the Americas. Then you've studied an advertisement from a travel agency encouraging you to visit a foreign country.

See how these tie together with a common thread? Before you even look at the prompt, you need to be thinking about how the pieces of the triplet relate. How are they similar? How might they might be different? Think about how you would feel entering a new place or situation or relationship. Would you be scared? Excited? Curious? Would you trust your first impressions, or would you hold off judgment until you understood more?

An Example

Now, suppose that this was your prompt:

> **Write an essay in which you explain the validity of a person's first impressions.**

Analyze the question. Are you sure what *validity* means? Remember you have access to a dictionary, so don't take any chances. Look it up. As you read the definition, more ideas will develop until you begin to get a firm hold on the prompt.

 Be sure you understand the prompt before you start writing.

If not, if you are still struggling, scan the triplet again, looking for connections. The preparatory work you do will help your words to flow easier once you start writing. It is worth every minute it takes.

Prewriting

By doing this thinking, you have already started the prewriting stage of your work, which may be the most important part of your paper. The test booklet will have several pages where you can jot down notes and organize ideas. Once you understand what the prompt is suggesting, though, it is time to begin.

First, write down how you think the pieces of the triplet illustrated first impressions. Because you've already thought about this, these notes will be easy. You won't need to use them in your final piece, but they might help you get started.

Then relate the topic to yourself. All prompts are carefully selected to apply to a student's life, so you should have no problem. Think of an occasion or two when you made a first impression. Was it accurate? If not, when did you realize your impressions were wrong? Were there adverse consequences of your misjudgment? Be as detailed as you can in recording the memory. If you can make this connection between your experiences or observations and what you have read, your writing will sound more believable, and authenticity is something the graders want.

 Think: How can you link the prompt to your own life?

Next, think of other pieces of literature, of songs, and of movies or TV shows that have touched your life. Can any of these be related to a first impression? If so, jot them down. How about a time in history, in science, or in technology that first impressions played a big role? Write down what you remember.

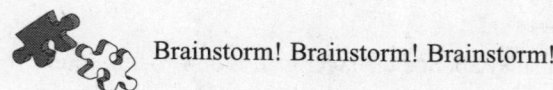 Brainstorm! Brainstorm! Brainstorm!

Now, go back and examine these ideas. Is there a general statement they all seem to suggest? Is there a common idea they share? Can you express that? If so, write it down and you're on your way. If not, go back to your notes and think. Was there ever a time when someone you know was fooled by a false first impression? Or how about adults? What kind of first impressions do they tend to make about teenagers?

Of course, you won't use all of these. What you are working toward is a focus for your writing, something that will tie it all together. In ELA TAKS terms it is called "focus and coherence," and it is something that the judges specifically look for. One controlling idea should be threaded throughout your piece, holding it together. So the time you spend here is well spent. Stay with it until you find a commonality. Remember that you are laying your foundation, so you want it to be sturdy, something strong enough to hold the paper together.

Organization

Next, consider the order in which you will present this information. The writing has to flow easily from one thought to the next, and this comes from planning before you begin to write. You want the reader to become effortlessly involved in your writing; you don't want to make them work.

So you must use some kind of organizational pattern. Order of importance, order of categories, and order of time are all patterns you have probably practiced in class. One of these might work, or you might come up with your own design based on the thread or focus you've chosen. As the author, you can choose whichever strategy you think will best support what you want to say, but you must have a plan to help your reader stay with you. (Refer to chapter 12 to review these organizational patterns.)

 Choose an organizational plan before you start writing.

Drafting

Once you've done your mental planning, know your focus, have picked your organizational plan, and have jotted down ideas to support your theme, you are ready to write. This stage is called drafting. Using the ideas generated in your prewriting notes and following the organization pattern you've selected, you begin to write. Because you've spent a good deal of time preparing, your ideas should flow easily from one to the next.

The Opening

This is the time when you want to think about your attention-grabbing opener. A journalism teacher might call it a lead. The ELA TAKS graders call it engaging the reader. In any event, you need to think of something that will immediately capture your graders' attention—a question, a quote, a word, a brief narrative—something that will quickly set your essay apart from all the other juniors writing on the same prompt. But the opening must be relevant. It needs to hint at, or announce, what will come, inviting the reader into your piece. Within the construction of the composition, this opening idea will need to be fully developed, with depth and insight, not just explained with examples. So be sure to think through this stage carefully.

For example, if you were writing on the prompt mentioned above, discussing the validity of first impressions, you might open your essay as this student did.

> "'How primitive!' I thought to myself when I searched through the night club for a restroom. Our ship had just docked in France for our yearlong stay—our Junior Year of College Abroad—and the only restroom available to foreign students was a hole in the floor. Both sexes used it, one group at a time. I was disgusted. I thought the French had no idea of civilized behavior, until much later in my stay when I began to realize that a different way of living was not necessarily a bad thing."

The writer opened with a brief narrative, yet hinted at the idea that first impressions can be changed. Such an essay could easily sustain the theme that "a different way of living was not necessarily a bad thing" through insight and description. Thus, this would be an effective beginning for a reflective piece.

Transitions

But any beginning is just the start. Once you have your opening, continue drafting the essay, paying close attention to the links, or transitions, to use between sentences and paragraphs. When correctly used, they should go unnoticed, pulling the reader along from one idea to the next. Some, for example, tell your reader that you are continuing to give more ideas along the same line. *Next*, *another thing*, and *in addition* do this. Others, like *however* and *although*, tell your reader you are switching to another thought. You can use transitions to show contrast, to indicate that the ideas are building in importance, or to show that there are other categories to consider. For example:

 For similarities use *also, similarly, just as*

 For contrasts use *but, however, on the other hand*

 For cause and effect use *therefore, thus, consequently*

 For time use *before, during, earlier, then, later, meanwhile*

 For examples use *for example, for instance*

 For conclusions use *in conclusion, finally, thus*

Although using good transitions may seem like a small detail, it is what separates a good writer from an ordinary one, or a choppy essay from a flowing one.

 As your write, plan your transitions carefully.

As you continue to write, use information from your prewriting notes as a launch pad for your ideas. When drafting you must go beyond your first noted recollections and details to come up with fresh observations and conclusions. This is what is meant by *development*. Your writing must show depth and substance, not just examples and details. You must make some emotional connection to the prompt by offering your feelings, thoughts, and impressions.

As you write, say the following to yourself:

 This is important because . . .

 This is true because . . .

 I believe this because . . .

 This will make a difference because . . .

 Ask yourself: Why? Why? Why?

Ending

And don't forget the conclusion. The ELA TAKS must sound like a finished piece of writing, so make sure you leave yourself enough room at the end of the essay to tie everything together. Wrap up your thoughts crisply and neatly, connecting your ideas to the opening paragraph so that the essay comes full circle. You mustn't leave your reader hanging.

For example:

> Even though sharing a restroom with both sexes will never be comfortable to me, I recognize that it is part of French culture. I regret wasting the first few weeks I lived in France during my junior year of college with a disdainful attitude. My first impression based on this one experience was certainly neither accurate nor indicative of all I was to learn and appreciate from the French. Regretfully, as in my case, sometimes first impressions can be deceiving.

 All essays must have a strong conclusion.

Revising and Editing

Once you have completed your draft, you are now ready to get down to the core of writing and revise your essay. This is where the thesaurus and dictionary will come in handy. If you feel like you are saying the same thing over and over again, find other words to convey the same thoughts or refine your ideas. Professional writers keep these reference tools at hand as they work, and they use them. You must, too.

This is also the time to rethink your conclusion, to be sure it is effective. Ask yourself some questions. Will the reader clearly understand my message? Have I provided enough information to show that I believe what I've said? Have I written from the heart?

If so, great!

If not, you can still add ideas, change words, or reorganize. Until you commit your words to the answer document, your essay is still a work-in-progress. Keep rereading and rewriting until you are completely satisfied.

Proofreading

You are now ready for the final step: proofreading. This is the time that you go back over your draft looking for anything that might stand out as an error. (This topic will be covered in detail in chapters 14 and 15.) But it goes without saying that your spelling and capitalization have to be correct. You need to be sure you have not confused homonyms (e.g., their, they're, there). You need to use your thumbs to check sentence boundaries. Place one thumb at the beginning and one thumb at the end to make sure that the information from period to period is a complete thought. Even reading your composition backward—from the last sentence to the first—to see if each sentence is complete can help. And remember, you can still use those reference books. Don't leave anything to chance.

Finally, it is time to transfer what you have developed, carefully and neatly, onto the answer document. Clearly indicate your introduction and conclusion with paragraph breaks. Write carefully and neatly. Judges might be negatively influenced if handwriting is illegible. Be sure the reader will see and understand every one of your developed ideas.

Then sit back and relax.

You did it.

You've written an ELA TAKS essay that you know will meet the standards of the grader. You have prewritten, drafted, revised and edited, proofread, and finalized. Your work has a great opening, which is strongly supported throughout with insightful writing, and you've concluded well.

You are done.

All your hard work has paid off.

The ELA TAKS composition is over, and you are heading home.

To get to this point, though, you must practice. Write as often as you can about everything going on around you. If you've never before kept a journal, now is the time to start. Try turning journal entries into essays. Ask others to read your pieces and tell you what they think.

In this case, as in most, practice really does help.

 Good writing takes practice.

Practice, Practice, Practice

But now it is time to pick up your pencil and see what you can do.

Remember the imaginary triplet previously mentioned? It was based on a literary piece about a teenager new to this country, struggling to embrace it as home, followed by an excerpt from Christopher Columbus's diary, where he recorded his first impressions of the Americas. Then an advertisement from a travel agency encouraging you to visit a foreign country was presented.

When you have at least an hour, sit down with a dictionary and thesaurus and write an essay based on the prompt we've been discussing, just as you would for ELA TAKS: prewrite, draft, revise and edit, and proofread. Be sure to develop a specific focus and plan your organization. Check your writing for development, transitions, and correct grammar. These are the elements that the graders will evaluate when you take the real test.

Below you will find some questions to help you get started. When you are done, compare your answer to the sample essay that follows.

> **Write an essay in which you explain the validity of a person's first impressions.**

Questions to ask about the prompt:
  What is validity?

  What are first impressions?

  When have I formed first impressions?
    Example 1

    Example 2

  When have I witnessed an initial first impression being formed about me or someone else?
    Example 1

    Example 2

What other things could I say about first impressions based on:
A book I've read

A movie I've seen

Songs I've heard

A TV show I remember

How does the idea of a first impression relate to history?
Example 1

Example 2

How does the idea of a first impression relate to modern times?
Example 1

Example 2

When I look at my notes above, I could write about the following:

This would be a good thesis statement:

Describe the organizational pattern you plan to use to develop your ideas.

What transitions would help support the organizational plan described above?

Now use the planning space and lined pages to write your essay.

Prewriting/Planning Space

Sample Response

First, let's look at a sample another student wrote and evaluate it.

We all make judgments based on first impressions. Sometimes they are correct; sometimes they are misleading, but it is what we choose to do with these instinctive reactions that gives them validity.

I remember my first day of high school. The halls seemed to disappear into a never ending maze. We had only five minutes to get to our lockers, exchange books, visit the restroom, and find our next class. The numbers above the doors didn't make sense, and after a fiasco where I ended up in first hall when my Spanish class was in third, I wanted to run away. My first impression of high school made me think that I was looking at four miserable years.

In history class, though, I learned that first impressions can be deceiving by thinking about what happened to the early settlers who landed at Jamestown. Only one-third survived the first winter, eating the sparse plants, nuts, and fish. Only half of the Pilgrims who arrived at Plymouth survived their first winter. If they were relying on Columbus's enchanted description of the new world, his first impressions had misled them.

Another group of settlers arrived ten years later, and came prepared for this new venture. Their ships were loaded with food, clothing, and livestock. Although they were perhaps intrigued by first impressions, they studied the situation, applied their learning to their needs and made the provisions necessary to adapt.

So, if I have first impressions, how can I make them work for me? Like the Jamestown colonists, perhaps I should be cautious of what I initially hear and see and be willing to make adjustments as need be. Perhaps, too, I could show more tolerance to adverse scenarios, asking for help when necessary from the more experienced traveler.

Fortunately for me, my first impressions of my high school were quickly changed. My first week I was adopted by a more experienced traveler. My Big Sister walked me through the building and filled me in on all the short cuts. I now easily maneuver from classroom to classroom. The numbers of the rooms make perfect sense. I even have time to stop by the restroom and quickly say "hi" to my friends.

We all may make judgments based on first impressions, but I am glad I learned to give a second or third look a try. First impressions are valid. They give us an initial perspective upon which to build, but they mustn't be absolute. Their only truth lies in a momentary imprint, providing us a foundation for growth.

ELA TAKS-like analysis: This student has maintained a central theme throughout the piece, stating that although first impressions can be true, they are only the beginning of an experience. The progression of ideas is logical and smooth, and effective word choice adds interest and insight to the essay. Personal experience offers a unique perspective, and the coherence of the essay is further strengthened by the conclusion. Overall this composition would probably be awarded a high 3 or a low 4.

Now go back and analyze your own piece. Review the rubric at the end of the chapter (page 60). Highlight the differences as the evaluations move from 1 to 4 in each objective. Have you met all the requirements for 4? Does your piece progress in a smooth and coherent way? Did you have a strong organizational pattern? Were your transitions clear? Did you connect and hold the reader's interest? Was your writing error free?

Remember that the graders are expecting a polished draft, so at this point you would want to refine all the good things you have written and throw out the bad.

Describe your attention grabber. Does it work?

What was your theme? (If you can't state it, you probably don't have one)

How did you keep this theme alive throughout your writing?

How does your organizational pattern affect the rest of the writing?

Did your transitions work? Why or why not?

How do you show depth or insight in the writing?

How does your writing apply to your own life or observations?

What are your original ideas—that is, ideas unique only to you?

Have you used a dictionary to check your spelling, word choice, and usage?

Final Thoughts

On ELA TAKS test day, only when completely satisfied with your essay, only when you know there is not one thing more you could do to improve your composition, would you write it onto the two pages provided on the answer document. If you've taken your time and thoughtfully composed your answer; if you've checked your dictionary, used your thesaurus and carefully edited your first draft; if your theme is clear and your writing sincere; then you can smile.

You are done.

All your hard work has paid off. You have succeeded on the ELA TAKS essay in your own way, with your own style.

And it does feel good.

Review Box
→ Practice writing on a daily basis.
→ Pay attention to life around you. Notice how things affect you.
→ On test day, take your time. Prewrite, draft, edit and revise, and proofread before committing your essay to the answer document.
→ Use your dictionary and thesaurus when writing.
→ Study the rubric. Know how to earn a 4.

Writing Rubric

	1	2	3	4
Focus and Coherence	• paragraph and/or composition is unfocused • little, or no, sense of completeness • poorly developed, does not answer prompt	• paragraph and/or composition is slightly focused • some sense of completeness • poorly developed, redundant wording	• paragraph and/or composition is mostly focused • sense of completeness • most writing contributes to development	• paragraph and/or composition is focused • sense of completeness, meaningful introduction and conclusion • most, if not all, writing contributes to development
Organization	• progression is illogical, with no transitions • no organizational pattern; ideas presented in random manner • wordiness or repetition hinders understanding	• progression not always logical and smooth • organizational pattern ineffective • some wordiness or repetition, but ideas clear	• progression is generally smooth and controlled • organizational pattern is generally effective • progression is not hindered by minor wordiness or repetition	• progression is smooth and controlled • organizational pattern enhances presentation of ideas • words flow smoothly and coherently
Development of Ideas	• presents ideas, but no development • presents ideas, but development is too vague to understand • presents a plot summary of another published work • omits information that hinders understanding	• attempts development by listing ideas • attempts development but too general and inconsistent • omits small pieces of information, which creates holes but does not prevent understanding of ideas	• attempts development of all ideas included • some ideas thoughtful, but little compositional risk	• thorough development • presentation of ideas is thoughtful or insightful; willingness to take compositional risks enhances understanding
Voice	• writer does not connect with the reader • little or no sense of the writer's personality • unique perspective not expressed	• connection to readers established but not maintained • some sections sound original; has difficulty expressing individuality	• reader is engaged throughout most of the composition • most of the composition sounds authentic; generally expresses individual perspective	• reader is engaged and sustained throughout composition • sounds authentic and original; individuality or unique perspective is expressed
Conventions (spelling, capitalization, punctuation, grammar, usage, sentence structure)	• little or no evidence that writer can correctly use the English language • misused or omitted words; awkward sentences • mistakes interfere with effective communication of ideas	• errors in conventions indicate a limited control of language • may include some simple or inaccurate words and phrases • mistakes weaken the effective communication of ideas	• generally demonstrates a good command of conventions; few disruptions in the flow of the composition • words and phrases are generally appropriate; ideas effectively communicated	• the strength of the conventions adds to the composition • words and phrases enhance the effectiveness of communication

Part Three

Mastering Objectives 1, 2, and 3

Chapter 6

Identifying Literary Elements

You are sitting in a movie. The lights are low and the popcorn fresh. The music begins. You hear a quick beat and a perky melody. The camera pans into a scene of a classroom where students are throwing paper wads and chewing gum. And you *know* that the story is a comedy. Why? Because the director's choice of certain sounds and images pull from us an expected response.

Writers do the same when they write, but not with music, lights, and visual pictures. Writers use words to convey their ideas, and it is by connecting with these words that you, the reader, mentally form the picture the author has penned.

Descriptive Details

Are the main characters wearing blue jeans and team sweatshirts? Is their hair braided? Is it long? Short? How do they walk? Talk? Do they slur their words? Use a minimal vocabulary? Or do they ramble on, making absolutely no sense?

Does the author open the story in a graveyard or a mall? At the prom or on the basketball court? Is the team winning or losing? Is the viewpoint that of a player or a cheerleader?

It is through a specific choice of descriptive words that the author immerses the reader in a scene. The author shapes his character into a personality the reader can understand, and then places a stumbling block in the character's path. And it is the handling of this obstacle, or conflict that evolves into a plot. Through the main character's specific response, the conflict is resolved, and the outcome reveals an underlying theme.

Story Structure

Setting, characterization, plot, conflict, and theme, are all literary elements you have been studying in English classes for years. And through these studies you have developed an ingrained sense of story structure. To do well on ELA TAKS, though, you have to step back a bit and analyze exactly how a writer does what he does. You must take the text apart and look separately at the techniques a writer uses. Then you can apply what you already know, and answer the questions well.

For example, there are many different ways an author can show characterization. Physical description, of course, is one. But how characters dress, what they say or even don't say, the way they walk, carry themselves, live, the jobs they have and the cars they drive all define nuances of personality, as does their reaction to and treatment of those around them.

Characterization

What can you tell about the character below from this brief description? [All excerpts from *The Devil and Tom Walker* by Washington Irving]

> He reposed himself for some time on the trunk of a fallen hemlock, listening to the boding cry of the tree toad, and delving with his walking staff into a mound of black mold at his feet. As he turned up the soil unconsciously, his staff struck against something hard. He raked it out of the vegetable mould, and lo! a cloven skull with an Indian tomahawk buried deep in it, lay before him. The rust on the weapon showed the time that had elapsed since this death blow had been given. It was a dreary memento of the fierce struggle that had taken place in this last foothold of the Indian warriors.
>
> "Humph!" said Tom Walker, as he gave the skull a kick to shake the dirt from it.

No physical description is given, but you do get a glimpse into the character's personality. This is certainly not someone who is shy or particularly superstitious. When the skull turns up, he simply bats it away, and the reader learns a great deal in that tiny action.

These are the types of details an observant reader notes, and these are the fine points that can lend validity and interest to an answer. If, in an open-ended response you said, "Tom Walker's disregard for the relics of the dead is evidenced when he tosses the skull away," it has a much more powerful impact than, "Tom Walker didn't respect the dead." The latter may be true, but without supporting details drawn from the text the statement falls flat.

Setting

Let's take another look at Irving, this time at his depiction of setting.

> One day that Tom Walker had been to a distant part of the neighbourhood, he took what he considered a short cut homewards through the swamp. Like most short cuts, it was an ill chosen route. The swamp was

thickly grown with great gloomy pines and hemlocks, some of them ninety feet high; which made it dark at noonday, and a retreat for all the owls of the neighbourhood. It was full of pits and quagmires, partly covered with weeds and mosses; where the green surface often betrayed the traveller into a gulf of black smothering mud; there were also dark and stagnant pools, the abodes of the tadpole, the bull-frog, and the water snake, and where trunks of pines and hemlocks lay half drowned, half rotting, looking like alligators, sleeping in the mire.

No doubt, this is not a place you'd want your junior class to hold the prom! Through carefully penned details, you get a picture of a dismal, threatening environment. Words like *ill chosen*, *gloomy*, *dark*, *quagmires*, and *stagnant* conjure up images of doom, not to mention the simile that compares tree trunks to sleeping alligators.

If you were responding to an open-ended question that asked, "What effect did the environment have on Tom Walker?" you would not want to say, "It was scary." You would want to add the same details Irving used to draw you into his chilling swamp, and then contrast them with Walker's nonchalant attitude.

Literary Terms and Techniques

For ELA TAKS you will have to not only recognize various literary terms but also understand the way they influence the writing. Just remember, nothing an author does at this level is by chance. If there is an ant in the story, it is there for a reason. Ask yourself, "Why?"

Because questions on the exam referring to literary techniques are many and varied, it is important that you take the time to understand what is being asked. It is possible that a question will be worded differently from what you are used to. Rather than asking for the *conflict* the question may ask for the *obstacle* or *problem*. Rather than asking for *characterization* the test may ask for a *character trait*. Or, you may be asked to identify a simile, a metaphor, a flashback, the antagonist, a stereotype, or imagery. If you think of all the things that your English teacher has covered, the list could go on and on.

 Be sure you read each question carefully.

Remember, though, that you don't have to memorize the definitions to all these terms, because you have your dictionary. Look up any word that leaves you feeling the least bit doubtful. Get comfortable with the definition, and then think, analyze, and evaluate. The ELA TAKS test is not going to ask a simple, elementary school–type question like, "Who is the main character?" Rather, it is going to ask you to apply the information from the dictionary to the literary piece.

For example, a question might ask, "What motivates the main character to respond bravely?" To answer, you would not only have to identify the main character but also understand his or her inner motivation and how it applies to the act of bravery.

Literary elements are dealt with on both the multiple-choice portion of the test and the open-ended question. In both sections, you must think about why the author has chosen to present the material in a specific way. Ask yourself, what does the author want me to think?

On the other hand, an objective question might ask why the author used a particular literary technique, like a simile, in a certain paragraph or line. Using the testing strategies discussed in chapter 4, first verify the definition for a simile (using the dictionary, if you are unsure), and then examine the question to be sure you understand what is being asked. Find the line or paragraph in the passage, reread, answer the question, and move on. You've done it a thousand times in English class, so it should just be another day's work.

So let's practice.

Practice, Practice, Practice

Below are two literary passages, similar to but shorter than the ones that will appear on ELA TAKS. Read them both, then answer the questions that follow.

"Ripe Figs"
by Kate Chopin

Notes

1   Maman-Nainaine said that when the figs were ripe Babette might go to visit her cousins down on the Bayou-Lafourche where the sugar cane grows. Not that the ripening of figs had the least thing to do with it, but that is the way Maman-Nainaine was.

2   It seemed to Babette a very long time to wait, for the leaves upon the trees were tender yet, and the figs were like little hard, green marbles.

3   But warm rains came along and plenty of strong sunshine, and though Maman-Nainaine was as patient as the statue of La Madone, and Babette as restless as a humming-bird, the first thing they both knew it was hot summertime. Every day Babette danced out to where the fig-trees were in a long line against the fence. She walked slowly beneath them, carefully peering between the gnarled, spreading branches. But each time she came disconsolate away again. What she saw there finally was something that made her sing and dance the whole long day.

4   When Maman-Nainaine sat down in her stately way to breakfast, the following morning, her muslin cap standing like an aureole about her white, placid face, Babette approached. She bore a dainty porcelain platter, which she set down before her godmother. It contained a dozen purple figs, fringed around with their rich, green leaves.

5   "Ah," said Maman-Nainaine arching her eyebrows, "how early the figs have ripened this year!"

6   "Oh," said Babette. "I think they have ripened very late."

7   "Babette," continued Maman-Nainaine, as she peeled the very plumpest figs with her pointed silver fruit-knife, "you will carry my love to them all down on Bayou-Lafourche. And tell your Tante Frosine I shall look for her at Toussaint—when the chrysanthemums are in bloom."

[Thoreau is a nature writer who went to live at Walden Pond in a very simple dwelling in an effort to discover the meaning of life through the study of nature. His introduction explains that he wanted to learn what nature had to teach.]

"Spring"
from *Walden* by Henry David Thoreau

1   One attraction in coming to the woods to live was that I should have leisure and opportunity to see the Spring come in. The ice in the pond at length begins to be honeycombed, and I can set my heel in it as I walk. Fogs and rains and warmer suns are gradually melting the snow; the days have grown sensibly longer; and I see how I shall get through the winter without adding to my wood-pile, for large fires are no longer necessary. I am on the alert for the first signs of spring, to hear the chance note of some arriving bird, or the striped squirrel's chirp, for his stores must be now nearly exhausted, or see the woodchuck venture out of his winter quarters . . . .
. . .

2   The change from storm and winter to serene and mild weather, from dark and sluggish hours to bright and elastic ones, is a memorable crisis which all things proclaim. It is seemingly instantaneous at last. Suddenly an influx of light filled my house, though the evening was at hand, and the clouds of winter still overhung it, and the eaves were dripping with sleety rain. I looked out the window, and lo! where yesterday was cold gray ice there lay the transparent pond already calm and full of hope as in a summer evening, reflecting a summer evening sky in its bosom, though none was visible overhead, as if it had intelligence with some remote horizon . . . .

Multiple-Choice Questions

1. In "Ripe Figs," Chopin uses a simile in paragraph 2 to—
   A indicate the sheen of the figs
   B help the reader understand how long Babette would have to wait
   C indicate the size of the figs
   D emphasize that the figs were hard

2. In "Ripe Figs," Chopin uses what literary device in the dialogue between Babette and her godmother in paragraphs 5 and 6?
   F Setting
   G Allusion
   H Alliteration
   J Irony

3. Which of the following lines expresses a theme in "Ripe Figs?"
   A There is a time and place for everything to happen.
   B Patience is a virtue.
   C Pleasing adults is difficult for young people.
   D Some people really enjoy figs.

4. In "Ripe Figs," what is Babette's attitude toward Maman-Nainaine?
   F She resents her authority.
   G She rebels against her.
   H She tries to please her.
   J She follows Maman's restrictions, learning to celebrate patience.

5. In Chopin's story, what do ripe figs symbolize?
   A They symbolize the tyranny of adults over youth.
   B They symbolize ripening fruit.
   C They symbolize young people maturing.
   D They symbolize the errors in the decision-making process.

6. In the second sentence of "Spring," Thoreau uses sensory images to—
   F demonstrate the changing season
   G describe the texture of the pond
   H explain what he was feeling
   J make the reader visualize the season

7. Why does Thoreau write "Spring" from the first person point of view?
   A He was afraid people wouldn't understand unless he made it personal.
   B He knew that if it were written by an observer it would be too technical.
   C He wanted to present his own philosophy and share his observations.
   D He needed the money to support himself.

8. Why did Thoreau use contrast in the second paragraph?
   F He wanted to prove what he observed by living in nature through several seasons.
   G He wanted to show the positives and negatives in nature.
   H He wanted to heighten the drama in nature.
   J He wanted to confuse the reader.

9. Why did Thoreau choose Walden Pond as the setting for "Spring?"
   A It was a quiet place where he could focus on nature.
   B That is where he was living.
   C He thought it would please his mentor, Ralph Waldo Emerson.
   D He had already observed other seasons at that same location.

Answer Explanations

Now let's look at the answers.

Question 1: From either your memory or by using the dictionary you know that a simile is used to make a comparison, so ask yourself, what two things are being compared? What connection does the author want us to make between figs and marbles? Marbles are shiny, hard, and about ⅜" in diameter. All of the answers seem to be reasonable responses.

What if you are not familiar with a fig? Look for other information given about this fruit in the story. Note that at the end Babette presents twelve purple figs. Also note that the godmother peeled the plumpest with a fruit knife. You could guess from this that the change from hard, shiny green marble-sized fruit to a plump, purple fruit large enough to peel with a fruit knife would require time. Chopin creates meaning (the passing of time and how hard it is to wait when you really want something) with this comparison, so the best answer is **B**.

Question 2: First, if you don't know the meaning of *allusion*, *alliteration*, or *irony*, look up the word in the dictionary. Then, when you are confident of your terms, review the passage. Note that Maman-Nainaine said the figs had ripened early, whereas Babette replied they were late. This is a contrast in the opinions of the two characters, and one definition of *irony* is saying one thing and meaning another. In the banter between the two characters, neither seems to be saying exactly what they mean. Rather, the dialogue seems intentionally used in this brief story to point out the difference between the two characters, the irony of the contrast of their characters. Of course, the story has a setting, but it is not emphasized in the dialogue, nor are allusion and alliteration. So your best answer is **J**.

Question 3: Answers **C** and **D** can be eliminated because they are too limited to one part of this story. Remember a theme must relate not only to the whole story but also to those who read it. **B** can be eliminated because it is too broad. It goes beyond the story. So the best choice is **A**. The story suggests that Babette must wait for the right time. Just as the figs ripen in due season, timing plays a role in peoples' lives as well.

Question 4: Both **F** and **G** can be eliminated immediately. Although resentment and rebellion would be possible reactions, nothing in the text indicates that Babette has these negative feelings. Answer **H** is possible. She does wait patiently for the figs to ripen and is constantly looking for the first signs. But, **J** is better. It states exactly what Babette does.

What she finally saw on the branches was something that made her heart sing and dance the whole day long. She took the ripened figs to Maman-Nainaine the next day just as requested and presented them to her on a porcelain platter with their leaves prominently displayed. She was demonstrating and celebrating the restrictions.

Question 5: You can eliminate **B** because both *figs* and *fruit* are concrete things that the eye can see. A symbol generally goes beyond physical references. This seemed to be a positive story, so tyranny and errors in **A** and **D** can be eliminated. Answer **C** is the best answer because we can see that Babette's godmother wanted her to wait until the time was right for her to go on her trip. Just as Babette knew when to pick the figs to serve to her godmother, her godmother knew when Babette was ready to move on.

Questions about symbolism generally relate to the text as a whole. Usually, the symbol is something the eye can see and what it represents something the eye cannot see. You can probably eliminate one or two answer choices through the positive-negative approach here: Is the object used a good or positive one? If so, the unseen should also be good or positive. If the object has negative connotations, so should what it represents.

Question 6: Although the term *sensory imagery* might throw you at first, use your strategies. Look up *sensory* and then *imagery* in the dictionary. From this, you can draw the conclusion that sensory imagery is something that appeals to the five senses and makes a mental image.

Then go back to the paragraph or line cited and reread. Which sense is being used in the description? Taste? Smell? Is there more than one sense? Who is experiencing the sensation?

Note that once again you have been asked to recognize how a literary technique enhances the meaning. So you have to go beyond mere description. Think of what you know about ice—how it has a slick, cold, smooth finish. Then ask yourself what you know about a honeycomb. If you don't know what a honeycomb is, look it up. Then think about how bees enter and exit a honeycomb, through holes that form a rough surface.

The sensation Thoreau alludes to in this sentence is touch, or texture. He is not talking about emotions but about physical sensation. So the best answer is **G**.

Question 7: Answer **D** can be immediately eliminated because there is no mention of finances in the piece or in the introduction. **A** can be eliminated because there is no mention or allusion to fear on Thoreau's part. Answer **B** can be eliminated because there is no reference to that in the text, the explanatory material, or that period of history. This leaves **C**, which fits. Overall, this seems to be a philosophical piece, wherein the author's observations of nature offer his individual interpretation of life.

Questions considering point of view might relate to the effect of using that particular point of view. What if another person told the story? How would it change? Come up with your own idea, and then look at the possible answers. Just because yours is there, don't eliminate the others. Chances are yours is correct, but the test makers may have had another answer in mind. Because you can't defend your answer here (like you can in the open-ended responses), be sure you give fair consideration to the other options.

Question 8: Answer **J** can be eliminated immediately. Why would Thoreau want to confuse anyone if the introduction said that he wanted to learn? Answers **F** and **G** are both possibilities, but "Spring" talks about only one season. On first glance, **G** seems obvious, but remember that the introduction said Thoreau wanted to learn, and this answer doesn't show learning. So ask yourself, why did the author use contrasts? What is the impact on the piece as a whole? With this line of thinking, the best answer is **H**, because the use of contrasts definitely "heightens the drama in nature," something that Thoreau seems to have learned.

A question might consider why a certain reference or allusion was made. These allusions are probably well known to you in history, literature, politics, current events, or the fine arts, but check to see if they have footnotes explaining them or if there is an explanation before or after the piece. If there is, it is because it is important. Use it. Remember that the correct answer has to be reasonable. Think like the test makers think, or think like your teacher. How did the symbol or allusion clarify the writing?

Question 9: Answer **C** is not evident in the text or the introductory material, so it can be eliminated even though it is reasonable and shows that you know the time frame and literary community. Answers **A** and **B** seem to both be correct, but remember you are looking for the *best* answer. Answer **D** shows the effect of using this particular setting as supported in the introduction, and so **D** is the correct answer. It goes beyond the obvious and shows analysis. Therefore, it is the *best* choice.

Open-Ended Response Practice

Finally, let's look at how an open-ended question might include a literary element. The basic strategies to use for answering this type of question were covered in chapter 5, but it is always good to practice.

A short answer question for these two pieces might ask:

What was the effect of the similes in paragraph 3 of "Ripe Figs?"

First, go back to that paragraph. Do you remember what a simile is? If not, look it up. Once you understand that it is a form of comparison between things that are basically unalike, using *like* or *as*, go back to the passage. Highlight where you think the simile falls. Then think of how that comparison helped you to better understand that character or idea.

Practice answering the questions here:

> **What was the effect of the similes in the paragraph 3 of "Ripe Figs?"**

Planning Space

_____
_____
_____
_____
_____

Did you see that Maman was "as patient as a statue?" What did that suggest? Does a statue ever change? Is a statue frozen in time? In contrast, then, did you note that Babette "was as restless as a hummingbird?" Do you know that a hummingbird is a small bird with wings capable of beating very rapidly, and it is named for the humming sound that these vibrating wings produce? You would have, if you had used your dictionary. A mental image would be forming, and with it the contrast.

 You must reference the text to receive credit for an open-ended answer.

Sample Answer

Your answer might have been something like this:

> In the third paragraph, Babette was compared to a rapidly and constantly moving hummingbird. Maman was compared to a statue. This suggests a significant contrast of their personalities and goals. This is the conflict that opens the plot of the story.

This response shows that you have not only identified the similes but also analyzed how they have impacted this piece of literature, and that you know the elements of the development of the plot in a narrative piece.

Another question might involve the literary devices in both pieces. For example, what was the importance of the passing of time in these two pieces?

As this question covers both pieces, you would have eight lines in which to respond, and remember, you must reference both pieces.

Go back into the pieces and use the side-note space to make notes about time. Then practice answering below.

Practice, Practice, and More Practice

> What was the importance of the passing of time in these two pieces?

Planning Space

"Ripe Figs" covered a growing season for fruit, from spring (leaves were tender) to sometime during or following "hot summertime."

"Spring" began with the ice in the pond beginning to honeycomb, finally transitioning to a "transparent pond already calm and full of hope."

So ask yourself, what do these two pieces both say about time?

Sample Answer

Your answer might have been:

> Both "Ripe Figs" and "Spring" talk about the passing of time. In "Ripe Figs," it was necessary for time to pass for the figs to grow to their full size to be enjoyed, just as it was necessary for Babette to grow and mature to appreciate her role as a young woman; it made her "sing and dance the whole day." In "Spring" the change from "Dark and sluggish hours to bright and elastic ones" made Thoreau feel as if nature "had intelligence with some remote horizon." Both pieces therefore suggest that the passing of time is a natural process and necessary for a fulfilled life.

Do you see how this response uses information from both pieces to evaluate why the passing of time was important in each and in what they shared?

Be sure to check you answer with the rubric on page 41. Make sure you have added everything to earn a 3, or exlempary.

Final Thoughts

And there you have it.

An author makes conscious choices in writing, choices that bring out an expected response from the reader. Answering questions that include literary elements isn't any harder than answering other kinds of questions. Just remember to take your time and think like a writer.

It is that simple.

Review Box
→ Carefully read each question so you know exactly what is being asked.
→ Refer to your dictionary to clarify the literary terms.
→ Be sure to reference the triplet when answering the open-ended questions.
→ Look for what the author wants you to believe.

Chapter 7

Utilizing Reading Strategies

Ever since you first recognized the Golden Arches of McDonalds you've been reading. So you can read. You know you can read. What's the big deal?

Well, the reading section of the ELA TAKS test isn't so much about the physical aspects of reading, such as recognizing different words, as it is about comprehending what you have read. Understanding and grasping the meaning of written material, really getting to the core of what the words convey, is a talent that, with a little work and lots of practice, can be strengthened.

How?

Read.

It is as simple as that.

Read. Read. Read.

Think of it this way. When you take on any new activity, say a new sport or hobby, at first it seems awkward and perhaps even difficult. However, as you gain confidence and awareness about what you are doing, that activity becomes easier.

The same is true of reading. The more you read, the easier it gets. Your vocabulary becomes stronger, your speed improves, and you become grounded in common reading proficiencies. The skills you had to think about when you first encountered the written word become second nature. You don't even have to think about what you are doing. It just happens.

Sustained Reading

To improve, though, you must engage in sustained reading, that is reading for at least fifteen minutes or longer. The material doesn't matter. It could be a novel, a magazine article, information from an on-line site, or even a newspaper article. But you must read for at least fifteen minutes at a time.

Doing this consistently, once or twice a day, just as you would eagerly practice a new sport or take up a new hobby, is the best way to ensure success on the reading portion of the ELA TAKS test.

You can also prepare by specifically reviewing individual reading skills to sharpen your test-taking strategies. So let's start with a look at what teachers call cause and effect questions.

Cause and Effect Questions

Simply put, these are *what* and *why* questions on the ELA TAKS test. The *what* questions are almost always based on simple details that can be found directly in the text. Take your time. Look for the answer, and find it.

The *why* questions are not as obvious because the answers are typically based on an analysis of the reading. As with all answers, though, if you remember that your conclusion must be based on the offered triplet and that you should be able to defend any choice you make with information found in the passage, a reasonable answer can be determined.

 Construct your own answer before looking at the possible choices.

Questions on the test, however, may be camouflaged and not actually use the words *what* and *why*. For example, the following might be stated as a question: "In this passage, the author quotes from Thoreau in order to—"

Essentially, this question is asking what effect the Thoreau quote has on the author's message. So you might ask yourself, "Why does the author quote from Thoreau?" Although the words *what* and *why* are not evident in the question, it is still asking you to apply cause and effect thinking skills.

Words that might appear in a cause and effect question:
because, as a result of, since, in order to

Also, wording in the question will sometimes take on a different form than that found in the passage. For example, the passage may have a reference to the year 1903, whereas the question may ask, "What occurred at the beginning of the twentieth century to change the author's life?" As a reader, you have to connect 1903 to the beginning of the twentieth century.

In thinking back to "Up from Slavery," from chapter 4 (see page 36), a multiple-choice question covering cause and effect might be something like:

Example A: Washington states that slaves took on new names because—
A new names conveyed a sense of the complete person
B they didn't like their old names
C it was a sign of freedom
D they needed new names to enroll in school

This question is simply asking *why* the slaves took on new names, so it is a simple *cause* question. The answer, of course, is **C** and is stated directly in the passage.

A possible open-ended question might be:

> **What was the significance of a slave changing his or her name?**

This question is asking for the outcome or *effect* of a name change. What impact did it have on a slave's life?

A possible answer might be:

> Washington points out in "Up from Slavery" that for many slaves a name change was "one of the first signs of freedom." It marked a new beginning, one that would become the foundation of a heritage to come and encourage generations.

The key is to always read for meaning. Be careful of questions where wording and paraphrasing disguise the intent. Cause and effect questions will always ask you to make a connection between one event and another, and if you can justify your answer with information in the triplet, you will be okay.

Always base your conclusions with information in the passage.

Sequencing

Sequencing is another skill that might be tested on ELA TAKS. Any time a question asks what happened first, last, or third, for example, it is a sequencing question. Also, any question hinting at the need to follow directions falls into this category.

Generally these questions are pretty easy, unless there is a flashback in the passage or the writing doesn't follow a normal time sequence.

 Words that might appear in a sequencing question:
after, before, first, second, third, last, finally, later than, next

If the time sequence is chronological—that is, it flows from the beginning to the end in a successive pattern—the easiest way to answer the question is to find each possible response and mark it on the passage. Then you can clearly see the order.

If the time sequence is not chronological, though, as in a flashback, draw a time line. Mark each event on the time line in relation to when it occurs. Then you should be able to pick out the correct answer.

For example, read the passage below, paying special attention to the sequence of events.

Changes

1   Michael stared at Kara's reflection in the mirror. She looked so, what was the word? Distant?
2   No, more like unaware.
3   But that was okay. Today was her day, not his, her time to shine. And she looked magnificent, ready to take on the world.
4   But, then, she always had it together. Like the day he'd slid into second base and broken his arm when he was eight. They'd been playing alone in the back lot, just the two of them, and she'd raced more than a mile to Mrs. Morrison's to get help.
5   How many years had they been friends? Ten? Twelve?
6   No, they'd known each other since before kindergarten. It was Kara who'd held Michael's hand the first day of school, leading him into the building to introduce him to his teacher. Then, before he could cave, she'd given him a big hug and bounded off for her own adventures in first grade.
7   Their families had always lived side by side, at least for as long as either could remember. The two had played T-ball in spring, soccer in summer and baked cookies at Christmas time. Two little kids, together, battling the world.

Notes

8   When Kara began to change, grow in ways that defied explanation, he'd laughed and teased her, but he didn't know why. They still rented movies and popped corn on Saturday afternoon. They still went to the opening day of baseball season.

9   Even Cody hadn't come between them. Oh, he'd tried, not out of meanness, more out of confusion. Eventually, though, he'd learned to accept their friendship as an essential part of who Kara was.

10 "So how do I look?" she asked, adjusting her cap.

11 "Great," Michael said. "But I think the tassel goes on the left side." He reached up and flipped it over the square rim, and she beamed. This was indeed her day. She was graduating, going off to places unknown, going away, leaving him to finish his senior year alone.

12 Her eye caught his.

13 "Are we okay?" she said turning toward him.

14 He started a bit. Kara unsure?

15 "Why wouldn't we be?" he asked, and her only answer was a shrug.

16 "Hey," he said, surprised by the look of uncertainty in her eyes. "Remember when you went off to high school, and I was still in junior high? It didn't change a thing, did it?"

17 She shook her head.

18 "Besides, as soon as you get settled, I'm coming up to check out the freshmen girls."

19 "Promise?" she asked.

20 "Promise," Michael said, and they both grinned. Graduation would bring about changes, but good things were happening, too.

21 "This is not a big thing," Michael added. "We're going to be friends in the old folk's home."

22 "Yeah. I've always wondered what you would look like without hair."

23 "And you with those tight gray curls and no teeth."

24 Kara gave one last look in the mirror and then held out her hand.

25 "Come on, guy," she said. "Let's do it."

26 And, just as she had taken him into kindergarten, they walked hand in hand out of the room.

Notes

To find the correct sequence of events in this narrative, you would have to make a time line like the one below:

—————	—————	—————	—————	—————	—————	—————
Families live	Kara takes	Michael	Kara goes to	Story	Dialogue between	Kara leaves for
side by side	Michael to	breaks	high school; Michael	opens	Kara and Michael	graduation
	kindergarten	arm	to junior high			

A typical ELA TAKS question on this type of passage might be, "What was the second thing Kara did to illustrate that she is someone who usually controls the situation?" On the time line you can easily see that the first time Kara takes charge is when she takes Michael to his kindergarten room. The second time is when he breaks his arm, although in the passage this order is reversed. The time line helps you keep the chronological sequence clear.

Also, notice that the connection between the group of shared life events and the continuation of the friendship between Kara and Michael could be woven into a cause and effect question. For example, the following might appear on a ELA TAKS test: "Why does the author include Michael's remembrances of the past?" The answer would be because it strengthens the idea that their friendship is solid and will continue. The cause (why) is that they have many shared experiences that will affect (what) their future as friends.

Summary

Some ELA TAKS questions ask you to find a summary for either the passage or a section of the passage. The best way to do this is to first cover the possible answers. Then write *who*, *what*, *where*, *when* and *why* in the margin of your test. Answer as many of these questions as you can about the requested section. You may not be able to come up with all 5Ws, but do as many as you can. Then write a sentence that includes all of your answers. Now uncover the possibilities and see which one matches what you've written.

Try it for the narrative above.

```
WHO _____
WHAT _____
WHERE _____
WHEN _____
WHY _____
```

Did you have "Michael and Kara" for the *who*; "share concerns about the future" for *what*; "standing before a mirror" for *where*; "on Kara's graduation day" for *when*; and "because they are friends" for *why*? If so, you could easily recognize a summary like, "Two friends share concerns that their friendship might be influenced by one's graduation" as a good answer.

Main Idea Questions

Questions that ask for the main idea can be solved in this same manner. And remember, the response to any question asking for a detail can be found directly in the triplet.

 Answer the reporter's 5W questions to find either a main idea or a summary

Fact and Opinion Questions

Now let's look at fact and opinion, as it might be presented on the test. For the purpose of ELA TAKS, a *fact* is defined as something that can be verified or proven by an outside source. It doesn't mean that *you* have to be able to prove it by yourself, but that someone, somewhere, can verify the information in a scientific way. It could be found by reviewing some record, interviewing a witness, or checking statistics, or in some such manner. If information cannot be verified by a second source, then it is opinion.

It doesn't matter if the information is true or if you believe it to be true. It only matters that it can be proven and is contained within the text. You need to be on your guard, though, because test makers will put in information that a teenager naturally believes to be true but that is unproveable.

Say, for instance, a possible answer choice might be, "A curfew of 10 P.M. is too early on a weekend." Although most adolescents would heartily agree with this, there is no way to scientifically prove how early is *too* early. Be careful of any word that qualifies, like *many*, *all*, *some*, *more*, *best*, or *most*. Also, statements that refer to the future are always opinions, because until the event occurs, it cannot be proven.

Look at the statements below, and see if you can identify whether they are a fact or opinion.

 Kara and Michael have known each other since before kindergarten.

 Kara and Michael will be friends in the old folk's home.

The first statement is a fact. A check of school records and family history could identify when the two first met. The second one is an opinion because it speaks to a future event.

 A fact can be verified in a scientific manner by an outside source.

Vocabulary

Vocabulary is another skill that ELA TAKS tests, and this is where your fifteen minutes a day of reading will come in handy. The more familiar you are with word usage, text structure, and context clues, the easier the vocabulary section will be. The test is not measuring how many words you know or how great your vocabulary is, but instead whether you can recognize if a word is used correctly in context. Somewhere in the passage there will be a clue that directly links to the word in question.

Again, you must always be thinking. Although a word may be familiar, on the test, it may be used in a way that goes against its more common usage. The passage may use a connotation, or indirect, suggested meaning of a word, rather than the direct, specific meaning, or denotation.

Did you see how that worked? The sentence above gave you the definition of *connotation* (the indirect or suggested meaning of a word) and *denotation* (the direct, specific meaning of a word) through the use of context clues. And the way you can tell whether a word is being used in a direct, specific way or in a suggestive, indirect way is to look at the words that surround it in the passage. So you must go back to the triplet to check how the word in question is being used.

 The denotation of a word is its dictionary meaning.

For example, in the narrative above it says, "Then, before he could cave, she'd given him a big hug and bounded off for her own adventures in first grade." The word *cave* is usually defined "as natural underground chamber," but it can also mean, "to fall apart." In this case, the words surrounding *cave* indicate that Kara left before Michael emotionally collapsed.

In many passages, though, the context clue may not appear next to the word. You may find it in the sentence above, the sentence below, the paragraph above, or the paragraph below. It may be an antonym, a synonym, or maybe even an example. But it will be there.

Take your time and find it.

 Always check surrounding words and phrases to determine how a word is being used.

Compare and Contrast Questions

You may also be asked a question dealing with comparing and contrasting two texts or two parts of the same text. In answering these questions you will be looking at the relationship between two ideas, or items. You will be considering how they might be the same and how they might differ.

 Words that might appear in a questions dealing with a contrast or comparison: *however, but, also, on the other hand, yet, common idea,* or *theme*

As always, you must read the question carefully to determine exactly what is being compared. Then ask yourself, "What is the relationship between these two items?"

For example, you may be asked how a character changes during the story. First, you would determine the character's attitude or personality at the beginning of the passage, and then you would redefine it at the end. Say to yourself, "Has the character changed? If so, how? If not, what is my proof?" You must analyze the information from both the beginning and the end of the passage before the correct answer will be evident.

Sometimes a graphic, such as the one below, can be helpful.

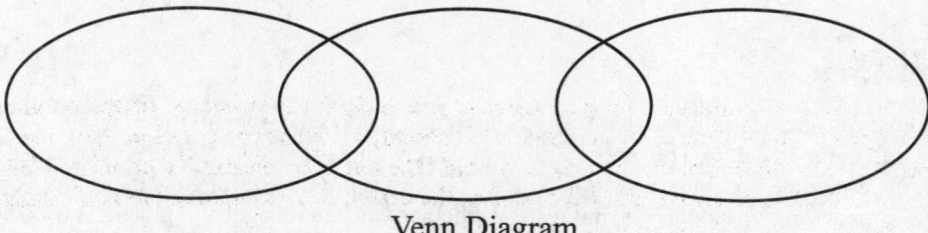

Venn Diagram

In the left circle, you would jot down details about the characters from the beginning of the passage; in the right, information about the characters from the end of the story. The overlapping area in the middle would indicate areas in which the character remained stable. So to answer the question, you would draw from the right and left circles.

Character Traits

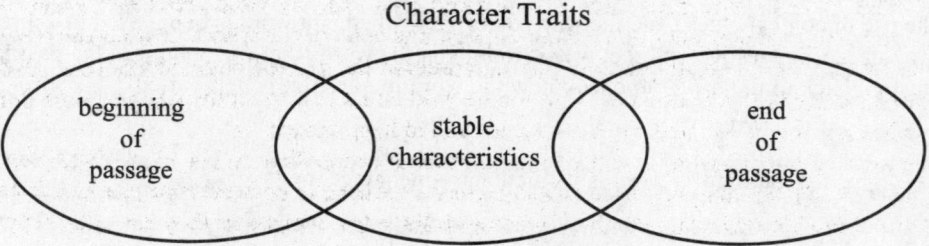

It is not uncommon for test makers to include possible choices from only one part of the passage to fool you. Don't fall into the trap.

Predicting

Some test questions might ask you what you think will happen next, and those that do are asking you to predict an outcome. You won't find the answer to this directly stated in the test. Rather, you must draw on information found in the triplet to make a reasonable guess. These kinds of questions are a lot like cause and effect questions, and if you think of them this way, it may seem easier. The text will specifically describe or explain something (the *cause*, or *why*), which will directly hint at an outcome to follow (the *effect*, or *what*).

Try to get some idea of the answer before you look at the choices so you won't be confused. Remember, like all responses, your conclusions must flow logically and smoothly from the text. It must be a reasonable guess based on the triplet, not something that seems right, but isn't actually a part of the passage.

For example, in the narrative about Kara and Michael (see pages 76–77), a prediction question on ELA TAKS might be:

> **Example:** You can tell from this passage that Michael is most likely to—
>   **A** go to the same college Kara has chosen
>   **B** visit Kara in fall
>   **C** be in the same old folk's home as Kara
>   **D** e-mail Kara once she is away at school

All answers are reasonable, but **B** is the only one that directly flows from the passage. There is no indication that Michael is even considering college, so **A** can be ruled out. And although **C** is in the passage, it is stated in jest. Answer **D** may be a reality, but again nothing in the passage indicates whether either Michael or Kara has a computer.

 All answers must flow logically from the passage.

Inference

Finally, let's look at inference. If a question asks you to draw a conclusion, interpret a graph, or make a judgment about what you have read, it is probably an inference question. Note the key words in the sentence above: *about what you have read*. The test is not examining prior knowledge. Always, always, always, the answer must be based on the triplet, so it is important to read carefully and to thoughtfully mark your passages as you go.

More likely than not, inference questions require you to think about information from two or more parts of the triplet. But if you remember that your answer must be logical, and must be based solely on the passage, you should do fine.

Summing Up

Okay. A lot of terms have been thrown around and reviewed, but these aren't new ideas. Not only have you been practicing such skills from the first day you started school, you actually began to build the foundation for reading before you encountered the printed page. When your grandmother shared a story before bedtime or your mother told you a tale about the day you were born, you were analyzing, verifying, and wondering what would happen next.

So memorizing the names of specific skills isn't what succeeding on the ELA TAKS test is about. However, being familiar with what is being tested establishes a comfort zone that builds confidence. Thus, although reviewing common reading skills helps, remember they are valid only as they relate, in context, to a whole literary piece.

On the ELA TAKS test, questions probably will not directly use the common terms for specific skills. They may not ask for a main idea or for you to predict. They may not even use the word *why*. Rather, most questions appear to be more literary, referring to the passage in such a way that disguises the reference to a specific proficiency. *But it is there*. Look at the possible questions below and see if you can figure out what reading skill is being tested:

1. What is paragraph 3 mostly about?
2. Which word in paragraph 18 helps you understand the meaning of the word *catastrophic*?
3. What is the best summary of the passage?
4. What are paragraphs 6 and 7 are mainly about?
5. A dictionary entry is given, and the question is: Which definition best matches the meaning of a certain word used in paragraph 27 of the story?
6. What ideas do the authors of both passages share?
7. How did the main character's feelings toward another character change after a certain incident?

Questions 1, 3, and 4 can be solved by using the 5Ws method. Questions 2 and 5 involve looking for context clues, and questions 6 and 7 require you to compare the two passages or two sections of one passage. Once you understand the question, finding the answer is just another day's work.

Practice, Practice, Practice

So let's put into practice what you've learned. Below are two selections, a fictional piece and an essay. Read each passage carefully, and then answer the questions that follow.

[In her novel, Promises, *Katie Cobb tells the story of Marti, a teenager frustrated because her parents never seem to acknowledge her accomplishments. They always fuss at her for small, inconsequential issues, rather than recognizing that in the overall picture she is far more reliable than her peers. In this chapter, after a morning argument with her father, Marti has stopped by the mall with a friend, mainly to avoid going home.]*

Boone
by Katie Cobb

Notes

1. Devon tugged the heavy outside door open and bounced into the mall, grabbing Marti's wrist to coax her along.
2. "Is that as fast as you can go? Wait 'til you see the boots in Macy's window. I saw the exact same pair in *Seventeen*."
3. The way Devon embraced a mall was beyond Marti's comprehension. Why get worked up over pushy salespeople, tiny dressing rooms and elevator music? When Marti needed clothes, she shopped, out of necessity, not enjoyment, not like Devon who was jabbering about this skirt and those earrings. If she'd tried on everything she admired on the way to the Food Court, the mall would be closed long before they could order.
4. "Find us a place. I'll get us some drinks," Devon said as soon as they spotted the stalls brimming with culinary treats. Quickly she disappeared into the crowd, weaving in and out like a pro, leaving behind a sense of fluttering calm.
5. Marti blinked once to clear her head before looking around. The mall was surprisingly crowded for a Monday night, but she found a table off in a corner and sat down next to the wall. Nearby a young mother struggled with a stroller, trying to unload packages she had stacked inside and replace them with her sleeping child. Marti scooted to the edge of her seat and stretched out her long legs, steadying the wheels with her feet. The mother mouthed a silent thanks, finished her task, and

dropped wearily into her chair. Marti grinned. She'd babysat enough to know how much energy it took to keep up with a little one.
6   "Marti, this is Boone."
7   Marti's eyes leapt to the right and moved up. Before her stood a Nordic god, in the flesh, blonde, muscular, and oh, his smile!
8   "And Boone, this is my friend, Marti."
9   Marti forced herself to look at Devon, who was trying hard to swallow her grin. She set two medium drinks onto the table and quickly settled into the chair furthest from Marti.
10 Boone eased his six foot frame down in the only seat left. "It's good to meet you."
11 "You, too," Marti squeaked, wondering why her voice sounded so strange.
12 Boone picked up Devon's Coke and in one deep swig finished it off. Her grin collapsed into a deep pout.
13 "Boone Daniels! I was thirsty."
14 "Easy now." He reached into his shirt pocket and produced a ten dollar bill. "How about if you get us another round, and some popcorn, too?"
15 "Okay." Devon sprang up, ignoring Marti's wide-eyed plea to stay put.
16 "She's been after me for weeks to meet you," Boone said, watching Devon's back. "I'm glad she kept pushing."
17 Marti's ears felt hot. She'd just come from practice, her hair was a mess, her knee was skinned and good grief, what if she smelled? She would kill Devon, strangle her, no, skin her alive.
18 She picked up her Coke and took a sip, a *long* sip while her eyes darted around desperately.
19 "If you're looking for Devon, she's going to be a while. I saw her duck into the Cookie Shop with Phillip."
20 *Wonderful*, Marti thought playing with the straw.
21 Boone's face suddenly lit up. "You didn't know about this, did you?"
22 He didn't wait for an answer. He threw his head back and laughed so hard Marti thought she would skin him alive, too. She didn't see anything funny.
23 "I'm sorry." The words were weakened by his body's acute need for oxygen. "Devon's blindsided me so often I should have seen this coming." He took a deep breath, ran his fingers through his hair and stood up. "How about if we start over. Hi, I'm Boone Daniels. Mind if I join you?"
24 Marti waved her hand at the empty chairs.
25 "And you are?"
26 "Marti Lawrence. Is Boone your real name?" *What a dumb thing to ask*, Marti thought, but Boone smiled, so easily, so handsomely.
27 "Uh-huh. I have six brothers, and Daddy said that by the time they got to me he'd run out of Jasons and Joes."
28 "S-s-six brothers?"
29 "And three sisters." Boone laughed at Marti's shock. "How about you?"
30 "I'm it." Conversation was definitely running thin.
31 Boone took her hand. "You know, Marti, I'm sorry Devon did this to you. You seem nice, and I'd like to get to know you better. I have two tickets to the state fair for Saturday night. Would you like to go?"

Notes

32   "Maybe." She wanted to scream 'YES,' but she couldn't, not until she and her father had had their little chat. "I need to clear it with my folks first."

33   She felt like a little girl having to ask to go out to play, but Boone accepted the news without pause.

34   "No problem. I'll call you tomorrow."

35   And so it went, an exchange of phone numbers, small talk, popcorn, sodas, goodbyes, and it was over, in a snap, leaving Marti confused and warm and bubbly, all at once. Boone was so—what was it? Laid back? Charming? Cute? No, it was more than charisma. He'd mentioned goals and ambitions, he had energy and wit, and he'd asked *her* out, Marti, Miss Conservative-of-the-Senior-Class.

36   If only her father let her go.

First Dates

1   First dates.

2   Doesn't the mere sight of those words make your palms sweat? Your mouth turn dry?

3   When you think someone likes you, and it's time to hook up, don't you want to pick up the remote and fast forward? Get past the opening credits and on with the story?

4   Unfortunately, that's not real life. Before you can establish a comfort zone with a new significant other, before you can even think, "Maybe this might be *the one*," you have to get through the dreaded first date.

5   What should you wear?

6   Where should you go?

7   Wait. Back up.

8   Who to ask?

9   Meeting someone is no small task in today's world. Oh, we are all surrounded with prospects, but finding the right one, the person who shares the same interest, morals, goals is tough. School is a good source, but you've known some of the kids since first grade. Do you really want to go out with Sally, who threw up all over Ms. Carpenter? Or will you ever be able to forget that Tosha was Mark's girl for three years?

10   Of course, there are always the newbies who transfer in from other schools, but it is not like you are the only one looking. Swarms form around any fresh face like fans at a rock concert.

11   Work is a good meeting ground, and so, of course, is church. Anywhere you hang out can bring opportunities to meet new people, but how often do you find yourself attracted to another, in a way that makes you zing? And even if you get to that point, don't you wonder, "Is the feeling mutual?"

12   So you've got to check it out, arrange for those "chance" meetings where you run into each other "accidentally" with a greeting and a smile. Flirt a little, not so much that your heart is visible, but enough to sense the chemistry. Ask around to be sure you aren't treading onto shared territory, and if things still look positive, brave up and make THE REQUEST.

13   Sometimes it's best to start simple. Just say, "Hey, would you like to hang out sometime?" If the answer comes back "No," then dust off your dignity and move on. But if a spark lights, set a time, place and give it a go. What do you have to lose?

14   Well, money, hope, pride, self-esteem.

15   Nobody said it would be easy.

16   I remember one of my first dates that happened about seven years ago. Now at my high school the only place to be on Friday night was under the lights. I'd met this girl, Julie, at the mall where I worked, and I liked her a lot. She was an assistant manager at the store across from where I sold shoes. Not exactly a glamorous job, but somebody had to do it.

17   Now Julie's store and the one where I worked were owned by the same company, and her store shared storage space with ours. So once or twice a shift she'd bring over a few boxes, or retrieve some inventory, and we'd chat and smile and kind of bump into each other when we could.

18   Things were going along good, though, so I decided to step up the pace and ask her out. It took a few tries. She'd come over and put up a box, and I'd asked if she'd had many customers. Finally, when the thought of asking her out played with my mind more than thinking about food, I knew I had to do something. I jammed my hands into my pockets to dry them off and said, as casually as I could squeak out, "Wanta go to the game Friday night?"

19   She smiled, said yes, and suddenly I was Mr. Smooth. We made plans like I was prepared, or something, when actually everything was off the top.

20   Friday afternoon rolled in and seemed ordinary enough. I'd passed my vocabulary quiz and finished all my homework before I left school. The evening was full of promise, and I was ready to go—until I got home.

21   First, our car had broken down. I'd like to call it "my car," but truth is, it belonged to my mom. We shared. When it broke down I was glad for this arrangement. Mom would pay to have it fixed. But when it was somewhere between our house and the garage being towed, and I had a date, it didn't matter whose car it was. I was stuck.

22   So I called my brother. I knew he was doing his National Guard thing over the weekend, and he wouldn't be needing his car. Besides, he'd been young once. He'd understand.

23   He did. Only he needed a ride to the armory.

24   I called Julie. She said she'd just catch a ride to the game, and we could go out after.

25   Cool.

26   So I dressed in a T-shirt and blue jeans, threw on my letter jacket, checked my money twice, then checked it again, and my brother and I headed out.

27   Now his National Guard unit is only about an hour away, and only in the heart of the city, and it was only 5:00, when all the arteries leading from here to there were clogged.

28   By the time I hit the stadium the lot was full, and I was in the south forty. I'd missed kick-off and maybe my chance to kiss Julie good-night, but I had to let her know I hadn't stood her up.

29   I threw the car into park, jerked the keys out of the ignition, and took off jogging for the stands. I really didn't have to run. I'd called Julie on her cell, and she sounded okay. But it was a good way to shake my nerves.

30   First date.

31   Late.

32   What else?

33   Well, we lost the game, a close game aided by bad refs missing clear calls. It put our chances to make the playoff in jeopardy, but I didn't know if Julie was really into the game or if she was just being nice, so I had to act like it was no big deal.

34   Only it was.

35   It wasn't until we were sauntering out of the stadium with a million other disgruntled fans, that I realized I had no idea where I'd parked. The lot had been full, and I'd been funneled into the auxiliary lot, the one in the pasture beside the school, way away from the lights. It was a moonless night, the car was black, and I had no idea of the tags.

36 What next?
37 Do I admit it?
38 Or do I find some excuse to walk up and down the aisles on uneven ground on a moonless night looking for a black car?
39 I decided to be tough. I admitted it. What else was there to do?
40 Julie just laughed, not a vengeful, ugly, "stupid you" laugh, but a sweet, "it's okay, I understand" laugh.
41 And I laughed, too, not a "I'm so stupid that I can't remember where I parked the car" laugh, but a relieved, "I'm glad she understands" laugh.
42 We lingered for a while at the concession stand, letting the fans who knew where they were parked leave. Then Julie took my keys and ran off, lightheartedly dancing up and down the aisles, clicking the "unlock" button on the remote control until we saw far away interior lights come up. I grabbed her hand like we were in kindergarten, and we skipped over to the car, giddy with life.
43 She held my heart for a long time, until college and distance took us down different paths. We're still friends though. I see her when I get home on breaks, and we email when we can. I don't think I'd ever want to date someone who couldn't laugh about losing a car on a moonless night. That much I did learn.
44 Just as I've learned from others I've gone out with what I want in a date.
45 I'm in college now, and first dates aren't any easier. My palms still get sweaty and my mouth dries up. But I've learned that is just part of the game, something you have to go through at regular speed.
46 Besides, I met a fine looking lady in my study group last week. We've been talking quite a lot. She's witty and intelligent and—
47 I think I'll go make a call.

Use "Boone" to answer questions 1–4

Multiple-Choice Questions

1 Marti might have reacted differently to Boone if—
   A she hadn't been so thirsty
   B she'd known she was going to meet him
   C he hadn't bought her a soda
   D she hadn't been arguing with her father

2 The author uses the description in paragraph 5 to show that—
   F Marti doesn't like to baby-sit
   G she was tired after practice
   H her nature was accommodating and helpful
   J the mall was full of shoppers

3 Paragraph 3 is mostly about—
   A Marti and Boone getting acquainted
   B Boone coming from a big family
   C Boone having an unusual name
   D Marti being frustrated with Devon for introducing Boone

4 The author includes the statement, "If only her father let her go," at the end of the selection to show that—
   F Marti has no freedom
   G Marti's parents are too strict
   H Marti is frustrated by her parent's boundaries
   J Marti is angry about her father's control

Use "First Date" to answer questions 5–8

---

5 Paragraph 12 is mostly about how—
   A difficult the author finds dating to be
   B first dates are more difficult than second or third ones
   C important it is to know something about someone else before you ask them out on a date
   D chance meetings are a good way to meet a prospective date

6 What word in paragraph 42 helps the reader understand the meaning of the word *giddy*?
   F vengeful
   G lingered
   H lightheartedly
   J sweet

7 Which quotation from the selection best summarizes the author's view of first dates?
   A "Just as I learned from others I've dated what I do and don't want."
   B "Meeting someone is no small task in today's world."
   C "But I've learned that they are just part of the game, something you have to go through at regular speed."
   D "Nobody said it would be easy."

8 The author develops his essay mainly through—
   F citing an example from his own life
   G describing the common difficulty of asking someone out on a first date
   H using questions to involve the reader
   J revealing his relationship with his family

Use both "Boone" and "First Date" to answer questions 9 and 10

---

9 What is one theme shared in both "Boone" and "First Date?"
   A Girls are hard to understand.
   B Dating is a normal part of adolescent life.
   C Making a date with someone for the first time can be an emotional experience.
   D Just when you want things to go well, they don't.

10 Unlike the author of "First Date," the character Boone seems—
   F more confident about going out the first time
   G less educated
   H older
   J more of a flirt

Answer Explanations

Now for the answers.

Question 1: This question is a basic cause and effect question. So first ask yourself, "Why did Marti react as she did?" Your answer would probably be along the lines that she was flustered and embarrassed about her looks, because she wasn't expecting to meet anyone new. Then look at your answers to see which one fits best with your own thoughts. There is nothing stated about Marti being particularly thirsty. The explanatory note said she stopped by the mall to avoid going home, so **A** cannot be supported by information from the passage. And Devon bought Marti the soda, not Boone. Thus **C** is incorrect. While Marti had argued with her father, it was before school and probably not something that impacted her first reaction to Boone. Answer **B**, however, does fit with your own conclusions, and it is also supported when Boone laughs about Marti being blindsided. So **B** is the best choice.

Question 2: This is an inference question. It is asking you to read information in the passage and then draw a conclusion based on your understanding of what you have read. Before you look at the answer choices, ask yourself what the paragraph says about Marti. It shows her to be helpful and considerate in a situation that did not demand or require her to participate. Although Marti may have been tired after practice, it is not mentioned in paragraph 5. This rules out **G**. And while babysitting is mentioned, the paragraph says nothing about her feeling negative toward this activity. So answer **F** is incorrect. The young mother does have packages, but Marti seems to have a choice of tables. So there is no indication that the mall is overly full. Thus, your best answer is **H**, which matches your own conclusions.

Question 3: This is a main-idea question, so ask yourself the 5Ws. Who is the paragraph talking about? (Marti.) What is happening? (Marti is trying to keep conversation flowing but is messing up.) Why is Marti feeling frustrated? (She didn't know she was going to meet Boone.) Where does the action take place? (At a table at a mall.) When does it happen? (After school.) Then put it all together. (After school Marti met Boone at the mall, but she kept messing up because she didn't know he'd be there, catching her off guard.) If you do this, the only possible answer, the only one that matches your 5Ws is **D**. Answer **A** is too broad, and **B** and **C** are not addressed in paragraph 5.

Question 4: This question asks you to predict a possible conclusion. But remember, although you are being asked to make a guess, it must be based only on what is written in the passage. While you may think that her parents are too strict, so far we have seen no evidence of that. This would rule out **G**. And, although Marti may wish for more freedom, we know she is able to go to practice and stop by the mall after school, so she isn't totally confined. This rules out **F**. *Anger* is a strong word, and we know to be careful of words with intense meaning, so **J** is out. *Frustrated* is more in line with what the reader has seen in the passage. Therefore, the best choice is **H**.

Question 5: Because this question asks you to determine what a paragraph is mostly about, you know you need to summarize or find the main idea. So use your 5Ws, just like you did for question 3. Who? (The author.) What? (Tells how to check out a possible date.) When? (Before asking the person out.) Where? (This one isn't relevant because the setting doesn't affect the essay.) Why? (So you know if you want to go on a date.) When you put it all together you have, "The author suggests that before asking someone out on a date, you check them out." When you read the answer choices, **C** fits well with your conclusions. Read all the possibilities, and then, if still satisfied, go with **C**.

Question 6: This is one way vocabulary is presented on ELA TAKS. If you previewed your questions before you began reading, you should have highlighted *giddy* in the passage. Go back and read the section where this word is found. The couple is happy, enjoying the evening, glad just to be together. Also, remember to use your dictionary. The question asks what *other* word helps you understand the meaning, so compare the dictionary definition with the possible choices. *Vengeful* is a negative word, and therefore wouldn't apply, and while *sweet* is a positive word, it doesn't imply light-headedness. *Lighthearted*, however, shows the abandon that seems to go with someone feeling light and happy. So the best answer is **H**.

Question 7: This question is directly asking for a summary. When you go through the 5Ws, you come up with the idea that the author (who) believes that while first dates (what) are often awkward, you just have to get through if you want to meet someone (why) in today's world (where/when). Answer **A** is too narrow. The passage isn't solely about what the author learned on dates or about meeting people. So **B** can also be ruled out. Answer **C** matches well with the statement derived from using the 5Ws, whereas **D** is too broad. Therefore, you go with **C**.

Question 8: A question that asks you how an author develops his topic is asking you to recognize how details are used to support the main idea. The essay is about more than asking someone out, so **G** is too narrow. And, although the author's family relationships are mentioned, they serve only as background material, which rules out **J**. The questions do engage the reader, but they do not provide the details to illustrate the point that dating can be awkward and difficult. This eliminates **H**. The core of the essay is the story that is told. Therefore, **F** is your best answer.

Question 9: This question is asking you to find a similarity between both the fiction and nonfiction selections, so you must compare them. Ask yourself, how are they the same? What ideas do both writers share? *Boone* doesn't deal with girls being hard to understand, so **A** is out. Dating is a normal part of adolescent life, but both passages go further than that. So you can eliminate **B**. And, although both passages deal with the unexpected happening at an inopportune time, this is not a dominant theme, so you can rule out **D**. The awkwardness of making a first date is shared in both pieces and mentioned in the title of *First Date*. Therefore, the best answer is **C**.

Question 10: This time you are being asked to identify shared details of the two passages. Nothing is mentioned about age or education. So **G** and **H** can be eliminated. The key words seem to be *confidence* and *flirt*, and neither the author of *First Date* nor the character Boone seems to be a flirt. So you can cross off **J**. Rather, the best answer is **F**. Boone appears to be confident about asking Marti out, whereas the author of *First Date* displays a sense of nervous hesitation when he considers asking a girl out.

Final Thoughts

So there you have it.

The reading questions on the ELA TAKS test really aren't anything new. If you take your time and trust your instincts, you shouldn't have problems finding the correct answer.

You *have* been reading all your life. All you have to do is to buckle down, get to work, and take care of business.

Review Box
→ Read a minimum of fifteen minutes every day.
→ Include a variety of materials in your reading selections.
→ On test day, take your time and read carefully.
→ Analyze each question to be sure you understand what is being asked.
→ Either justify or verify all answers with the information specifically stated in the text.
→ Trust your instincts.

Chapter 8

Detecting Historical Impact on Literary Texts

It's a new school year, full of fresh beginnings and good intentions, and the Student Council has designated a week of theme days to encourage spirit. Monday is College Day, which is way cool. You know exactly which T-shirt you are going to wear, the one from the University of Texas. Tuesday is Dress for Work Day, and you have that old apron from Joe's Chicken Shack, which should get a few laughs. Wednesday is Class Day, and the juniors have voted to dress in all black. And of course Friday, the day of the first pep rally, is Western Day.

Howdy, y'all!

The problem is Thursday is Decades Day, and you have no idea what to wear. You could go as someone from the '50s and wear a poodle skirt, or maybe jeans with a white T-shirt and leather jacket. Or, you could throw back to the '60s, dig up some bell-bottoms, paint a peace sign on your face, and put flowers in your hair. The problem is deciding, because it all sounds good.

Each decade had a distinctly different flavor that influenced clothing styles, music, art, furniture, and even food. This historical impact, the environment in which life existed, is also reflected in the literature, and whether or not you can recognize the impact of a certain time period on a piece of writing is something ELA TAKS tests. This is what is meant by the impact of history on literature.

Historical Influences

Just as historical events influence the people who live during their occurrence, the setting of a story shapes the characters. If an author wants to emphasize a particular theme, sometimes a time period in which that theme was obvious is selected to form the backdrop to the plot.

 Setting is the time and place in which a story takes place.

For example, during the Civil War people had strong feelings about the issues of slavery, of states' rights, and of what was morally right and wrong. Thus, writing dating from this period might reflect the unrest that enveloped the nation at that time. The Civil War also provides a prime setting for stories dealing with the worth of the individual, politics, the military, and soldiers facing the reality of their own mortality. Although these are general topics and could apply to any age, using a time when our country was emotionally torn and divided might enhance an author's theme.

Questions on the historical context of a piece might refer to the descriptive details that reveal the cultural beliefs and attitudes of the time. If you were reading an American story written during World War II, for example, expressions of negativity against Hitler could be articulated because he was an enemy of the United States at that time.

However, a modern author might set a particular story in World War II, using details of that time period to add fictional realism, but bring into the text modern themes. Perhaps a writer wanted to explore the complex issue of the randomness of war—why one soldier lives and another dies, and what responsibility to life the surviving soldier must assume. Add to this a mix of heroism, issues of military obedience and personal rebellion, and you have *Saving Private Ryan*. The story is set in World War II, but it touches a human chord that did not exist in 1945 because veterans of that war had yet to age.

So some literature reflects the age in which it is written, whereas other literature echoes the background in which it is set. In either case, though, the test does offer hints about the time period and the situation surrounding the literature.

Descriptive Details

As you read, pay attention to the small details. Be sure to note the introductory material, the information that often precedes the actual reading, because sometimes hints are given there that can aid your understanding of the passage. If a historical event is presented, ask yourself, "How did what happened influence the characters?" But also note the author's attitude toward and depiction of that historical event.

For example, a question might ask, "How did the writer's past experience affect the attitude evident in this story?" To answer this question you would have to think about where an author lived, during what time, and if that historical era had an impact on the literary piece.

Or, say a question asked, "How does the setting make a difference in this piece?" You would have to ask yourself how the time period, the place, or both influenced the outcome of the character's experience.

Historical context will reflect the cultural time period in which a piece of literature is set by using descriptive details.

Historical Questions on the ELA TAKS

Questions about historical impact can occur throughout the test in the multiple-choice section, the open-ended response section, or even the writing section. They might refer to one piece or both, or they may be addressed in the crossover open-ended question. Or, they might not appear at all.

If, however, they do appear, you need to be able to connect the piece of literature to what was happening at that time. This context will either be obvious in the selection, very well-known, or will be accompanied by a short, explanatory paragraph. You won't be asked about the historical event itself. That is secondary. What you will be expected to do is to evaluate how a certain situation or time period contributed to the meaning of the piece. Can you appreciate the story better because you understand the background surrounding when it took place? Did placing the story in a specific time period clarify the theme?

Okay. Time to practice.

Practice, Practice, Practice

Read the following passage, which deals with a historical event, and then answer the questions that follow.

[Born into slavery in upstate New York, Isabella Baumfree, later known as Sojourner Truth, became known as a powerful speaker. Drawing on personal experiences, she advocated for women's rights and against slavery. The following is a rendition of an extemporaneous speech given in Akron, Ohio, in December 1851.]

"Ain't I a Woman?"
by Sojourner Truth

1 Well, children, where there is so much racket there must be something out of kilter. I think that 'twixt the negroes of the South and the women at the North, all talking about rights, the white men will be in a fix pretty soon. But what's all this here talking about?

2 That man over there says that women need to be helped into carriages, and lifted over ditches, and to have the best place everywhere. Nobody ever helps me into carriages, or over mud puddles, or gives me any best place! And ain't I a woman? Look at me! Look at my arm! I have ploughed and planted, and gathered into barns, and no man could head me! And ain't I a woman? I could work as much and eat as much as a man—when I could get it—and bear the lash as well! And ain't I a woman? I have borne thirteen children, and seen most all sold off to slavery, and when I cried out with my mother's grief, none but Jesus heard me! And ain't I a woman?

3 Then they talk about this thing in the head; what's this they call it? [member of audience whispers, "intellect"] That's it, honey. What's that got to do with women's rights or negro's rights? If my cup won't hold but a pint, and yours holds a quart, wouldn't you be mean not to let me have my little half-measure full?

4 Then that little man in black there, he says women can't have as much rights as men, 'cause Christ wasn't a woman! Where did your Christ come from? Where did your Christ come from? From God and a woman! Man had nothing to do with Him.

5 If the first woman God ever made was strong enough to turn the world upside down all alone, these women together ought to be able to turn it back, and get it right side up again! And now they is asking to do it, the men better let them.

6 Obliged to you for hearing me, and now old Sojourner ain't got nothing more to say.

Use "Ain't I a Woman?" to answer questions 1–4

Multiple-Choice Questions

1 In paragraph 2, to what was Truth referring when she said that she could bear the lash?
   A Her days as a slave
   B Her difficult work
   C Her anger
   D A disease of her skin and eyelashes

2 In paragraph 4, to what woman was she referring?
   F Herself
   G Her mother
   H Mary
   J Eve

3 In paragraph 5, what was the event caused by the first woman God made that turned the world upside down?
   A The flood that Noah escaped
   B Sojourner Truth giving birth to thirteen children
   C Mary giving birth to Jesus
   D Eve convincing Adam to eat an apple

4 In paragraph 1, Sojourner Truth says, "The White Men will be in a fix pretty soon." What does she mean by this statement?
   F She is expecting an outright rebellion to overcome the white man's rule.
   G She believes that if the Negroes of the South and women of the North combine efforts, they will be successful.
   H Both women and Negroes are slaves.
   J White men will soon be able to appreciate the beauty of both women and Negroes.

What was the purpose of Sojourner Truth's speech?

Planning Space

_____
_____
_____
_____
_____

Answer Explanations

Okay. Let's look at the answers.

Question 1: You can immediately delete **D** because eyelashes are not mentioned in the text. Then ask yourself, did the author seem angry when she was comparing herself to men? No, she seemed proud that she could keep up with them. So eliminate response **C**. She was working very hard. She was not *referring* to that; it was *stated*. So you can rule out **B**. What she was referring to was the practice of whipping, or lashing, the slaves. The correct answer is **A**. The answer is given in the introduction to the text when you are told she was a slave for her first 31 years. You could have looked up the definition of *lash*, if you were uncertain. You would have found that one definition refers to whipping.

Question 2: Truth says nothing to link Christ to herself or her mother. Both **F** and **G** can thus be eliminated. Your historical knowledge tells you that Eve was in the Old Testament and that Christ and Mary were in the New Testament. Thus **J** is incorrect. If you didn't know this, you could have looked up *Eve* in the dictionary and found that she was the wife of Adam in the Old Testament. In the dictionary in one of the definitions, *Mary* is defined as the mother of Jesus. The obvious correct answer is **H**, and you can back this up with the dictionary and your reasoning powers.

Question 3: Again, you can immediately eliminate **A** and **B**. The flood Noah escaped had nothing to do with the first woman, nor did Sojourner's having babies. The account of Mary giving birth to Jesus appears in the New Testament, which comes later than the story of Adam and Eve. Remember that Eve convinced Adam to eat the forbidden fruit, and the world was turned upside down. So the only possible response is **D**.

Question 4: With answer **F**, no rebellion is indicated. Answer **H** is both wrong (not *all* women were slaves) and too broad to be correct. In answer **J**, *pretty* has nothing to do with beauty, but rather with describing the kind of fix, or bad situation, white men would be involved in if they didn't recognize women and Negroes. The correct answer is **G**. Sojourner understands the value in a number of people making an impact.

Open-ended Question: This question directly refers to the purpose of the speech. The introductory material clearly states that Truth was responding to a speech that opposed women's rights. It is probably a good guess that she was trying to persuade the listener that the opposition was wrong. So, as you read, you should have looked for and highlighted what she said in favor of women's rights. It is from this information that you would form your answer. A good response would have been similar to this.

To convince the people to support women's rights, Sojourner Truth used personal examples comparing the work she had done to the work men had done. She also used historical examples of Eve and Mary, proving women have been and still are important contributors to the world.

This response directly ties in information found in the reading to the fact that the speaker was trying to gather support for women's rights. It states her purpose and then supports it with specific examples from the text. Be sure to check your own answer against the rubric for open-ended responses on page 41.

The idea of historical impact can also be addressed in the composition. For example, a prompt might say:

> **Often the events going on around a person will determine how successful that person might become. Write an essay in which you establish the validity of that statement.**

or

> **People are often affected by what is happening around them. Write an essay in which you explain this.**

or

> **To what extent do experiences determine a person's future?**

Each question is asking you to think about current events (things going on around you) and evaluate the effect they have on the individual. Because literature is writing about life, this is nothing more than talking about the impact of history on life or literature. The background information will be provided in the text or in the introductory material. How you interpret the impact is up to you.

Final Thoughts

Throughout your life you have seen how your friends, family, and classmates have responded to different situations. You will have your dictionary, which gives you historical background and information. You know to be on the look out for historical influences.

So, questions that fall into this category shouldn't be difficult. All you need to do is apply your observations to the pieces of literature read, support your ideas with information from the text, and you have it made.

It is as easy as that.

Review Box
→ Carefully read the triplet, including all introductory material.
→ Look for hints that identify the time period reflected in the writing. List these hints as you discover them so you can see the "big picture."
→ Ask yourself, how does the time and place, or setting, impact the writing?

Chapter 9

Determining an Author's Purpose

Juan sat at the computer, fingers poised over the keyboard. His assignment was due tomorrow. Tomorrow. And he hadn't even started.

"Write something persuasive," the teacher had said. "Convince somebody else to think like you do."

But how?

Juan had been worrying for days, trying to come up with an idea, any idea, but the only thing he felt strongly about was how dumb the assignment was. What difference did it make if he could or couldn't persuade anyone?

He had better things to do with his time.

He typed the word *assignment*, then the word *dumb*.

His fingers picked up momentum as he began to write about what he wanted to learn and what was important in his life. He told how little time he had, what with working, and practice, and hanging out with his friends. After all, everyone needed a little diversion. And then he wrote about how much he loved to read, not stories from the literature books, but Stephen King, Dean Koontz, and Robert Jordan. And he asked why English assignments couldn't be based on more modern works. He talked about how much better it would make him feel to write about something he wanted to read, and—

He had it.

His persuasive essay.

He could expand what he'd written, include an interview or two with his friends, and he'd be done. And who knows? Maybe he could actually convince his teacher to do things differently.

Understanding Written Text

Everyone who has ever been in high school has been right there with Juan, worrying about the assignment that is due tomorrow—that really dumb assignment.

But did you see what happened? Even subconsciously Juan followed the pattern of prewriting (worrying), drafting (which began when he wrote the first word), elaborating (adding interviews), and eventually concluding his paper. He had a valid idea all along. All he had to do was uncover it.

The same thing is true when you read, only the process is reversed. Rather than coming up with an idea that will then be put on paper, the reader is looking to discover an idea that has already been penned.

Behind every written word is a human being, whether it is a story that is trying to make you laugh, an essay that is aimed at informing you, or an ad that is trying to persuade you. Your task is to understand the author's message, and the only way to do this is to become a word sleuth. Pretend that you are a detective looking for clues and that your only source of information is a written passage. What would you do?

Noticing Words

Ask yourself, what words did the writer pick? Big words? Complicated words? Emotional words? Do they have a specific tone? Are they funny, gloomy, angry? How do they make you feel? Good? Bad? Indifferent?

 Analyzing word choice helps determine an author's intent.

Appeals to envy (using words like *wealthy, happy, self-confident*), fear (using words like *danger, harmful, painful*), hatred (using words like *stupid, wimpy*, or any number of ethnic, religious, or sexual slurs), and pride (using, for example, the American flag) all tend to rouse our feelings. Be aware of such words and the emotions they evoke.

Also, remember that questions on the ELA TAKS test are expressed in a literary style. You probably won't be asked directly to uncover the author's purpose. Rather, wording will be more along the lines of the following:

The underlying message of this flyer is—

or

The author of this passage most likely wants you to believe—

or

You can tell from this passage that the author feels—

or

The author's main purpose in writing this passage is—

or

A quote might be given, and a question like: What sentence best describes the author's attitude toward the speaker?

or

If it is the crossover question, it might say: The two authors probably agree on—

or

The two passages were probably written to—

What lies behind these words are the writer's ideas. If the question is, "You can tell from this passage that the author feels—," then you are being asked, "What does the author believe?" Remember that the author reveals his beliefs through what is said or stated in the passage.

A writer presents a sense of theme through subtle hints and clues dropped along the way. Many of these are emotional associations, linking the reader to the author's view. These emotional reactions, when analyzed, reveal the author's purpose.

Fiction or Nonfiction

Sometimes knowing whether a passage is fiction or nonfiction can help you understand what an author is trying to do. A fictional passage, which evolves from the writer's imagination, is almost always meant to entertain, to make you laugh, cry, or simply feel empathy with the writer. However, nonfiction, or writing that is based on truth, can fall into many categories. It can inform the reader (using a balanced approach of presenting neutral facts), or it can attempt to influence the reader's thinking. Although some nonfictional pieces, such as letters or journal entries, are merely means of self-expression, the writer is still making a point, if only to vent private feelings.

 Ask yourself, am I reading fiction or nonfiction?

What Does the Author Want Me to Believe?

In any piece of writing, you need to think about what the author wants you to believe and why. Is any proof offered to support what the writer is saying? Is this proof based on fact or opinion? Can it be separately verified? What tone or mood has the author chosen? What feelings do the adjectives and descriptive phrases convey?

If you learn to recognize how a writer manipulates words, when you see a question on the test that asks for an author's attitude or purpose, it will not throw you off.

 Ask yourself, what does the writer want me to believe?

Summing Up

People all over the world are different. Some are kind; some are crazy. Some are honest; others are not. Some are tall; some are short. Some have blue eyes; others have brown, and still others have shades in between. We look differently, think differently, smile differently, talk differently, and all of these differences merge together to make each of us unique—the only human like us on this earth.

Remember this when you are reading. Someone with a unique set of ideas, values, opinions, hopes, desires, and dreams wrote the passage—someone who was short, or maybe tall; someone who likes salsa music, or maybe rhythm and blues; someone who is married with lots of kids, or maybe a high school student like you; someone unique and individual wrote each and every word.

Then ask yourself, "What is this someone saying to me? And how is he or she saying it?"

Practice, Practice, Practice

Okay. Time to practice.

Now let's take a look at how the ELA TAKS test might assess you on an author's style and purpose. Below are two passages which are shorter than the ones that will actually appear on the test. Read both, answer the questions that follow, and then check your answers with the explanations to see how you did.

My Brother's Keeper

Notes

1   Calvin fingered the money on the dresser. Fifty bucks. More cash than he'd seen in a long time. Seems every time he got some together, it had a way of flying off. His moms was short on the rent, or his car needed gas, or something was happening at school. But now he had fifty dollars, his own fifty dollars, and it had been so easy.

2   Buy wholesale, sell retail.

3   Wasn't that the way of the world?

4   And he wasn't even handling anything illegal. All he was selling was a little sugar. Candy. An afternoon high. The sweetness of life.

5   Of course, it was against school rules. The Student Handbook clearly stated that nothing was to be sold on campus unless it was sponsored by a club or something. But so what? He was just providing an opportunity to a few friends and classmates. No one would tell. No big deal.

6   And now he could use the profit he'd made to buy more from the wholesaler, and he could keep on rolling. He wouldn't have to ask his moms for a thing. He could get his own prom ticket, rent his own tux, and maybe even hire a limo.

7   He was his own man.

8   And it felt cool.

9   "Hey, what you got there?"

10 Calvin swung around, spilling the bills on the floor. Quickly he bent over and scooped it up, stuffing it in his front pocket.

11 "Hey," the voice continued. "I want some." A hand reached out going after the money, and Calvin slapped it away.

12 "Stop it, Nick. I'm tired of you playing around."

13 "Moms know about this?" Nick asked.

14 "No. And she ain't gonna, either."

15 Nick studied the possibilities with a grin. A big brother with this much money surely had some to spare.

16 "I'm not kidding, Nick. I don't wanta haf't ask her for money all the time. So I got me a job."

17 "Doin' what?" Nick asked, settling onto the bed. He grabbed a pillow out from under the blue and green plaid spread, threw it back against the wall and propped himself up.

18 Calvin scowled, fastening his eyes on his little brother.

19 "Why you all in my business?"

20 "Doin' what?" Nick asked again.

21 Calvin picked up his brush and began smoothing out his hair.

22 "I'll tell."

23 "And you'd be wishin' you hadn't," Calvin replied evenly.

24 "You selling drugs?"

25 Calvin's hand stopped in mid air, forgetting its task, and he turned away from the mirror to face Nick.

26 "You know better 'n that. Ain't I the one told you I'd take care of you personally if I caught you doing stuff?"

27 "Then what?" Nick whined.

28 "I'm selling candy. Candy. Twix and Snickers and things. Not drugs."

29 "I thought you wasn't supposed't do that." Nick said. "At the junior high you can't."

30 Calvin searched for a way to make Nick understand. It was against the rules, but the rule was dumb. He wasn't hurting anyone.

31 Or was he?

32 Calvin had been Nick's mentor, protector, counselor, babysitter, big brother, friend for years. Ever since their dad had left, it had been the three of them. He, his moms, Nick.

33 His moms.

34 He didn't want her to know.

35 Why?

36 Because he knew what she'd say, that a rule was a rule, and if everyone made their own rules the world would be a mess. Calvin smiled a little. That was easy for his moms to say. She didn't have to put up with high school.

Notes

37   But she did have to put up with a job she wasn't crazy about, and she did have to work overtime when she'd rather be home with her boys. What would happen if she just up and decided not to do what the boss said?

38   She'd get fired, and they'd be living out of a car.

39   What would happen if Nick decided not to do what his teacher said?

40   Calvin didn't even want to go there. He studied his brother hard. He could back him down, keep him from telling, but was that what he wanted? What message would it send, this year, next, when Nick had his own decisions to make?

41   "You know," he began, knitting his forehead into a puzzled frown. "I think you're right. Guess I'd better not do't anymore." He made a final pass over his hair and set his brush on the bureau.

42   Nick looked surprised. He'd dug in for an argument, but he didn't feel like he'd won.

43   "How 'bout some ball?" Calvin asked. He put out his hand and pulled Nick off the bed. "I think we got time 'fore Moms gets home."

44   Nick jabbed a move toward Calvin's pocket. "Sure wish I had me some new Jordans."

45   "Get," Calvin said, pushing his brother out the door. "I'll be down in a minute."

46   He stood for a long while listening, waiting for the sound of fading footsteps to change into the squeak of rubber soles pounding against cement before removing the cash. Carefully he spread each bill out on the dresser.

47   Fifty bucks.

48   More money than he'd seen in a long time.

49   He'd done the right thing, though, telling Nick he'd stop selling. And he would. He didn't lie to Nick.

50   But it sure would have been nice to have made a little more, maybe enough to buy Nick that new pair of shoes.

51   He opened the top drawer and neatly laid the cash on top of his socks. Next week was the first of the month. He knew his moms was short for the rent.

52   Maybe the money would help.

53   For now, though, he had a game.

Notes

Chopping Down the Cherry Tree

1. What's your favorite explanation when you forget to do your homework? Do you say you left it in the printer? Or maybe that your sister spilled jelly on it and it got stuck to the dog?

2. Excuses. Something we all use.

3. "Why are you late?" Your mom asks after you've missed curfew. How you answer, what you say, reflects deeply on who you are. It tells the world, "This is what I think of myself. This is who I am." You are saying to the world that you are someone who values and respects the self-image you present.

4. And there is a long-standing tradition for feeling this way. Some ancient cultures believed that words were a part of the essence of a person, and as they left the mouth they sent forward all that that person embodied. Once released they took a part of the speaker with them, going forward with a will of their own, never to be retrieved. Thus, when a person gave his or her word it was binding, whether for good or evil, because it contained an essential part of the sender. A handshake and one's word were all that were needed to seal a contract.

5. In today's society, however, making excuses has become all too easy. It is never our fault. Something happened that made us act a certain way. We had to do it.

6. But did we?

7. Were we forced into breaking curfew? Or did we leave the party too late to make it home on time? Did we really forget our homework? Or were we too tired after work to care?

8. What is the honest answer? And what, for that matter, is honesty? Do small lies really hurt?

9. That depends, perhaps, on your own personal sense of morality. For some, shading the truth is the better of two options, perhaps even sparing another's feelings. For others, standing for truth is a matter of ingrained pride. And sometimes we even manage to convince ourselves that we really haven't told a lie because we've answered a question truthfully, even though perhaps not honestly.

10. The story goes that as a child, George Washington, our first president, chopped down a cherry tree with his rusty, trusty ax. When asked by his father if he'd done the deed, he fessed up, admitting to the infraction, and because of his honesty was not punished.

11. Think of how differently the story would be if Washington had thought, *Dad asked if I chopped down the tree with my ax, but I used a hatchet, so I can say 'no' and still be truthful.* Or perhaps he thought, *It really wasn't a tree because it was only four feet tall. A tree is much taller, so I only chopped down a sapling.*

12. Actually, the story of Washington and the cherry tree is nothing more than that, a fictional tale made up by biographer Mason Locke Weems who, in an effort to make his hero seem more real, used pure fabrication. Yes, the story that for centuries exemplified moral fortitude was nothing more than a lie. Even after the tale was proven to be false, biographers held on to it for its motivating value.

13   In all, even historically the concept of truth seems to be a muddled mess, preached about on Sundays and mulled over in the mind. Yet when we are alone with our thoughts, struggling with our own heart, somehow the answer is clear. We all know what truth is. We all know how to answer, because we know what makes us feel good inside.

14   So the next time you forget your homework, or come home late from a curfew, think about what you say. Are you going to accept responsibility and fess up?

15   Or will you send out small parts of yourself to the world, clad in strange garments, presenting a false image rather than who you really are?

16   The choice is yours.

Use "My Brother's Keeper" to answer questions 1–3

Multiple-Choice Questions

1. You can tell from this passage that the author of "My Brother's Keeper" feels—
   A big brothers make good role models
   B in certain circumstance, it is okay to ignore a rule if it doesn't apply to you
   C role models often have to make difficult decisions
   D sometimes it is okay to break a rule for a short period of time if it will help the family

2. The author indicates that the family is struggling financially by—
   F saying that the father left
   G having Nick complain about needing new shoes
   H visiting Calvin's worries about the rent
   J saying that the mother sometimes had to work overtime when she didn't want to

3. By end of this piece it is clear that—
   A Calvin is used to adjusting to life's little surprises
   B basketball is something that the brothers use to bond
   C Calvin has only temporarily stopped selling the candy
   D Calvin would be buying Nick new Jordans as a means of keeping his brother from telling their Mom

> Use "Chopping Down the Cherry Tree" to answer questions 4–6

4 In this piece, why does the author open with questions about homework and curfew?
   F To persuade the reader that excuses are an ordinary part of everyday life
   G To explain that sometimes, as hard as you try, getting homework done is difficult
   H To connect to the teenage reader by asking about adolescent life
   J To illustrate that teenagers are more prone to lying

5 The author used the anecdote of George Washington and the cherry tree to—
   A remind the reader that even as a child our first president never told a lie
   B explain to the reader that if someone as famous as George Washington didn't lie, then neither should the reader
   C suggest that even historical traditions may not be accurate
   D make the reader feel patriotic

6 Which of the following lines best expresses the theme of this essay?
   F "In today's society, however, making excuses has become all too easy."
   G "Excuses. Something we all use."
   H "You are saying to the world that you are someone who values and respects the self-image you present."
   J "We all know what truth is."

> Use "My Brother's Keeper" and "Chopping Down the Cherry Tree"
> to answer questions 7 and 8

7 What is one method both authors use to convince the reader of the consequences of being less than truthful?
   A By indicating that there may be something to gain from telling a lie
   B By showing the emotional connection between lying and feeling bad
   C By hinting that no one is perfect
   D By showing that sometimes the outcome of a deception is worth the consequences

8 The underlying message of both pieces is that—
   F telling lies often leads to trouble
   G integrity is something that comes from inside
   H being a positive role model is everyone's responsibility
   J deciding what is right and wrong is a constant dilemma in an adolescent's life

Answer Explanations

Now for the answers.

Question 1: This question is asking for you to draw a conclusion, or to guess the author's theme. By presenting an emotional situation wherein Calvin must make a difficult decision, the author seems to be saying that being a role model is sometimes a difficult position. Not all big brothers make good role models, so **A** is too general. And, although the story does discuss the validity of following rules, initially Calvin was selling the candy for himself, not the family. This rules out **D**. Answer **B** is discussed, but dismissed. So the best answer is **C**.

Question 2: Again, this question deals with the underlying method the author is using to reveal his theme that maintaining inner integrity is not always easy. By contrasting the family's need with the ease with which Calvin has obtained the money, the author is making an emotional appeal that connects to the reader. Although **F**, **G**, and **J** all indicate that the family may have financial difficulties, the author shows the depth of the family's concerns through Calvin's worries about the rent. Therefore, the correct answer is **H**.

Question 3: Throughout this piece the author uses inner dialogue to show Calvin's struggle with making easy money at the cost of breaking the rules. He is shown as serious in his effort to be a good role model for Nick, and there is no indication he will go back on his word. So **C** can be scratched off. Also, while basketball may be a means the brothers use to bond, in this passage it is a minor point. Calvin seems able to influence his brother without resorting to bribery, so it is doubtful that he would buy a new pair of shoes just to keep Nick quiet. On the other hand, the author shows that Calvin is almost resigned to the fact that he has lost his money when he puts it in the sock drawer. This indicates that he has long learned to deal with life's disappointments. Therefore the best answer is **A**.

Question 4: First, you have to ask yourself, What is this passage about? Certainly, it is not about homework, so that rules out **F** and **G**. Next, **J** can be ruled out because there is nothing in the passage to suggest that teenagers are *more* inclined to lie. Remember to be careful of any word that qualifies. This leaves **H**. Asking questions is a means of connecting to the reader's thought, because our usual response to a question is to think of an answer. By centering on everyday events in a teenager's life, the author is hoping to draw the adolescent reader into the essay through an emotional reaction. Therefore, **C** is the best answer.

Question 5: First, if you aren't sure of the word *anecdote*, look it up. It may take time to use the dictionary, but it is time well spent because it will help you get the answer right. Then ask yourself again, what is this essay about? It isn't about George Washington, so why is this short, illustrative narrative included in the essay? The answer seems to come in the words, "In all, even historically the concept of truth seems to be a muddled mess, preached about on Sundays and mulled over in the mind." So the author seems to be using the anecdote to indicate how difficult it is to understand, even historically, what is truth and what is a lie. The essay comments that the whole story of Washington chopping down the cherry tree is a misconception, which rules out both **A** and **B**. And although using a patriotic symbol may stir the heart, the essay isn't about being an American. This rules out out **D**, leaving **C** as the best choice.

Question 6: The main thrust of this essay seems to be about being truthful, not making excuses. This rules out **F** and **G**. Answer **H** is well supported by the comments about ancient culture, but it is only one part of the essay. On the other hand, **J** is a point that permeates the whole essay, either stated or unstated. Therefore, **J** is the best answer. When the author says, "We all know what truth is," he is identifying the reader as an ordinary, intelligent, clear-thinking individual. This sense of identity helps persuade the reader to think as the author does.

Question 7: Both authors make a positive emotional connection with telling the truth, and a negative emotional connection with lying. Therefore, the best answer is **B**. Answers **A**, **C**, and **D** are hinted at or discussed in on or both pieces, but only **B** identifies the emotional link.

Question 8: Asking for an underlying message is another way of asking for a theme, and there is no doubt that both passages are trying to influence the reader to tell the truth. Being a role model is not mentioned in "Chopping Down the Cherry Tree," which rules out **H**, and **F** is too vague to be correct. **J** is a statement with which most teenagers would nod their head in agreement, but it is not specifically mentioned in either passage. Therefore, the best answer is **G**.

Final Thoughts

And there you have it.

To be successful answering questions about an author's intent, all you have to do is to put yourself in the writer's shoes. Think about the *why* behind the words. Imagine what the author was thinking, and back up your ideas with information from the text.

And success will be yours.

Review Box
- → Always remember that behind every written word is a human being.
- → Notice the author's unique word choice. Be aware of any feeling or mood the author's words evoke.
- → Notice whether the passage being read is fiction or nonfiction.
- → Remember to answer each question yourself, before looking at the possible answer choices.
- → Always ask yourself, "What does the author want me to believe?"

Chapter 10

Comprehending Visual Representatives

Oh, no. Not again! Your face is growing a pimple that is bigger than the cafeteria, and your big date is only 3 days away. Quick! To the drugstore for InstaZit Remover.

But why? Where did you learn about InstaZit Remover? How do you know it will work?

Thinking About Influence

Usually, the answers to these questions aren't simple. Somewhere, maybe yesterday, maybe a year ago, Miss Pretty Face told you on TV that InstaZit Remover is just what you need, and Mr. Skin-so-Clear admitted that he uses it, too. In the millions of seconds, minutes, hours, you've sat in front of the TV, listened to the radio, or leafed through magazines, advertisements have permeated your brain. Marketing is big business because it brings in the money that provides the financial foundation for much of what we enjoy in everyday life—movies, yearbooks, football games. But just how do advertisers persuade you to buy their product? Why do you think of InstaZit Remover instead of Grandma's home remedy when you get a pimple?

Because the people who design and make commercials, people who deal everyday with methods of persuasion, know exactly how to fool you into buying their product. They use time-proven techniques to make you think you've made an independent decision, when in reality you've been caught in a well-crafted web.

Advertising doesn't happen accidentally. People involved in the business understand the power of persuasion, and they use this knowledge effectively. Pretty girls with curvy bodies and straight teeth and handsome boys with gorgeous hair and appealing smiles invite you to buy a product by offering vague promises that your life will be better if you do. We all want the good life, and advertisers know this. Even though many ads are filled with unrealistic people and vague promises, we still buy.

Why?

Techniques used in persuasion are not hit and miss methods. They have been proven to sway us toward a particular view—they are specific psychological approaches that over the years have proven to be successful. And these same strategies are woven into the visual representation section of ELA TAKS. In this part of the test, as with any media, it is important for you to understand the message, or impact, being delivered. Is it to entertain, inform or persuade? What is it you are supposed to believe?

 Remember a human, trying to persuade you to think a specific way, lurks behind each instance of advertising.

It is also important to remember that, as with written works, behind every chart, drawing, or Web page is a human being, someone who made a choice as to which image to use and where to place it on a page. Someone wrote the message and defined the purpose. Someone decided what to put into the piece and what to leave out. And the more you know about these strategies and methods used, the better able you will be to make your own informed decisions.

Common Propaganda Techniques

So let's look at a few techniques commonly found in various forms of media.

Bandwagon: This form of persuasion encourages you to join the group, to do something because it is the fad, because everyone is doing it. It makes you think that you won't be cool unless you are like everyone else, and therefore you need to use a certain product. For instance, if an ad shows a group having fun at a party, and they are all drinking the same brand of soft drink, the implication is that if you sip the soda, you, too will have fun.

Transfer: When advertisers apply this form of persuasion, they use someone just like you, a teenager, and they identify that person with a product in a beneficial way, hoping that these positive feelings will encourage you to buy. The suggestion is that if you also use the product, you will have, for example, the same perfect teeth and beautiful hair that the model has. For example, a beautiful girl is seen flirting with a guy wearing a certain brand of blue jeans. The subconscious association that the advertiser hopes you will make is that if you wear this brand of blue jeans, good-looking girls will notice you, too.

Name-calling: This propaganda technique uses a negative word or saying, implying that you will be part of an unacceptable group if you do not use a certain item. For example, it might be implied that if you don't use Product X you are stupid, or dumb. Usually the negativity is subtle, but it easily persuades those who like to be thought of as cool.

Celebrity endorsement: This one is simple. Well-liked celebrities tell you that they use a certain product, inviting you to use the same thing. The person can be an athlete, a recording star, a Hollywood heartthrob, or someone else who is easily recognized. Michael Jordan selling hot dogs or J Lo recommending shampoo would be examples of this type of advertising.

Exigency: Almost all forms of persuasion have exigency to some degree. This is when pressure is put on you to do something, or you will forever lose an opportunity. The simple word *sale* implies this, because if you don't act during the sale, you will miss out on something, such as saved money or availability of a certain product.

Glittering generalities: Sometimes an advertiser will string certain words together, even though the words themselves are vague and lack specific meaning. For example, a certain medicine might be "fast acting," a beverage "warm and smooth," or a cruise "fabulous and fun." But what do these words actually mean? The connotations are positive. If you pay money for a cruise, you want to have fun. In themselves, however, the words lack a clearly definable definition.

Plain folks: This strategy is a lot like celebrity endorsement, but instead of using famous people, the one pitching the product is an average, ordinary person, just like the buyer. That is why on Saturday mornings the commercials on TV often feature youngsters, whereas ads for denture cream focus on the elderly. Even solid, well-known companies have different ads for different broadcast times. It is all a part of the game to persuade you to buy their product instead of the competitor's.

Over the next few weeks as you are preparing for the ELA TAKS test, be aware of the ads you see and the articles you read. Try to analyze the various influences that touch your life, and see if you can figure out what persuasive method is being used.

The techniques mentioned above are the most common, but they aren't the only ones. There are also approaches that twist thinking, making statements that are illogical sound right. This approach uses logical fallacies, and it is why there are advanced college degrees in marketing. It is a complicated issue. But no matter what name is given to an approach, the idea is always the same. If advertisers can somehow tap into your emotions, they have a good chance of influencing your thinking and perhaps selling you their product.

Practice, Practice, Practice

So let's take a look at a few generic ads, just to see how these propaganda techniques might appear on the ELA TAKS test.

Example 1: Several things are going on at once in this ad. First, there is a sense of exigency. The prom is only ten days away, and more money is needed. These factors create a sense of urgency.

Next, the invitation to come out and enjoy the fun uses the bandwagon technique. Everyone will be there, and so you should turn out, too.

The words *Be there or be square* are a subtle type of name-calling because most of us would not like to be considered square.

Finally, there is an appeal to an underlying sense of fear in the implication that the prom may be canceled if $500 isn't raised.

In ads of this kind, various propaganda devices work together for one purpose: to persuade you to do what the designer asks.

Now let's look at a second example.

ABC academy

Juniors!

Now is the time to plan for life after graduation

- Personal counselors
- Refreshments served
- Financial plans available

When: Tuesday night, April 24th
Where: Cafeteria   **Time:** 6:00

Example 2: This ad is a lot like the first, but much of the emotional impact is conveyed through the picture. The scene of a successful graduate, wearing a cap and gown, is an image with which most high school students would connect. Therefore, a sense of bandwagon and transfer are being communicated. The message is that if you get on board with the ABC Academy, then you, too, will be successful like the person in the picture. Also, although it is subtle, the word *refreshments* hints that a good time will be had by all. If the ad had said "warm cola" and "stale chips" students would not have been enticed to come, but the word *refreshment* simply sounds inviting.

Final Thoughts

In the big picture, interpreting the visual representation is not much different than thinking about an author's intent. You are simply analyzing relationships, ideas, and purposes of various forms of media. You may be asked to determine the main idea or intent of a piece, or perhaps identify the theme. Again, questions will be worded in a more literary way. They might say:

The slogan of the announcement is—
or
The underlying message of the flyer is—
or
The author of the advertisement hopes to persuade you to buy the product by—
or
The theme of the Web page is—
or
Why is there a picture of a graduate in the ad?

Questions on the ELA TAKS test might ask you to evaluate how effectively a message has been in persuading the reader, but they will not ask you to specifically identify individual persuasive methods. Still, the more you know about how an advertiser sells the goods, the easier it will be to analyze the visual.

In some ways, figuring out the illustrative piece feels easier than answering questions on the written passage because you have been interpreting visuals all of your life. You read billboards, look at writing on T-shirts, check out Web pages, and notice the charts and graphs your teacher has hung around your classroom. All you need to do to prepare for this part of the test is to brush up on your skills and think a bit more about the purpose behind each message.

And you will do just fine.

Review Box
→ Remember behind every visual representation is a human being.
→ Ask yourself, "What is the purpose of the visual?"
→ Examine the visual for any persuasive methods that might be used.
→ Respond to the question with an impartial eye, seeing what is actually being presented.

Part Four

Mastering Objectives 4, 5, and 6

Chapter 11

Distinguishing Voice and Style

Describe yourself. Right now. What are you wearing? What are you not wearing? Is your hair short or long? Gelled or natural? Braided or in dreads? Are you tall, short, plump or thin? What makes you unique from all the other people on this earth?

Now ask yourself, how would you feel if you were forced to wear something else? Say the school board ruled that you had to wear a certain uniform to school. And say that uniform consisted of boys wearing skirts and high heels, and girls wearing a suit, tie, and heavy oxford shoes. Would you be comfortable?

Now think about what is in your closet. If you had to attend Cousin Lousia's wedding, what would you pick out to wear? If you had to go to a job interview at McDonald's, how would you dress? Would it be the same outfit you'd chose for a college interview?

Individual Style

Each person dresses differently. Even if two people wear the exact same pair of blue jeans, made out of exactly the same demin, purchased in exactly the same size from the exact same store, the look isn't the same. Some might want to pull the waist down low on the hips; others might want to wear a belt. Some might want to hang something out of the pocket; others might fringe the legs.

Uniqueness is reflected in every aspect of life, in choices about what to eat, when to go to bed, whether to challenge or accept authority, and yes, how to wear your clothes. It is style. It is a statement of how each of us sees ourselves and of how we want that world to see us. It is a statement of our distinctiveness.

Just as choices are made about the image each of us wants to present to the world, writing reflects this same individualism, through word choice and sentence structure, as well as how much or how little is said.

Writer's Voice

When a writer picks up a pen, what is said—and how—can be as distinctive as the way a person dresses. It is what is called writer's voice. In any given sentence, the noun, the verb, the modifiers used are the results of a conscious decision that results in a specific thought being communicated in a specific way. Like the clothes we wear, it makes a clear comment about who the writer is.

The sad thing, though, is that over years of trying to please others, teachers in particular, individuality sometimes succumbs to a sense of traditionalism because often it is dull conformity that wins the highest grade. Writing thus becomes something done to fit a specific blueprint, even if it is contrary to what feels comfortable. Students find themselves walking around in badly fitting uniforms, following a formulaic pattern that has worked in the past, producing an essay that sounds like everyone else's.

However, this conformity doesn't work on ELA TAKS. The graders of this test want to hear each distinctive voice. They want to meet the individual, the person who is walking in their own clothes, the student brave enough to stand alone and say, "This is me."

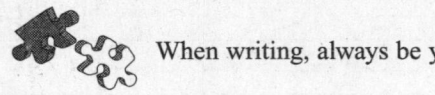 When writing, always be yourself.

But just how is this done?

Discovering a Writing Voice

Sometimes it takes unlearning things ingrained into your mind for years and years. It is okay to occasionally write with a fragment—if it is for a purpose and makes a strong point. It is okay to use your own words—even if it is appropriate slang. Of course, the essay shouldn't sound like a note being slipped to a friend during passing period, but it does need to sound like you.

Just like a speaking voice, an author's voice should have rhythm, resonance, tone, and even pitch. The grader should be able to close his or her eyes and know that the writer is different from all the other kids who live in Texas, because of what has been said. The passion and feeling should come through and declare, "I am important. Listen to me."

But how do you do this? Just how do you show that you are unique?

One good way is to think of a trusted adult, someone you respect and you know respects you, someone who doesn't treat you too much like a kid. Then write specifically to that person. Write almost as if you were talking to a mentor, using a personal, intimate tone. Using your dictionary and thesaurus, pick the most specific words you can to say exactly how you feel about the subject stated in the prompt. Make your friend truly hear the real *you*.

If you have no adult friends, make one up. Pretend you have a favorite aunt or uncle, someone who is nonjudgmental, someone who really likes you.

Anne Frank did this in her diary. She wrote to an imaginary friend, Kitty, expressing confidences and emotions that have touched readers' hearts for over half a century. She did not pen her diary to be read, but rather to record thoughts, feelings, and dreams. Visualizing a trusted friend erased barriers to intimacy that allowed Anne to write from the heart.

It is this same kind of intimacy that you want to achieve on the ELA TAKS essay. You want the graders to feel you are speaking directly to them and no one else. So you pick the words you might say to a trusted adult, even an imaginary one, words meant only for that one, particular person. Put emotion and power into your writing. Talk with your pen, and make the words flow. Let the essay sound like you, no one else, just you.

And your voice will be heard.

Of course, you still have to do all the things mentioned in chapter 5. You must directly address the prompt, use appropriate word choice, and vary your sentence patterns. You must employ good writing skills, using imagery when appropriate to support your tone. You may choose an academic or a philosophic approach, or you may strive to be entertaining. You may want to sound lively, sarcastic, formal, or fun. Whatever you do, when you write you must do it with style.

Your style.

Practice, Practice, Practice

So let's practice.

Say you and your friends are coming out of a movie, and you decide to go get the car while they stop off at the restroom. As you approach the vehicle, though, you are mugged. The thief pushes you to the ground and takes your wallet. You are shaken up, but not physically hurt. A passerby sees the incident and calls the police from a cell phone. Help arrives within minutes.

In the box below, explain what happened, just as you would tell the police.

_____
_____
_____
_____
_____
_____
_____
_____

Now, you've dropped your friends off and gone home. Your mother is still up, and she immediately senses that something is different. She asks you what's wrong.

In the box below, explain what happened, just as you would tell your mother.

_____
_____
_____
_____
_____
_____
_____
_____

The weekend has passed, and it is Monday morning. You get to school and find the word has gotten around and everyone knows about the incident. You are a minor celebrity.

In the box below, explain what happened, just as you would tell your friends.

Now look back over what you have written. Are the various accounts different? Did you, perhaps, talk more casually to your friends than you did to the police? Did you tell your mother exactly what happened, or did you try to protect her so she wouldn't worry? Did you add more intimacy, perhaps seeking comfort? When you told your friends, did your words have more bravado?

 Your words must match your purpose.

Although the accounts differ, each should still sound like you. Each should reflect your style, rhythm, and your own unique way of looking at the world. Each should have the very essence of your author's voice.

An Example

The distinctive nature of a writer's style is well illustrated in the true account of Stephen King's Bachman books. From 1977 to 1984, King published several novels using the pseudonym Richard Bachman. He made up a biography for the author that appeared on the cover, had an actor pose for a picture, and in general had fun with his alter ego.

But in 1984, when an advanced copy of the novel *Thinner* was sent to bookstores, a part-time clerk named Steve Brown noticed the similarities between Bachman's style and King's. Living in Washington, D.C., Brown decided to see who copyrighted the book. He went to the Library of Congress and found documents connecting the novel to King. When Brown presented the information to King, the novelist admitted that he and Bachman were one and the same. His unique voice had been recognized by Steve Brown, and the ruse was up.

Like other writers, even though King had attached a different name to his words, he couldn't hide his voice. The rhythm of his language, the sentence structure, grammatical construction, and word choice said, "I am Stephen King."

In the same way, a friend may write you a note and not include a name, but you would still know who wrote it. Even if it were typed, you would know, because you know your friend's voice and style.

Practice, Practice, and More Practice

Once you begin to notice such things, an author's style is easy to recognize. Below are eight passages written by three different writers. Read each one carefully, and see if you can tell which ones were written by the same author.

Passage A: The first in time and the first in importance of the influences upon the mind is that of nature. Every day, the sun, and, after sunset, Night and her stars. Ever the winds below; ever the grass grows. Every day, men and women, conversing—beholding and beholden. The scholar is he of all men whom this spectacle most engages. He must settle its value in his mind. What is nature to him?

Passage B: I was feeling blithe, almost jocund. I put a match to my cigar, and just then the morning's mail was handed in. The first superscription I glanced at was in a handwriting that sent a thrill of pleasure through and through me. It was Aunt Mary's; and she was the person I loved and honored most in all the world, outside of my own household.

Passage C: Sometimes they of the infantry looked down at a fair little meadow which spread at their feet. Its long, green grass was rippling gently in a breeze. Beyond it was the grey form of a house half torn to pieces by shells and by the busy axes of soldiers who had pursued firewood.

Passage D: And so I do not admire the human being—as an intellectual marvel—as much as I did when I was young, and got him out of books, and did not know him personally.

Passage E: Travelling is a fool's paradise. Our first journeys discover to us the indifference of places. At home I dream that at Naples, at Rome, I can be intoxicated with beauty and lose my sadness. I pack my trunk, embrace my friends, embark on the sea and at last wake up in Naples, and there beside me is the stern fact, the sad self, unrelenting, identical, that I fled from.

Passage F: When the water begins to flow through one of those ditches I have been speaking of, it is time for the people thereabouts to move. The water cleaves the banks away like a knife. By the time the ditch has become twelve or fifteen feet wide, the calamity is as good as accomplished, for no power on earth can stop it now.

Passage G: And now as he lay with his face turned away he was suddenly smitten with the terror. It came upon his heart like the grasp of claws. All the power faded from his muscles. For an instant he was no more than a dead man.

Okay. Let's see how you did.

Passages **C** and **G** were taken from a Stephen Crane short story entitled, "The Mysteries of Heroism." In these selections the description is rich and detailed. The sentence structure is simple, and the words are specific and precise. You can see behind this writing an author who has carefully crafted his words, weaving a mental picture with his exact choices.

Passages **B**, **D**, and **F** were taken from various writings by Mark Twain. Unlike Crane, Twain writes using a complex sentence structure, relying on dashes, colons and semicolons to establish almost a conversational tone. The effect is that the reader feels as if an old friend is telling the tale.

Passages **A** and **E** were taken from Ralph Waldo Emerson's essays. The style is formal, precise, and strong. There is no hesitancy in his words. They are confident and somewhat haughty by today's standards, but appropriate for persuasive writing in his time. You can see behind this work someone with a conviction of belief, someone who has no doubt that what he has written is correct.

Final Thoughts

Each writer can be "heard" as distinctly as if he or she had spoken the words.

And this is what you must strive to do when writing your ELA TAKS essay. You must let your own personality come through. You must sound unique, like you and no one else.

This is like adding that last piece to the puzzle, the final touch that completes the picture.

And the picture that will be seen in your essay is you.

Review Box
→ Form a mental picture of a trusted adult and write directly to that person.
→ Pick appropriate words from your own vocabulary.
→ Write with passion, as if you really care about what you are saying.

Chapter 12

Investigating Organizational Patterns in Writing

Sonya burst into the classroom. "You aren't going to believe this," she said, breathing quickly. "I was in Ms. Jennings's class when someone noticed that the snake was loose. You know, the big snake. And, hey, did you get tickets to the Talent Show? You said you would. Anyway, everyone started freaking and asking when was the last time it was fed. Oh, did I tell you I saw Carter at the movie? When I was there with Dad? He said to say 'hi.' Anyway, Ms. Jennings, she told everyone to get quiet, only Thomas said, 'There he is,' and pointed up. Everyone just headed for the door. Didn't matter what Jennings said. Chris said Mrs. Blankenship wanted me to baby-sit Friday, but I told her 'no,' because you said you'd get tickets. Do you think Carmella will sing again this year?"

The warning bell rang, and Sonya piled her books on her desk and slid into her seat, still out of breath. Alberto smiled. If he gave her enough time, she would eventually make sense. Now, though, he had to concentrate on Mr. Ziegler's lesson.

Ever known anyone like Sonya? Someone who talks in bursts and spurts, running ideas together into a one-sided discourse, letting you pick and choose what you need to know?

Usually, given enough time, rambling conversationalists will finally offer enough tidbits so you can make general sense out of what they are trying to say. In writing, though, the same isn't true. Limitations of space and time often block understanding in long-winded, confused communications, and this is especially true on the ELA TAKS test.

The ELA TAKS Essay

As mentioned in chapter 5, on this test you will have the front and back of one page to pen your essay, fifty lines max. You will have to directly address the prompt, logically develop your ideas, and convince the grader that you have a distinct and unique voice.

Sound tough?

Not necessarily. The complexities of such a task are easily manageable if you carefully plan what you are going to say before you begin to write. Surrounding your ideas with a cohesive pattern allows you the freedom to say what you want clearly and distinctively, in your own style. Giving direction to your writing lets the reader hear your unique voice.

But organization isn't something you arrange after you have finished writing. It is something you have to think about before you start. From the beginning word of your essay, you must have some idea of how your ideas will be linked so that the theme threading your paragraphs together doesn't get lost. The essay should have a logical flow from beginning to end that seems effortless, but in reality has been well thought out.

 Plan you organizational design before you begin to write.

Organizational Patterns

Usually, the decision about an organizational pattern comes in the prewriting stages of the composition process. As you jot down ideas, generally a theme begins to emerge, some message you want to convey to the reader. And, as you look for relationships and connections in your notes, generally some indication of a pattern surfaces, hinting at a logical way to develop your ideas.

For example, say the two passages in chapter 9 were part of a triplet on an ELA TAKS test, and the prompt for the composition was as follows:

> **Tell about an instance in which you or someone close to you had to make a difficult decision.**

119

Now, let's pretend the following scenario. Say your father has been offered a job in a city a thousand miles from where you live. It is a fantastic opportunity, one that promises to advance his career and significantly increase his salary, making it easier for you to go to college. So your parents have agreed that the move is right for them, but they have given you a choice. You can go with your family, who you dearly love, and start over at a new school your senior year. Or, you could stay behind, live with your mother's distant cousin and his family, who you don't really know, and finish your senior year with your friends. You choose to stay behind.

With this in mind, think of how you would address the prompt. First you would jot down notes, perhaps including ideas about the importance of family life, acceptance of the responsibility for your decision, the way your decision will prepare you for college, and even thoughts on what you've learned about life. Although it isn't required, one way to enhance your essay is to refer to the triplet. So, you may decide to relate your own dilemma to Calvin's decision to give up his new candy business in order to model correct behavior to his younger brother and also address the need to accept your decision, even though you miss your parents.

 Referencing the triplet isn't required when writing the composition.

At this point you would need to make some decisions as to how you are going to organize your composition. You must identify the basic theme you wish to convey, maybe because your parents trusted you enough to make this choice you are determined not to let them down. Then think about how you want to present your thoughts.

Chronological Pattern

You might choose a chronological pattern. In this design, events are recorded in the time sequence in which they occurred. Transitions such as *first*, *second*, and *then* are commonly used to connect these events, and the flow of the writing is from the beginning to the end of the time sequence.

For example, you might open your essay at the point where your father was offered his new position and your parents decided to move. You could follow with your activities after you learned of the transfer, commenting on how you made your decision to stay behind. Perhaps you went over to your mother's cousin's home, or perhaps you talked to your friends. Again, in the essay it is not necessary to link to the triplet, but you may if it strengthens your theme. You could liken your decision to Calvin's resolve not to sell candy. Both were difficult decisions, and both required sacrifice. You might liken your dilemma to the comment in "Chopping Down the Cherry Tree," where it says you know in your heart what is the right thing to do (see page 101). But unlike the author in the essay, you might mention that your decision didn't feel all that good. You could conclude with what you felt as you waved good-bye to your family as they left for their new home.

 The organizational pattern should compliment the theme.

A chronological pattern works well for many essays that deal with the sequence of events in life, but sometimes ideas develop more in chunks. In this case, a causal or cause and effect pattern might work best. There are two ways to approach this type of organization.

Cause and Effect Pattern

The first way is to begin with the *cause*, or *reason*, for a particular event. The second way is to present the problem first, and finish with the reason.

If you were writing an essay on the situation above, you might start with the fact that your father has accepted a new job a thousand miles away. This would be the *cause*, or *reason*, for the fact that you are now living apart from your family (which would be the *effect*, or *result*, of the cause). You could then tell about the difficulty of making your decision, your feelings about the separation, or perhaps the way you plan to accept the responsibility for your decision by making the best of your senior year.

A second way you could approach this design would be to begin with the fact that as your senior year approaches, you are now living apart from your family. This would be the *result*, or *effect*, of the fact that your father changed jobs (which is the *cause*, or *reason*, for your circumstance). You could then convey your feelings, perhaps emphasizing the difficulty you had making your decision. Or, you might dwell on your family, indicating that the only reason you have been able to accept your independence is because of their strong guidance.

The difference between the cause and effect and chronological patterns is that with the former you do not have to follow a time sequence. Points can be presented out of sequence, in blocks or chunks of information, if that is the best way to highlight your theme. Transitions are still paramount, but they can be much more subtle. Links such as *again*, *even though*, *nevertheless*, or *in spite of* often fit well with cause and effect.

Spatial Pattern

If your writing is particularly descriptive, you might decide to focus on a mental picture, in which case following a spatial pattern would be effective. You would start at some point in the scene, depict what you see, and then move to the next point in an orderly sequence. You could move from left to right, right to left, top to bottom, near to far, or any pattern that fits your idea.

For example, you could describe your new room, filled with boxes waiting to be opened and things yet to be organized. You could start at the door and move around the room in an orderly fashion, linking certain images to thoughts of your family. You might end by commenting on your new life, waiting to be discovered. Transitions such as *by*, *next to*, *beside*, and *on top of* might prove helpful. Again, although it isn't necessary to link to the triplet, you could liken your feelings to those of Calvin, who finds that because of his decision not to sell candy, he must now find another way to deal with his finances. Or, you might quote "Chopping Down the Cherry Tree" where it says, "Yet when we are alone with our thoughts, struggling with our own heart, somehow the answer is clear." You would have to make the connection between telling the truth and your decision to finish your senior year away from your family, though. Perhaps you could indicate that you are being truthful with yourself by choosing to stay behind, but in a descriptive piece there are many options. Just be sure if you choose a spatial pattern that you stay true to the initial design.

Be consistent throughout your writing with whatever organizational pattern you choose.

Climactic Pattern

Still another way to organize writing is to use the climactic pattern. If, when you are looking at your prewriting notes, you find a particularly strong point that you want to use as the focus of your composition, this would be a good design to employ. As with the cause and effect pattern, there are two ways to make a climactic pattern work. The first way is to save your main point until the end, building gradually, using description and examples that finally peak with your thematic point. The second way is to start with your strongest idea, and then support it throughout the essay. This is the design used most often in newspaper writing. Generally it is not as effective in personal essays, because after the opening paragraph the writing takes on an anticlimatic feel and tends to bore.

Continuing to use our fictional situation, you might decide that the point to be made is the importance of letting an older adolescent be a part of the decision-making process, especially when it is something that impacts his or her life. You might open with the fact that to grow, teenagers have to be allowed to make independent decisions. You might talk about how good decision making isn't something that happens all at once, rather it is learned through gradually escalating steps. You might then give an example or two of times when you were allowed to make a decision and had to learn through the consequences of your choice.

If you choose to bring in a relevant comparison from the triplet, you might say that because Calvin's decision to sell candy conflicted with his desire to be a good role model for Nick, Calvin had to choose which was more important. Or, you might mention how the narrator in "Chopping Down the Cherry Tree" points out that, although the story of George Washington's escapade isn't true, it does illustrate the moral necessity of accepting accountability for actions. You could then link this to your essay by explaining that being allowed to be part of the decision-making process is one way to learn responsibility.

Good transitions are still a must. Words and phrases like *with this in mind*, *it was significant that*, *most important*, or *the negative/positive side was* might work well.

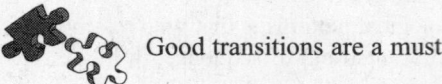 Good transitions are a must.

Order Pattern

If, in your prewriting notes, you decide to focus on the difficulty of making such a decision, you might use the order pattern of organization. This design is commonly used to explain something or to offer directions. If you wanted you could describe *how* you made your decision, perhaps by making a list of pros and cons, talking to your parents, talking to your friends, checking out your mother's cousin's home, doing research on plane fares and methods of visitation, or maybe even talking to an outside party, such as a minister or a counselor. In this essay, the process would be the focus. Transitions that are helpful here are those that indicate order, such as *next*, *another*, *as well as*, *again*, *further*, and *together with*.

Compare and Contrast Pattern

Finally, sometimes an essay falls into a compare and contrast pattern. This can be particularly effective if you find your prewriting notes indicate both similarities and differences you would like to discuss. You can use this method in two ways. One is to devote a good chunk of the writing to similarities and a second chunk to differences, wrapping up the essay with whatever conclusion you can draw from the comparison. The second method is to talk about each, the similarities and the differences, side by side. However, be careful if you choose this pattern. It can seem rambling and unfocused unless done well. A Venn diagram might help you decide if this pattern would work for your purpose (see page 80).

For example, you might concentrate on the decision you had to make, devoting one paragraph to the positive aspects of finishing your senior year without your family's support and another on the negative. You could draw a parallel to Calvin's decision to make money from the candy or find another method. And you could conclude with what you decided, and why you feel it is right. Simple transitions, such as *on the other hand*, or *besides*, or *also*, would move the essay along.

Practice, Practice, Practice

Now it is your turn. Have another look at "Chopping Down the Cherry Tree" in chapter 9 (see page 101), this time looking at the structural pattern. Then in the space below write a paragraph describing exactly how you think the author developed the theme.

_____
_____
_____
_____
_____

Did you notice that the author did not reveal the theme until the last line? The final words, "The choice is yours," offer a complete statement of all that the writer has said. By using the climactic pattern, the author uses a series of examples, comments, and descriptions that leads to the final thought that each of us is responsible for our actions.

 Organization is what holds writing together.

Final Thoughts

Organization is the glue that will hold your composition together. Of course, within each of these patterns, you must write well. You must have a strong opening that will invite the reader to continue. In the first paragraph you must establish the direction your writing will take. Then you may, if you want, bring in the triplet by either quoting or paraphrasing some section that relates to your theme. You must use good transitions that connect the essay together into one cohesive piece. And your conclusion must be confident and strong.

If you have succeeded in tying your ideas together smoothly, the reader will not even notice which design you've chosen. Yet, it is still there, connecting the pieces of your message until your message is revealed. It is the frame that ties everything together. Using a strong organizational pattern says to the grader, "I am in control."

And you are.

Review Box
→ Carefully read the triplet, marking notes of the major ideas you may wish to include in your essay.
→ Look for relationships and relevant links between these ideas.
→ Determine a pattern of writing that will best showcase your theme.
→ Note transitional words that would work well in your design.
→ Begin drafting your composition.

Chapter 13

Studying the Development of Ideas

"Boy, do I have juice." April's eyes sparkled with excitement as she slid onto her stool at the lab table. "I mean, this is too good."

Mia eagerly leaned forward on her elbows and raised her eyebrows expectantly.

"Okay," April said, stifling back a laugh. "You know Ms. Rose?"

"Yeah. The short, new teacher with those fancy, high heels."

April nodded.

"And those suits," Mia went on. "The one who acts like she's principal or something."

April leaned in closer. "Well, she was working first lunch, you know walking around acting tough, and she saw this kid wing a wadded up napkin at another table. So she took off to get him, only halfway there stepped right in the middle of a glob of Jell-O." Her words were interspersed among gales of laughter.

"And," she gasped, "that was all she wrote. One leg went this way, and the other that. She didn't stand a chance. She went down, slid right into the garbage can, hooked it with her heel, and it fell over, right on her head."

Mia joined in April's hysterics.

"When they pulled it off she had mashed potatoes in her hair, gravy on her pretty pink suit, and peas in her ears. It was too much."

Mia's head fell onto the table as tears streamed down her face. She motioned for April to finish.

"Everyone jumped up to see. It was better than a fight."

Both girls screamed in delight. After all, it wasn't every day a teacher wore a trashcan as a hat. The image was too cool.

Can't you just imagine that scene? See the teacher, half sitting, half lying with a gray trashcan on her head? Hear the cafeteria explode with energy as everyone craned for a look?

Think of how differently it would be if April had simply said, "Hey, you hear Ms. Rose slipped and fell at lunch?" The picture just wouldn't be the same. To be blunt, without the excitement and color of the first account, the story would sound boring. And if there is one thing you do not want your finished ELA TAKS composition to do it is bore. When your paper is picked out of the pile of thousands and thousands of essays written by students across the state of Texas, you want the grader to sit up, take notice, smile and say, "This is good."

But just what makes a piece of writing special?

Connecting with the Reader

You already know that your composition must directly address the prompt in a reasonable and relevant way, follow a well-defined organizational pattern, and echo your individual voice. But these are not the things that make writing exciting. To catch the grader's attention, your writing itself must be vibrant, must sail off the page and paint a clear mental picture, conveying ideas from your mind to the reader's. In a seemingly effortless manner, your words must make the mental connection between what you are thinking and what you want your reader to know.

And the way this is done is through elaboration.

When you are telling a tale, adding details and expanding are things that flow naturally from the structure of the story itself. But in ELA TAKS writing, when you are worried about doing your best, elaboration is often a conscious activity, something you carefully and actively incorporate into your piece.

It begins in the drafting stage. After you make your notes, clarify your theme, and pick your organizational pattern, it is time to write. Although your first attempt is merely a draft, you must write it as carefully as you can so in the revision stage you can turn a good initial effort into an excellent final. Remember, ELA TAKS isn't timed. So prepare yourself to work. Roll up your sleeves and dig in.

Using Careful Word Choices

First, as you write, take time to note word choice. Use the most specific word you need to convey your ideas. Don't say *walk* if you mean *stroll*. Don't say *run* if you mean *race* or *flee*. Rarely use adverbs. The same is true of exclamation points. They tend to look contrived, as if you are trying too hard, and if you pick the correct verb and noun, modifiers and extreme punctuation aren't necessary. The words can stand alone.

Don't forget, you will have access to a thesaurus. Use it, but don't overdo it. Always stay within your own voice, relying on words you know and understand. Be unique, in your own special way.

 Be conscious of your word choice.

Adding Specific Details

Next, as you are writing, be sure to expand your ideas, offering in-depth support for your thoughts. This is called extension. It is better to make fewer claims and establish them well, than to have many poorly developed ideas floating around. So after you establish a major idea, ask yourself, "What else can I add to clarify my point?" And when you respond to that question by inserting new information say, "Is there anything more I can say?"

When used correctly, extension adds substance and depth to writing. It not only helps to clearly convey your ideas, but it also helps maintain the reader's interest.

 ELA TAKS writing should show evidence of depth and substance.

For example, read the following excerpt from Bret Harte's "The Luck of Roaring Camp," taking time to notice how the author paints a clear picture of a motley group of miners.

> "The assemblage numbered about a hundred men. One or two of these were actual fugitives from justice, some were criminal, and all were reckless. Physically, they exhibited no indication of their past lives and character. The greatest scamp had a Raphael face, with a profusion of blond hair; Oakhurst, a gambler, had the melancholy air and intellectual abstraction of a Hamlet; the coolest and most courageous man was scarcely over five feet in height, with a soft voice and an embarrassed, timid manner. The term "roughs" applied to them was a distinction rather than a definition. Perhaps in the minor details of fingers, toes, ears, etc., the camp may have been deficient, but these slight omissions did not detract from their aggregate force. The strongest man had but three fingers on his right hand; the best shot had but one eye."

Note how specific the words are? He says *reckless* not *wild*. Both connote a degree of unruliness, but the word *reckless* carries an air of uncontrolled abandon. Note that he doesn't say that Oakhurst was sad and depressed. He gets this message across by making a comparison to Shakespeare's Hamlet, a famous dramatic character distracted by depression and contemplations. Even his subtle understated comment about the missing body parts ("Perhaps in the minor details of fingers, toes, ears, etc., the camp may have been deficient. . . .") packs a distinctive punch because it seems to imply that the living in the camp had been hard.

Everything in the paragraph answers the question, "What else can I say about this assemblage to help my reader really know this group?" First Harte talks about their past, then how they looked, extending his description to include specific details about one or two. There is no doubt by the end of the paragraph that this is one rough crowd.

Sensory Description

Still another way to enrich your words is to use sensory description. When you do this you explain how something feels, sounds, looks, tastes, or smells. Again, it is important to choose the most specific word possible. Don't say something is *bright* if *sparkles* would convey a clearer mental picture. Don't say the pollution was *bad*. Explain how it burned your eyes and stuck in your throat.

Again, let's look at words from "The Luck of Roaring Camp." In the story the miners are awaiting the birth of a child. And here is how Harte describes the first sound of the infant's voice.

> "Above the swaying and moaning of the pines, the swift rush of the river, and the crackling of the fire, rose a sharp, querulous cry—a cry unlike anything heard before in the camp. The pines stopped moaning, the river ceased to rush, and the fire to crackle. It seemed as if Nature had stopped to listen too."

Notice how specific the words are: *crackling, moaning, rush*. And notice the clear silence rings when Nature also stops to listen.

Sometimes when referring to the five senses, comparisons such as metaphors and similes are useful. You don't want to go too far out with these. The comparison must be something appropriate and known to both the reader and the writer, but using comparisons as a means to extend through sensory description is an excellent way of showing support.

 Using sensory words makes writing more vivid.

Using Comparisons

In the same story, as the child grows, the miners begin to change. Here Harte uses a comparison to describe a character named Kentuck's clothing.

> "It was a cruel mortification to Kentuck—who, in the carelessness of a large nature and the habits of frontier life, had begun to regard all garments as a second cuticle, which, like a snake's, only sloughed off through decay—to be debarred this privilege for certain prudential reasons."

By relating Kentuck's garments to a snake's shed skin, Harte gives the reader the image of tattered, worn garments while maintaining the flavor of the West.

Final Thoughts

Granted, when you write for ELA TAKS you will be responding to a prompt, not telling a story about a child born in a desolate mining town. But good writing is good writing. Elaboration adds spice to the text, giving it flavor and life. Without elaboration writing seems empty, but any description you use must fit your own style, just as Harte's fit his.

Be careful about sounding artificial. If a simile or metaphor seems to stand out or looks obvious, it isn't yours. Sometimes there is a tendency to overwrite, or overstate by using symbolism that is awkward and sounds contrived. Just write truthfully from the heart, saying things that only you would say as precisely and descriptively as you can.

When you have finished your initial draft, ask yourself, is there any part of the essay that seems dull? If so, fix it. Add sensory description and details. Ask yourself, is there any part of the writing that is unclear? If so, fix it. Add extensions. Ask yourself, have I picked exact, specific words to make my point? If not, fix it. Use your dictionary and thesaurus to refine and elucidate your message. Ask yourself, does my piece need more description? If so, add it.

This is where the *work* of writing comes in. This is where the pieces of your picture come together to form a complete image.

You will choose words unlike any other student in Texas. Realizing that each and every one is important, you will carefully place them together in your own special pattern, in your own unique way. Then you will analyze and review them until you are satisfied that they have done their job. Your writing will be vivid, explicit, and effective. It will convey exactly what you want to say.

And your grader *will* sit up and notice.

Review Box
→ Write your first draft, carefully choosing specific words to illustrate and clarify your message.
→ Add as many specific details as appropriate.
→ Use sensory description, making references to things that can be seen, felt, heard, tasted, or smelled.
→ Use comparisons when appropriate to enhance understanding.
→ When revising, look for any part of the essay that is dull or lacking, and spice it up. Take out the dead words and add new ones.
→ And remember, always, always be yourself.

Chapter 14

Reviewing Mechanics and Usage

A worried frown creased Cari's forehead as she ran her fingers across the page. Where to from here? She'd written her composition. She could identify an organizational pattern, and she'd used good description. What else did she need to do?

She took a minute to relax, let her mind wander back into the classroom, to yesterday and the day before, as they'd prepared for the ELA TAKS. What was it her teacher had said? That there was an art and a craft to writing?

Aw, yes, that was it.

Her teacher said that the art side of writing was the message, what makes each and every piece unique, the creative voice behind the written work. Cari smiled at that. She knew she had written from the heart, offering her unique perspective and ideas. And, yes, there was a theme. No other student in Texas would say the things she had. She was satisfied with the art side.

But the craft part, what was that?

Her frown deepened as she remembered her teacher saying, "The craft side of writing is the grammar. It is the nuts and bolts of the structure that makes your message clear."

Okay, Cari thought, mentally rolling up her sleeves. *Time to get busy*.

She knew that she had work to do, that as she proofread her piece there would be certain things she needed to think about, things that sometimes tripped her up. Her ideas were good, and she didn't want them to be muddled. She'd studied for the last eleven years to get this composition right, and she wanted the graders to notice her writing, her style.

A smile overtook her frown. She knew she had to check her mechanics and usage, challenging each and every word to be sure it was correct. She had to inspect all the little things her teacher harped about, to carefully revise her work as if she were someone else looking at it for the first time. She wouldn't be finished until she'd done this, perfected the craft of her writing, to illuminate her art.

Then she could copy her essay into the answer document, check it over, and be done with the ELA TAKS test forever. So with renewed determination, she went to work.

Pay Attention to Details

One of the hardest things you will have to do on testing day is to maintain focus, particularly when composing the open-ended answers and writing your essay. It is so easy to feel done, to want to rush on and write your composition onto the answer document before you've taken care of the details. After all, you have your ideas, you know the answer, and your original thinking is completed.

But, like Cari, you still have work to do. You still have to tighten up what you've written, add the structure that will hold your words in place and carry the weight of your original thinking and creativity.

Compare it to a futuristic car you dreamed up, drew out on paper, and then modeled with clay for art class. Or compare it to a dress you first sketched, and then your aunt cut and stitched for the prom. Or think about the way you designed your bedroom, planned the homecoming party, composed a rap or song or a letter for a special someone.

Whatever you imagined and constructed could not be completed if you didn't pay attention to the fine details—the glue and tape, the thread and fasteners, the rhythm of the words. No matter what the creative effort, after all the thinking and designing is finished, you have to check the fine points. You have to verify the measurements or, in the case of writing, use the language correctly so that your creative vision can be seen. English teachers refer to these details of language as mechanics and usage, and getting them right is an essential part of being successful on the ELA TAKS.

Mechanics

The mechanics of writing are spelling, capitalization, and punctuation. As previously mentioned, you will have use of reference materials to verify your spelling and capitalization in the open-ended responses and in the composition. However, the other place that mechanics and usage will be checked is in the revising and editing section, when you will no longer have access to these resources. Still, it is generally easier to see someone else's mistakes than your own, so as long as you have a good feeling for the basics of mechanics and usage, you should be okay.

So, let's start by taking a look at spelling.

Spelling

For your own composition, all you have to remember is to use your dictionary. You won't have to look up every word, of course, but be careful not to get tripped up on words that are commonly missed. You can find lists of these posted on the internet by searching under "misspelled words." Take the time to do this before test day, and learn your weaknesses. You don't have to be a champion speller; you do need to know which words might be confusing and need to be verified. Make a list of your errors. When it comes to spelling, everyone has blind spots, and you need to know yours.

A good strategy to use on test day is, as you draft your essay, put a dot over words you want to check. Then, when you are in the editing phase of your work, look them up. This won't slow down your creative process, but the dots will serve as a reminder that you do need to pay attention to specific words.

 Always be aware of your own spelling weaknesses.

Another area to check for spelling problems is with words that sound similar but have different meanings for different spellings, like *affect* and *effect*. With an **a**, affect means influenced—or made **a** difference: *His sore elbow affected his game*. With an **e**, effect means a caus**e** or to bring about: *The effect of his sore elbow was that he scored fewer points*. Other words commonly confused are *set* and *sit*. With an **i**, sit means **I** put myself down, or someone is in a seated position: *She was sitting on the sand* or *I decided to sit down*. With an **e**, set, means to do it to **e**verything else: *She set the book on the table*. Same thing with *rise* and *raise*. **I** (the doer) do it myself: *The sun will rise*. With an **a**, **a**nother thing does it: *He will raise his hand*. *Lie* and *lay* are other favorites to test: **I** put myself in a reclining position, or *I lie down*. The past tense of this, though, has an **a**, as in yesterday *I lay down* (**a**fter the current time). This is easily confused with the present l**a**y—what you do to **a**nother object: *He had to reach over Melany to lay the book on his desk*. Laid is the past tense of what you did to something else: Yesterday he laid the book on the table.

Another favorite thing that the test makers like to do in the revising and editing section is to see if you can distinguish between the three words, *their*, *there*, and *they're*. Remember t(*heir*) shows ownership, just as someone is the heir of something; t(*here*) is a place, just as here is a place; and *they're* is a contraction (they are). Other common errors in spelling happen when we confuse *who's* (who is) for *whose* (asking for ownership); or *lose* (you cannot find something) for *loose* (not tight); or *passed* (succeeded) for *past* (happened already); or *already* (quick in time) for *all ready* (as opposed to not ready).

 Be careful of words that sound the same but have different meanings.

If you were quizzed on these commonly confused words, you'd probably do fine. However, sometimes in your own writing mistakes go unnoticed, so be sure to take a second or even third look at any of these you use.

Also, don't let the little things trip you up. You know *a lot* is not a four letter word, just like *a little* (they are both two words) and *all right* cannot be one word, just as *all wrong* cannot be one word. Commit these pairs to memory. They are such common mistakes that the test makers love to throw them in.

To review, get familiar with your own weaknesses before the test and use your dictionary to sift out any confusion, and you should do fine.

Punctuation

Next, let's look at punctuation.

Always, always, always designate your sentence boundaries with the proper punctuation. If the sentence is a question, use a question mark. If you intend to show emotion, use an exclamation point, but use this punctuation mark sparingly. Usually, stronger words are more effective than an exclamation point. And if the sentence is a plain, ordinary statement, use a period.

One common mistake is when you think of a question in your mind but write a period out of habit. Also, when you are copying over from the polished rough draft to the answer document, clerical errors can occur. So don't overlook the small details.

Commas and Semicolons

Other punctuation marks that are common on the ELA TAKS are commas and semicolons used to separate two complete ideas (independent clauses). If used correctly in your own composition, they are signs of advanced writing skills. If used incorrectly, they stand out to the grader like a fire drill bell.

Commas are used with a coordinating conjunction (such as *for, and, nor, but, or, yet, so*) to separate complete ideas. But you need to be careful. You must have a subject and verb on each side of the comma-conjunction combination. For example:

 We are all especially happy today, *for* it is Friday.

 We don't have any homework tonight, *and* it is Friday.

 We have no classes tomorrow, *nor* do we have homework.

 It is the weekend, *but* we have homework.

 We will have a wonderful time, *or* it will rain too much.

 It was a rainy weekend, *yet* we were glad to be together.

 Friday has finally arrived, *so* we are all happy.

Notice how the comma comes before the conjunction. And if you put your left thumb at the beginning of the first word and your right thumb before the comma, you should see a complete idea. If you put your left thumb after that coordinating conjunction and your right thumb after the period, you should notice another complete idea, so you know you have used the comma-conjunction combination correctly.

A semicolon also is used to separate two complete ideas, but without the coordinating conjunction. For example:

 The weekend is finally here; we are all ecstatic!

 It is only Monday; the weekend is far away.

Knowing how to use both constructions allows you to add variety to your writing, something that the graders notice. But again, if you use a semicolon, you must use it correctly. Below are five sentences without the appropriate punctuation. See if you can correctly add either a comma or semicolon to clarify the construction.

1. The students were despondent Friday was 4 days away.
2. Studying for tests is traumatic not passing tests is worse.
3. They felt confident about the results yet they were anxious.
4. The students were ecstatic and the teachers were exuberant.
5. The mood was positive but it was only Monday.

Your teacher would have called these run-on sentences. The first two should have had semicolons added; the last three should have commas before the coordinating conjunctions. Correctly written the sentences would look like this:

1. The students were despondent; Friday was 4 days away.
2. Studying for tests is traumatic; not passing tests is worse.
3. They felt confident about the results, yet they were anxious.
4. The students were ecstatic, and the teachers were exuberant.
5. The mood was positive, but it was only Monday.

 During the editing process, check your punctuation carefully.

Remember that correctly joining independent clauses will be evaluated not only in your own writing but also on the multiple-choice questions in the revising and editing section of the test, so it is important that you get this concept down.

Joining Clauses

Let's look at joining subordinate clauses to independent clauses. Do you remember that a subordinate clause is dependent and cannot stand alone? The subordinating clause begins with a subordinating conjunction, such as *which, where, when, that, if, because*, and the list goes on. You can find a complete list of them in your grammar text. If the subordinate clause begins the sentence, it must be followed by a comma. A comma is not used if the subordinating clause follows the independent clause. That is what happened in the two preceding sentences.

Some teachers refer to these as *glue words*. Think of it this way: These words are strong enough to hook a subordinate clause to an independent clause by themselves if they are in the middle where these clauses join. However, if they are way off at the beginning of the sentence the "glue" won't be strong enough by the time the independent clause finally gets there and so a comma has to be added. Don't worry about remembering their labels; just remember what is necessary where they occur.

Check out these examples:

1. After all the commotion about having an open campus for the lunch hour ended, the students still found themselves eating lunch in the school cafeteria.
2. The students still found themselves eating lunch in the school cafeteria after all the commotion about having an open campus for the lunch hour ended.

Go back and circle the subordinating conjunction *after* in each sentence. When it began the sentence, the clause was followed by a comma. It did not need a comma when it was between the two clauses.

Look at the following sentences and add commas where necessary:

1. Many students take calculus although it is not required.
2. Although it is not required many students take calculus.
3. When the tardy bell rings all students must be in the classroom.
4. All students must be in the classroom when the tardy bell rings.
5. We are carefully practicing our writing skills because we want to graduate on time with our class.
6. Because we want to graduate on time with our class we are carefully practicing our writing skills.

Hopefully, you circled the conjunctions in each sentence (*although, when, because*). The sentences beginning with these words (#2, 3, and 6) required a comma after the subordinate clause; the sentences where these occurred between the clauses did not require a comma. They should be marked:

1. Many students take calculus although it is not required.
2. Although it is not required, many students take calculus.
3. When the tardy bell rings, all students must be in the classroom.
4. All students must be in the classroom when the tardy bell rings.
5. We are carefully practicing our writing skills because we want to graduate on time with our class.
6. Because we want to graduate on time with our class, we are carefully practicing our writing skills.

Nonessential Information

Sometimes commas are used to set off information that is not essential to the meaning of the sentence. Often, but not always, this is introductory information. For example, "Happily, all students were successful on the exam," or, "Because we had studied diligently, we were all successful." See if you can see where to place a comma in the sentences below:

1. We wanted to win the trophy our third this week.
2. We wanted to win our third trophy this week.
3. Our third trophy this week the statue was in the center of the case.
4. Our third trophy this week was in the center of the case.

Sentence 1 should have a comma after trophy because the central information being conveyed in the sentence is, *We wanted to win the trophy.* The fact that it was the third one that week is nonessential information. On the other hand, no comma was necessary in sentence 2 because there is no introductory clause. All information is essential. In sentence 3, a comma should follow *week* because it separates the introductory words identifying the trophy, which again are not essential to the meaning of the sentence (*the statue was in the center of the* case). The fourth sentence needs no other punctuation.

Apostrophes

When you are looking over your work for grammatical errors, be sure to check the apostrophes. These marks are used to indicate possession with nouns, but not with pronouns. Words like *his*, *hers*, *theirs*, *ours*, *its*, *yours*, and *mine* don't use apostrophes to show possession.

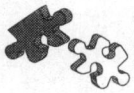 Apostrophes show possession with nouns, not pronouns.

While you are looking at apostrophes, remember that they are also used in contractions when letters are deleted, such as *don't* for *do not*, *we're* for *we are*, and so on. However, apostrophes do not show plurals. Watch out for these.

 Apostrophes do not indicate plurals.

Again, let's practice. See if you can place apostrophes in the appropriate places below:

Im glad we got his report from the teachers notebook. Its a good report, and its possibilities are numerous. Were in good shape compared to where we were last year.

You should have marked apostrophes on *I'm*, *teacher's*, *It's*, and *We're*. The lowercase *its* is the possessive and doesn't need an apostrophe, and the lowercase *were* is the past tense of the verb *to be*. The corrected paragraph should look like this:

I'm glad we got his report from the teachers notebook. It's a good report, and its possibilities are numerous. We're in good shape compared to where we were last year.

Quotation Marks

Quotation marks are great for identifying the exact words of a speaker, but be careful to make sure it is a direct quote that is being noted. If the piece uses the word *that*, as in *says that*, it is not referring to the exact words of the speaker. For example, look at the sentence below.

The article said that Mrs. Johnson had been a teacher for twenty-seven years.

In this case there would be no need for quotation marks because what is being recorded does not represent Mrs. Johnson's exact words. On the other hand, notice the difference in the following sentence:

Mrs. Johnson said, "I have been a teacher twenty-seven years,"

In this case you would need quotation marks because these are words actually spoken by Mrs. Johnson.

Again, see if you can correctly add quotation marks to the two sentences below:

1. The daughter loudly proclaimed that she was not going home at that early hour!
2. The daughter loudly proclaimed I am not going home at that early hour!

Did you notice that sentence 1 was not a direct quote (as indicated by *that*) and in sentence 2 the daughter actually said the words? Thus, in sentence 2 *proclaimed* should be followed by a comma and quotation marks, and quotation marks should also follow the end exclamation mark. The sentence should read as follows:

The daughter loudly proclaimed, "I am not going home at that early hour!"

Another place quotation marks are often tested is in titles. For a rule of thumb, if it is the title of something short—that is, it can be read in thirty minutes or so (like a short story, poem, song, article in a newspaper or magazine, or a chapter in a book)—the title is placed within quotation marks. Longer titles are underlined (such as titles of books, newspapers, magazines, movies, and albums).

Colons

Colons are another sophisticated punctuation easy to test on standardized tests. Of course, you know colons are used when expressing time (3:15 A.M.), lines from poetry (3:4 for stanza 3, line 4), or scripture from the Bible (Psalms 23:1). You will probably be tested on these with sentences that introduce a list or a long quotation. Examples include:

Our camp required we take the following:
sleeping bags, mosquito repellent, and water.

The principal told the teachers: "Station yourselves at the doors to your classrooms during all passing periods. Make sure you are there by the ringing of the first bell and at the last bell. There will be no exceptions. The security of our school depends on you."

Hyphens

Another concept easily tested is hyphens. Make sure you use them in numbers from twenty-one to ninety-nine, for fractions (one-fifth), and for compound nouns and adjectives (cross-country).

Capitalization

And it goes without saying that capitalization is important. You know to capitalize the first word of every sentence and the first and most important words in titles and proper names. Remember, too, that you also must capitalize directions when they refer to specific geographic locations. For example, "We traveled north last summer," should be, "We traveled to the North last summer." In the second instance, *North* is capitalized because it refers to a specific geographic location; the word *the* was your clue. Also, adjectives formed from proper nouns are capitalized, as in Mexican food (food from Mexico) or African dialect (dialect from Africa.)

By the time you've reached eleventh grade, though, understanding basic grammatical structure is more or less second nature. You've learned it directly, through classroom practice, and indirectly through your reading. If, however, you feel your background is weak in a particular area, ask your teacher for help or check out the internet. There are many good sites with exercises on sentence combining, punctuation, and revising, and any time spent in review will help bolster your confidence on test day.

 Surf internet Web sites for more explanations and examples.

Usage

The ELA TAKS also evaluates usage, which has to do with subject-verb agreement, pronoun-antecedent agreement, verb forms, and modifiers. It also deals with the use of active and passive voice, parallel construction, and sentence variety. However, usage isn't anything new. Like the grammatical structures just reviewed, it is exactly what you have been studying in your writing since kindergarten. Let's take a quick look at some problem areas.

Subject-Verb Agreement

First of all, with subject-verb agreement, remember that singular verbs take singular subjects, and plural verbs take plural subjects. The troublesome pairs are when *or* or *nor* are used. In these cases, the verb agrees with the subject closest to it.

For example, look below and see if you can tell whether the sentences are correct:

1 Tishara and Juan play basketball.
2 Neither Tishara nor Juan play basketball.
3 Either Tishara or Juan play basketball.

The first sentence is correct as is. The names *Tishara* and *Juan* form a plural subject that could be replaced by the pronoun *they*. Thus, the plural verb *play* is correct. In the second and third examples, though, the verb *plays* is correct because the subject closest to the verb in each sentence (*Juan*) is singular.

Think of it this way, in the third person (*he*, *she*, *they*), a singular subject takes a verb ending in **s**, whereas a plural subject's verb does not end in **s**. It seems backward, but if you remember this it may help.

Pronouns

Another problem area of usage commonly tested on the ELA TAKS is pronouns. Indefinite pronouns pose particular problems, and the easiest way to be successful is simply to memorize which pronouns are singular and which are plural. Common sense tells us that *everybody* and *everyone* sound like lots of people. However, both require singular verbs. Look at the makeup of each word. Every [single] body and every [single] one. Each will take a singular verb. Same thing with *anybody*, *anyone*, *each*, *either*, and *nobody*.

Likewise, *both*, *many*, *few*, and *several* are always plural.

See if you identify whether the following sentences are correct:

1 Everybody choose a favorite song.
2 Nobody choose a favorite song.
3 Many choose a favorite song.
4 Several choose a favorite song.
5 Anyone choose a favorite song.

Sentences 3 and 4 are correct; the others needed the verb *chooses* because each subject contains a singular pronoun.

As for modifiers, remember you need to place what you are describing as close as possible to the description. If not, the result can be humorous. For example:

1 Sunning on the riverbank, the fish could be seen as I looked in the water.
2 Sunning on the riverbank, I saw the fish swimming in the water.

In the first sentence, the fish are basking on the riverbank, whereas in the second sentence the speaker is the one sunning.

Parallel Construction

Another area you need to check is parallel construction, which means using matching grammatical forms. Not only does it make writing flow, it helps clarify your ideas. For example, you would say, "Brandon likes to swim, to fish, and to hike," rather than, "Brandon likes to swim, to fish, and hiking." In the first sentence all of the activities Brandon enjoys are described using the same verb form, an infinitive. In the second example, *to hike* became *hiking*, a form that is not parallel with *to swim* and *to fish*.

See if you can identify which of the following sentences make good use of parallel construction:

1 The students clapped, cheered, and were dancing when the last bell rang for the school year.
2 Do you prefer playing football, watching wrestling, or reading a good book?
3 The best place to have a picnic is in the shade, on a huge picnic table, and away from bugs.

If you guessed sentences 2 and 3, you are correct.

Sentence 2 correctly uses gerunds to name the three activities, and sentence 3 uses three prepositional phrases. On the other hand, sentence 1 shifts from using the simple past tense (*clapped* and *cheered*) to adding the helping verb *were*. Remember, though, that on the ELA TAKS test you don't have to use the grammatical names. You just have to be able to recognize the correct construction, and the more reading you do, the more language begins to simply sound right. So don't forget to keep up your 15 minutes a day of practice with various written texts.

Active Voice

Your teacher has probably told you that using the active voice, rather than the passive voice, makes your writing more vivid and alive. For example, look at the two sentences below.

1. Robert ate the hamburger.
2. The hamburger was eaten by Robert.

The first sentence is in the active voice because the subject (*Robert*) performs the action (*ate*). In the second sentence, the action (*was eaten*) was performed on the subject (*hamburger*). Although active voice is bolder and more direct, passive voice does have a place. It is commonly used in scientific reports and in sentences where the writer is being noncommittal. It is also used when the importance is being placed on the action rather than the actor, as well as when the actor is obvious, unimportant, or unknown.

For your ELA TAKS essay, though, when you want your writing to stand out and be concise and clear, you should use the active voice. Thus, when you are in the editing phase of your writing process, any time you see a form of the auxiliary verb *to be* (a quick indication of passive voice), try to recast the sentence.

Look below and see if you can pick out active or passive voice.

1. The boat crossed the lake.
2. The lake was crossed by the boat.
3. The game was won in the ninth inning.
4. We won the game in the ninth inning.

If you guessed sentences 1 and 4 to be the active voice, you are right; in both cases the subject (*boat* and *we*) performed the action (*crossed* and *won*). In sentences 2 and 3 the action (*crossed* and *won*) was performed on the subject (*lake* and *game*).

 Use the active voice for your ELA TAKS essay.

Sentence Structure

Still another area of consideration in usage is sentence structure. Sentences come in all shapes and sizes. They can be simple, compound, complex, or compound-complex, and how you use them determines your style of writing. If you consistently only use one or two structures, and if your sentences are generally the same length, your writing will come across as boring and elementary. Variety adds interest and helps to keep the reader involved, but if all your sentences are complex, your writing may be too complicated and confusing. They key is to use a combination of structures. Alternate beginning your sentences with prepositional phrases, participial phrases, and dependent clauses. This will not only add variety but also move your writing up a notch on the graders' scale. Instead of first saying who did what, you might start with *where* or *why* or words that describe the action or the persons or things doing it. Look at the simple introduction below.

It was a dark and stormy night. It was the children's first night away from home. The electricity went off. The children were scared. They waited and waited. Then it came on again.

All the sentences are the same, but adding a few descriptive words and varying the sentence structure adds much more interest.

On a dark and stormy night, the children's first away from home, the electricity went off. Terrified, they huddled in the darkness until they heard the hum announcing its return.

Also, don't forget that along with having various sentence structures, you need to use good transitions, making sure they are appropriate for the content. You don't want the reader to notice these. Their function is to seamlessly knit your ideas together, allowing your reader to see the logic of your original thoughts.

Okay. Time for some more practice.

Practice, Practice, Practice

Below you will find a diagnostic exercise that will help determine your areas of strength and weakness. See if you can correctly rewrite each sentence in the provided box.

1. the athletic booster club has invited coach sam mcgee to address the students in the english and social studies classes next monday when he returns from visiting the south on his civil war tour.

2. who said ask not what your country can do for you ask what you can do for your country

3. caught off gard we heard the whistle before we saw the referee

4. caught off guard the whistle was heard before the referee was seen

5 lashaunda did you see the horse running across wrigley football field without a saddle

6 when i started preparing for this test i knew I would do my best no matter how much time it might take me

7 every occassion to think about possible topics I can write about are definately helpful to i

8 reading writing and to practice are my goals for this year and I think I will be successful

9 there newest invention a remote controlled water gun might of been fun if it's inventer new how two tell time

10 knowing what I want to say is one thing saying it correct is something else

Answer Explanations

Sentence 1: Capitalize the following: The Athletic Booster Club, Coach Sam McGee, English, Monday, South, Civil War (If you missed these you need to review capitalization.)

Sentence 2: Who said, "Ask not what your country can do for you; ask what you can do for your country?" (If you missed this, you need more work on punctuation of dialogue, compound sentences, and punctuation with semicolons.)

Sentence 3: Caught off guard, we heard the whistle before we saw the referee. (If you missed this, you need help with capitalization, spelling, and introductory participial phrases.)

Sentence 4: When we heard the whistle before we saw the referee, we were caught off guard. (This sentence measures your understanding of introductory participial phrases and dangling modifiers.)

Sentence 5: LaShaunda, did you see the horse without a saddle running across Wrigley Football Field? (If you missed this, you need to review punctuation, misplaced modifiers, and capitalization.)

Sentence 6: When I started preparing for this test, I knew I would do my best, no matter how much time it might take me. (This sentence evaluates introductory dependent clauses and punctuation.)

Sentence 7: Every occasion to think about possible topics I can write about is definitely helpful to me. (If you missed this, you need help with capitalization, spelling, subject-verb agreement, and pronoun usage.)

Sentence 8: Reading, writing, and practicing are my goals for this year, and I think I will be successful. (If you missed this, you need to practice parallel construction, understanding run-on sentences, and spelling.)

Sentence 9: Their newest invention, a remote controlled water gun, might have been fun if its inventors knew how to tell time. (If you missed this, you need help with pronouns, nonessential elements, and homonyms.)

Sentence 10: Knowing what I want to say is one thing; saying it correctly is something else. (This sentence measures your understanding of run-on sentences and adverbs.)

Of course, this is not how questions will appear on the ELA TAKS; this is just a quick review of mechanics and usage. It can, though, measure your grammatical comfort zone. If you feel you need more help, look in the glossary, the quick-reference section, or the index of your grammar and composition text. And you can always ask your teacher for help, or, again, check out the internet. There are many good sites with exercises on sentence combining, punctuation, and revising.

Final Thoughts

The bottom line is before you transfer your composition onto the answer document, you must take the time to attend to the small details. If you do this, if you use the mechanics of the English language correctly, your message will be coherent and unified. It will show the grader that you know what you are doing, that you understand your response must be reasonable, relevant to the topic and reflect original voice. The grader should be able to see *you* in your writing, *your* attitude and personality revealed by your words. Your transitions, progression of ideas, and coherence will prove that your writing has depth of development and an authentic voice. The details—the small things that no one notices when they are done correctly—will hold your piece together.

And your composition will excel.

Review Box
→ Usage and mechanics will be evaluated on both Part I and Part II of the ELA TAKS
→ You will not have to know the names of specific grammatical forms, but you will have to know how to recognize whether or not something is written correctly.
→ Reading helps you learn to recognize good writing.

Chapter 15

Analyzing Proofreading Skills

Maria fingered her folder. How long had she worked on this paper? Days? Months? Years? No, it just seemed like years because she didn't get her first draft printed until after midnight. And now her teacher wants her to read over it and make corrections? Doesn't the silly lady realize that if she *knew* she'd made a mistake, she would have corrected it before she printed it out? Next they'd probably be exchanging papers, and she hated that part. Thomas was always so busy looking at the mistakes she found on his paper, he never even noticed any on hers, and Chelsea always got such an attitude, and Karen couldn't even spell.

"Oh, well," Maria said to herself. The whole assignment didn't make sense, but she needed the daily grade. So like it or not, she was going to have to give it her best try.

Ever feel like Maria? Wonder why, when you've done your best, you have to look at your paper again?

The Final Touch

This last picky part of the writing process is called proofreading. For some thinkers, those who have slaved over the creative process, it is the easiest; for others, those who find ideas flow easily from pen to page, it is agonizing. For both, though, it is crucial. It is your last chance to make your piece really stand out from everyone else's, your last chance to make it great.

Published writers write and rewrite and rewrite again.

And so must you.

Why? Because when you are creating, your brain can do funny things. It can *think* it sees something you have written because it *knows* that is what you meant to write. The closer you are to your writing, the more connected you feel to what you've said, the more this is true. That is why it is usually a good idea to plan ahead and allow some time to pass between when you write an essay and when you proof it one final time before printing the final draft.

Ideally, this would be a week or so. Realistically, the best-case scenario might be overnight. This gives your brain distance, allows it to "forget" what it *knows* you have written and actually see what is there. But as you know, the world of ELA TAKS is a world of its own, and you must learn to function within its parameters. Because you take the test in one sitting, you won't be able to let your composition rest, so you must learn the strategies that will enable you to be the most successful in the testing situation.

Proofreading on ELA TAKS

Your ability to catch errors can impact ELA TAKS in two places. First, your written piece and open-ended responses are being graded as polished drafts. You not only have plenty of space to plan out your answers in your test booklet before you commit them to the answer document but also are expected to use your dictionary and thesaurus. So the graders will be looking at your essay with this in mind. They will expect good word choice and organization, accurate spelling, and use of correct grammatical conventions; they will also be looking at content and style. If these things hinder your message, points will be deducted, so any mistakes you can find and correct by proofreading your own written composition will definitely pay off.

The other place where proofreading is paramount is in the revising and editing section of the test where you are asked to read a written piece and show how it can be improved. You need to look for things like spelling, capitalization, punctuation, subject-verb agreement, pronoun-antecedent agreement, verb forms, parallelism, sentence combining, organization of ideas, sentence structure, and word choice—all the things you've been learning in English class for the last 11 years. The difficulty is that at this point you will not be able to use a dictionary or a thesaurus.

The Written Composition

Thus, although both sections require good proofreading skills, they should be approached differently. On your composition and open-ended questions, no one will ever ask if you have proofread, just like no one will ask if you have prewritten or drafted your ideas in your test booklet before writing them in your answer document. However, you simply cannot achieve your best score if you do not do these things.

So this is where you start, by writing your answer in the blank space provided in the test booklet. Then, put on your editor's hat. As mentioned before, you won't have time to let the composition rest, as you would in an ideal setting. So you must tell your brain to let go, to look at the writing as if it were someone else's. What would you tell your best friend if he or she brought you the piece you've just written and asked you to find any mistakes?

Checking for Spelling Errors

One good way to find spelling errors is to read the composition backward. If any word doesn't look right, look it up in your dictionary. This is especially important for all those homonyms—their, they're, there; to, two, too; its, it's; your, you're; effect, affect; and choice, choose. When you see any of these words, automatically stop and make sure that you have used the correct form.

 Read backward to catch spelling errors.

Some are dead-on-the-page words. For example words like *a lot*, *nice*, *fine*, *very*, and *things* have little impact. Eliminate them wherever possible.

Checking for Complete Sentences

Next, check for complete sentences. Put your left thumb to the left of the first word of a sentence and your right thumb to the right of the last word. Carefully read the enclosed material. Does it constitute a complete thought? If so, you are okay. If not, correct it.

If more than one thought is given, make sure you have used the correct punctuation to join the two. What we are talking about here is joining independent clauses, but don't worry. You won't be asked to tell if a group of words is a phrase or an independent or dependent clause. What you will be expected to do is correctly join them. Remember you can join sentences together with either a semicolon or a comma and a coordinating conjunction. In elementary school, the acronym FANBOYS is commonly used to help students remember the coordinating conjunctions—*for*, *and*, *nor*, *but*, *or*, *yet*, *so*. Just be sure the connection logically links the two ideas.

Also, check to make sure that if you have asked a question that you have used a question mark and that if you have used quotations that you have correctly included the exact words of the speaker.

Checking Agreement

Next, think about agreement, starting with the subject and verb. Find only the verb of your sentence; then find only the subject. Do they sound correct? For example, if you said, "The main problem for all of the students are the books they have to carry," what you are really talking about is the problem (singular) and not the students. The verb should agree with the subject of your sentence (problem) and not with the object of the preposition (students). When you repeat only the subject and the verb, you would say, "problem is," so you would correct your sentence to read, "The main problem for all of the students is the books they have to carry."

 You don't have to know technical terms, but you do need to be able to recognize the right answer.

Checking Pronouns

Identify any pronoun, perhaps by circling it on your planning pages, and draw an arrow to the word to which it refers. Are they the same in number and gender? You can check whether you have used them correctly by consulting your dictionary. For example, you have said, "Anybody can see the advantages of summer vacation, and they will agree with me." You circle *anybody* and draw an arrow to *they*. You know you mean many people can do this, but the antecedent *anybody* is identified in the dictionary as singular, so the pronoun referring to it must also be singular. The correct rewrite is, "Anybody can see the advantages of summer vacation, and he or she will agree with me." You can look this up in the dictionary because you are still in the composing section.

Again, committing to memory this list of indefinite singular pronouns is helpful: anybody, anyone, anything, each, either, everybody, everyone, everything, neither, nobody, no one, nothing, one, somebody, someone, something. All of these must have singular pronouns referring to them.

Checking Gerunds, Participles and Infinitives

Another area of the test explores your proficiency in using gerunds, participles, and infinitives. Although you won't be asked to identify them, you will be asked to show that you know how to use them. You will be expected to make sentences sound smooth with similar construction and to place modifiers near the words they are referring to. For instance, if you wrote, "The main things I enjoy about summer are sleeping late, going to bed late, and I don't have homework," you would be expected to recast the sentence as follows: "The main things I enjoy about summer are sleeping late, going to bed late, and not doing homework." Here you have changed all phrases into gerunds. Or you could have said, "The main things I enjoy about summer are I can sleep late, I can go to bed late, and I don't have homework." Now you have changed these mismatched phrases into independent clauses. You won't be expected to explain that; just to do it. And you can see how your rewrite better matches the parts.

Or perhaps you wrote, "The teacher said when school is out for the summer the students should read novels." Did you mean that the teacher made that statement when school was out, or that the novels should be read when school was out? You would therefore correct it for clarity by saying, "When school was out, the teacher said that the students should read novels." A second interpretation would be, "The teacher said the students should read novels when school was out." See the difference? This is called placing modifiers near the words they are describing. Again, you aren't expected to identify the error or give it a name; you are simply expected to correct it.

Revising and Editing

When you have finished proofreading both the open-ended responses and the composition for sentence structure, spelling, capitalization, punctuation, agreement, and organization and you have copied all answers neatly into your answer document, it is time to move on. First, though, you must turn in your dictionary and thesaurus. Then you can read the pieces you are to edit for revision.

A typical question might ask you how to rearrange sentences or how to link thoughts. All sentences are numbered, and the question will identify each area to be corrected. So you would begin by rereading the section, substituting in the possible answer choices. If you need to add a connection, ask yourself which one would best fit.

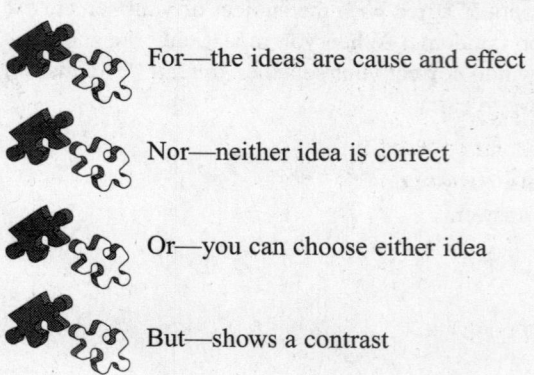

For—the ideas are cause and effect

Nor—neither idea is correct

Or—you can choose either idea

But—shows a contrast

🧩 Yet—shows you can reconsider

🧩 So—another way to show cause and effect

Okay. Let's practice.
Say your friend has written the following piece explaining how the school broadcast team decided to create a wall of heroes honoring military personnel.

The Wall of Heroes

(1) When our country recently went to war, we wanted to do something to show our campus that we cared that they had friends or loved ones in harm's way. (2) We decided to create a Wall of Heroes. (3) That wall would list everyone in the military who people on our campus cared about. (4) We wanted to display it. (5) We wanted to call attention to it. (6) We wanted to share our concern. (7) We wanted to show our campus that we cared. (8) We did not want it to become a political issue. (9) Or an emotional issue.

(10) We started this on the second day war had started. (11) Later we saw that several of the networks were doing the same thing. (12) Our biggest problem had been in keeping our list updated. (13) We were pleased that we were on the cutting edge. (14) Every day we would here of additional graduates serving in the military. (15) Our list then became so long that we were worried about it taking up to much of our production time. (16) Everyone seemed to be giving us names of all the people they know who had ever been in the military.

(17) Then a funny thing happened the fighting was declared finished. (18) Nobody was interested in it. (19) We started asking ourselves if Military Personnel are important to us only when a war is going on.

(20) That question has led us to the next phase of our project. (21) We now want to ask everybody to send us names of who they consider to be heroes for any reason. (22) And to tell us why. (23) We don't have to be at war to have heroes.

Clearly your friend is sincere, but the delivery is lacking because the ideas have not been coordinated. They sound choppy and childish.

On the ELA TAKS, this might be presented in the revision passage in the following way. See which answer you would pick.

Multiple-Choice Questions

1. What is the best way to combine sentences 1 and 2?
   A Add *so* after sentence 1 and add sentence 2
   B Add *yet* after sentence 1 and add sentence 2
   C Add *for* after sentence 1 and add sentence 2
   D Make no change

2. What is the best way to rewrite the ideas in sentences 4, 5, and 6?
   F By displaying it, we thought we could share our concern.
   G We wanted to display it, so we wanted to call attention to it.
   H Delete sentence 4.
   J By displaying it, our concern could be shared.

3 What is the best way to combine sentences 8 and 9?
   A We did not want it to become a political or emotional issue.
   B We did not want it to become a political issue, or an emotional issue.
   C We did not want it to become a political issue; or an emotional issue.
   D Make no change.

4 What change, if any, should be made in sentence 14?
   F Change *Every day* to **everyday**
   G Change *here* to **hear**
   H Change *graduates* to **graduate's**
   J Make no change

5 What change, if any, should be made in sentence 15?
   A Change *worried* to **worryed**
   B Add a comma after *now*
   C Change *to* to **too**
   D Make no change

6 What change, if any, should be made in sentence 17?
   F Insert a comma after *happened*
   G Insert a semicolon after *happened*
   H Insert *when* after *happened*
   J Make no change

7 What change, if any, should be made in sentence 18?
   A Nobody wasn't interested in it.
   B Change *interested* to **interested**
   C Change *it* to **the wall**
   D Make no change

8 Which transition should be added to the beginning of sentence 18?
   F Besides,
   G However,
   H Consequently,
   J Nevertheless,

9 What is the most effective way to improve the organization in paragraph 2?
   A Place sentence 12 after sentence 13
   B Begin with sentence 16
   C Delete sentence 14
   D Make no change

10 What is the best way to combine sentences 21 and 22?
    F Insert a comma after *reason*.
    G We now want to ask everyone to send us names of all their heroes and to tell us why they are heroes.
    H We now want everyone to send us names and reasons.
    J Make no change.

Answer Explanations

Now, let's look at the answers.

Question 1: The best combination of sentences is response **A**, combining them with *so* because this shows cause and effect. The sentences are correctly written, so answer **D** is grammatically correct, but the better and more sophisticated writing would be in combining them as in answer **A**.

Question 2: The best combination of sentences 4, 5, and 6 is **F**. There is no cause or effect, so **B** is incorrect. Sentence 4 contains necessary information, so it cannot be deleted. Answer **D** has a dangling modifier because it isn't clear what would be displayed.

Question 3: "Or an emotional issue" is not a complete sentence, so sentences 8 and 9 cannot be connected with a comma or a semicolon, making **B** and **C** incorrect. Answer **A** is correct.

Question 4: Answer **G** is correct; the homonym **here** refers to place, not sound.

Question 5: Answer **C** is correct; **too** refers to excessive amount.

Question 6: **G** is correct because two simple sentences (independent clauses) can be joined with a semicolon if the ideas are similar.

Question 7: **C** is correct because it clarifies what no one was interested in

Question 8: *Consequently* (answer **H**) indicates why there was no longer any interest in the wall of military heroes.

Question 9: **A** is correct. Placing sentence 12 after sentence 13 follows the chronologic organization.

Question 10: **G** is correct because it uses parallel construction of infinitive phrases. Again, you don't have to know those words; you know the comma with *and* is used when a simple sentence follows it, and you know that **C** left out important information. It wasn't correctly written because "And to tell us why" is not a complete sentence.

On the test, the problem areas have already been selected for you. All you have to do is find the section in question, examine it, try out all the possibilities, and select the best correction.

Final Thoughts

Many students find it effective to mark the mistakes they see as they read the passage through, before they even look at the questions and possible suggestions. You might try that on some of the passages in this book to see if it helps.

How you go about getting the right answer is not important. Being able to explain the problem is not being measured on this test, either. You only have to revise the passage in one of the ways already suggested, or, if you eliminated all the answer suggestions as having errors, select "make no change."

The revision is the last part of the test. You don't have to think of anything new or creative; you just have to select the best answer. The more you read, the more you practice, the easier it gets.

And once done, you can close your test booklet, check over your answer document, and then turn in your work.

You have completed the ELA TAKS.

And it is time to relax.

Review Box
→ You must proofread all open-ended responses as well as the composition, even though this is not stated in the test.
→ Proofread as if it were someone else's work.
→ Use your reference materials to help you with the open-ended responses as well as the composition.
→ In the revising and editing section, put each possible answer into the selected sentence to see if the change is better.
→ In the revising and editing section, look for obvious errors in the possible answer choices.
→ Trust your instincts.

COMMON PROOFREADING SYMBOLS

Symbol	Meaning	Example
ℰ or ɤ or ᵍ⁄	delete	take it out
⌒	close up	print as o ne word
ℬ	delete and close up	close up
∧ or > or ⋏	insert something	insert here (something
stet	let stand	let marked text stand as set
tr	transpose	change order the
¶	begin a new paragraph	
SP	spell out	set 5 lbs. as five pounds
cap	set in CAPITALS	set nato as NATO
lc	set in lowercase	set South as south
ital	set in *italic*	set oeuvre as *oeuvre*
rom	set in roman	set *mensch* as mensch
bf	set in **boldface**	set important as **important**
= or -/ or ⸗ or /H/	hyphen	multi-colored
ˆ	comma	
˅	apostrophe	
⊙	period	
; or ;/	semicolon	
: or ⊙	colon	
❝❞ or ˘˘	quotation marks	

Part Five

Practice Tests for the ELA TAKS

Chapter 16

Practice Test A

Reading and Written Composition

DIRECTIONS: Read the two passages and the visual piece. Then answer the questions that follow.

In her novel Happenings, *Katie Cobb explores a modern protest. The main character, Kelsey Blackwell, has joined in a sit-in with her friends, to object to her teacher's instructional methods. As she sits in class in a nonresponsive pose, her mind wanders around the room, trying not only to pass time but also to understand the significance of the event for her own life.*

Day One
by Katie Cobb

1 Seconds after the bell Mrs. Delaney rushed though the front door and worked her way to the back, picking a path around backpacks and long legs, using the side of her loafer to scoot Terrance's notebook under his desk.

2 *I wonder when she'll notice?* Kelsey thought. To be joined with others in a collective stand felt exciting, but Mrs. Delaney seemed to be a sensitive person. Had anyone considered that she might feel hurt?

3 Kelsey heard a rustle of papers, and her sympathy disappeared. She didn't even have to turn around to know that this class had begun like all recent ones. Mrs. Delaney had entered the room and walked straight to her station in the back, picked up the dreaded stack from the upper-left-hand corner of her desk, and started distributing her boring assignment, sending papers and more papers of monotonous questions up each isle. "Please read the following passage and select the correct answer for each multiple-choice question. Do the following sentence completions, analogies, vocabulary exercises."

4 Kelsey was sick of the same routine, day after day, week after week. What was wrong with Mrs. Delaney, anyhow? Why the change? No more prodding discussions and spirited debates; no more challenging essays. All she assigned any more were grammar exercises and reading passages and questions, questions, questions. Talk about dull.

5 In fact, the work looked like the same type of stuff Kelsey did when she took an SAT prep class. Only they weren't preparing for the SAT; they were signed up to take the AP test, the *advanced placement* test. So how were the SAT exercises helping. . . ?

6 Today it took less than three minutes for the correct number of pages to be distributed. There were five assignments in all: a grammar exercise, a vocabulary drill, a set of analogies, and two long reading passages with questions. As usual Mrs. Delaney was settled behind her desk, attendance taken, assignment given, in under five minutes.

7 Seconds later Kelsey heard the swishing of a moving skirt followed by a soft shuffle. She ached to know what was happening, but she didn't dare turn around. Like everyone else, she sat still, hands folded on top of the work sheets stacked neatly in the center of her desk. She felt, more than saw, her teacher's gaze wandering around the room. Finally Mrs. Delaney spoke.

Notes

8   "Okay. Someone tell me what is going on?"

9   Drew was ready for his five minutes of fame. "We're having a sit-in, protesting until you start teaching us like you did last semester."

10 "E-e-excuse me?" Mrs. Delaney sputtered. "*You're* telling *me* what to do?"

11 Kelsey chanced a quick glance. Mrs. Delaney's usual calm expression had taken on a sharp edge, like someone trying hard to regain control.

12 "This isn't a democracy," she said, color invading her cheeks. "Get to work."

13 No one moved.

14 Slowly Mrs. Delaney started walking, hands stuffed deep in her pockets, up one aisle, down another, until finally she stopped beside JJ's desk.

15 "Javier, do you agree with this?" she asked, touching his back.

16 JJ's neck turned red as he nodded.

17 "Ratasha," Mrs. Delaney said, moving over an aisle, "you've always prided yourself on your independence. Do you agree with this?"

18 "Yes, ma'am," came the soft response. "We want you to, you know, teach us like you did last semester."

19 "Well, you know what?" Mrs. Delaney said, addressing the whole class. "How I teach is my business, and yours is to get to work. Now." Her words rushed into the air, demanding attention, but still nobody moved.

20 "Whatever," Mrs. Delaney mumbled, returning to her desk. "Your assignment is due at the end of the period."

21 Five minutes down; fifty to go.

22 An unwelcomed sense of isolation seeped into Kelsey's heart, even though she was sitting in a room full of people. She took a deep breath and hunkered down for the duration. Her hands were jittery, her heart racing. She wanted out.

23 *Then why don't you get up and leave?*

24 *Right.* She answered herself. *Then I'd get written up for a cut and Russell would have a fit.* She frowned deeply at the thought. She hated being accountable to anyone, let alone a thirty-year-old sibling, but like it or not, their dad's will had clearly appointed Russ guardian. And she had no doubt her law-abiding brother would expect her to maintain a standard of conduct that did not include taking part in a sit-in.

25 *Well it's my life*, she told as her eyes roamed over the heads of her classmates, all staring forward, hands folded, idle. That was one advantage of sitting near the back—she could at least look around.

26 She'd never seen Terrance so still. Usually he was stretching his back or crossing his legs or any of a dozen other things in an effort to find comfort in a world built too small for his six-foot six frame. His mother would be about as pleased as Russ if she knew what was going on . . . .

27 . . . JJ said Terrance's greatest talent was his ability to blend with a team and strengthen the whole. "Smooth" was the word JJ used, though the only thing Kelsey knew was that she liked watching Terrance play.

28 On the flip side, JJ said he most repected Kelsey for her calm, logical mind, and then he'd laugh uproariously. No one who knew Kelsey would agree with such a description. It would be like calling a lioness a lamb.

29 Her eyes shifted slightly and found JJ's back. One of the most popular students on campus, JJ—Javier Juarez—was into everything. He played trombone in the band, soccer on the weekends, and was president

of the Student Council. He was treasurer of the Science Club and volunteered as a student translator—that is, when he wasn't working. He spent almost twenty hours a week helping his Dad in their family-owned auto shop, something he enjoyed almost as much as geology. JJ's dream was to open a jewelry store, maybe with a partner, one who could handle the business end while JJ dealt with the gems.

30 *If he gets to go to college.*
31 What a sobering thought. JJ's family was huge, seven brothers and sisters, and his best chance of continuing his education was pinned squarely on winning a scholarship. Even though he didn't seem as intense as some of the guys she knew, JJ had an inward determination that bordered on obsession. For him, testing out of freshman English wasn't just a lark; it was a financial perk he couldn't afford to lose.
32 Kelsey's attention moved on to Ratasha, who, like the others, sat erect with eyes straight ahead. JJ said she was one good-looking woman, but she ignored him the way she did everyone who flattered and teased. She didn't want to be derailed with sweet talk and promises because she wanted to make a difference. She was proud of her heritage, her culture, and it bothered her to hear others speak glibly of Martin Luther King in terms of a holiday or of Malcolm X as an excuse for disruption. She planned to major in education to be sure that the next generation understood the meaning behind the great leaders' words.
33 Again Kelsey scanned the room. How much time had passed? Ten minutes? Fifteen? Shoulders were now sagging, and occasionally a head drooped forward. Fifty-five minutes was a long time to do nothing. Had Drew considered that?
34 Probably not. Perhaps the most intelligent of the group, he had little ambition. Russ's word for Drew was "spoiled," and while she hated to side with her brother, in some ways Kelsey agreed. Once Drew's parents caught him smoking pot and told him they were disappointed.
35 *Disappointed?* What a deal! If Kelsey's father had caught her with pot, he would definitely have done more than tell her he was "disappointed." She wasn't sure exactly what. . . .
36 Russ, though, she could predict. As a state trooper he had no problems meting out consequences. He'd simply ground her for eternity, and then turn her over to their middle brother, Nathan. In his second year of medical school, Nathan had a way of getting into Kelsey's head and making her really think. . . .
37 The good news was that after staying stoned once for nearly a month, Drew sobered up on his own. He wanted to be a writer, and he used this as an excuse to do crazy, unacceptable things, supposedly to build up his "well of personal experience". . . .
38 The sound of the bell brought a stirring of relief as weary backs relaxed and stiff legs flexed. With exaggerated precision Drew gathered his papers into a careful pile, one page, two. When all five were stacked, crisp and neat, he walked to the back of the room and laid them on Mrs. Delaney's desk. She didn't even glance up. One by one the others did the same, crisscrossing the sets so that each remained separate. Kelsey stared in mute surprise at the regulated performance. It was as if they'd rehearsed! Still she followed along, too, more hurried than most, anxious not to be the last one caught in the room.

Notes

39 And suddenly it was over. Kelsey rushed through the crowded hall, weaving in and out, down the stairs, to the right. Lockers slammed; voices swelled; everything was the same, like yesterday. Right?

40 Wrong. Yesterday she hadn't just taken part in a sit-in, refusing to work. Yesterday she had simply done her assignment, turned it in, and walked on to her next class.

41 Surely tomorrow Mrs. Delaney would go back to the way she used to teach. Once she'd had a chance to think things over, she'd come around.

42 But what if she didn't?

43 Kelsey felt an uneasy emptiness settle deep in her stomach. She'd seen the backslaps as she left the room, heard Drew bragging about how tomorrow would be even better.

44 Tomorrow?

45 Wasn't it supposed to be a one-day protest? Something to get Mrs. Delaney's attention?

46 Even if he didn't like it, Russ would probably understand why Kelsey initially joined her friends, but he'd never agree that a second day or third was necessary. She hated it when Russ fussed at her, just hated it. But if the protest continues, she'd have to stick.

47 *Maybe Mrs. Delaney will get the message and start teaching like she used to*, Kelsey thought, settling in for her last class, but the words had a hollow ring. Mrs. Delaney hasn't reacted at all as they'd expected.

48 [An] alarm sounded, the one deep in her head, warning, and . . . . Kelsey shut it off, pushing it back where it could no longer be heard. After all, there was nothing she could do, not really, not until after their next class, after Mrs. Delaney had had a chance to think things through.

49 *No use worrying about what hasn't happened*, she told herself. Tomorrow would come soon enough.

In 1846 Henry David Thoreau was arrested and spent one night in jail for refusing to pay his poll tax. He saw his resistance to the dictates of state government as protest against both slavery and the Mexican-American war. He did not protest against highway taxes or school taxes, but felt that a poll tax put money into the government in an unfair and unjust way. The following is taken from Thoreau's essay "Civil Disobedience," in which he contemplates the one night he spent incarcerated.

From "Civil Disobedience"
by Henry David Thoreau

1   I have paid no poll tax for six years. I was put into a jail once on this account, for one night; and, as I stood considering the walls of solid stone, two or three feet thick, the door of wood and iron, a foot thick, and the iron grating which strained the light, I could not help being struck with the foolishness of that institution which treated me as if I were mere flesh and blood and bones, to be locked up. I wondered that it should have concluded at length that this was the best use it could put me to, and had never thought to avail itself of my services in some way. I saw that, if there was a wall of stone between me and my townsmen, there was a still more difficult one to climb or break through, before they could get to be as free as I was. I did not for a moment feel confined, and the walls seemed a great waste of stone and mortar. I felt as if I alone of all my townsmen had paid my tax. They plainly did not know how to treat me, but behaved like persons who are underbred. In every threat and in every compliment there was a blunder; for they thought that my chief desire was to stand the other side of that stone wall. I could not but smile to see how industriously they locked the door on my meditations, which followed them out again without let or hindrance, and *they* were really all that was dangerous. As they could not reach me, they had resolved to punish my body; just as boys, if they cannot come at some person against whom they have a spite, will abuse his dog . . . .

2   The night in prison was novel and interesting enough. The prisoners in their shirt-sleeves were enjoying a chat and the evening air in the doorway, when I entered. But the jailer said, "Come, boys, it is time to lock up;" and so they dispersed, and I heard the sound of their steps returning into the hollow apartments. My room-mate was introduced to me by the jailer, as "a first-rate fellow and clever man." When the door was locked, he showed me where to hang my hat, and how he managed matters there. The rooms were whitewashed once a month; and this one, at least, was the whitest, most simply furnished, and probably neatest apartment in town. He naturally

wanted to know where I came from, and what brought me there; and, when I had told him, I asked him in my turn how he came there, presuming him to be an honest man, of course; and, as the world goes, I believe he was. "Why," said he, "they accuse me of burning a barn; but I never did it." As near as I could discover, he had probably gone to bed in a barn when drunk, and smoked his pipe there; and so a barn was burnt. He had the reputation of being a clever man, had been there some three months waiting for his trial to come on, and would have to wait as much longer; but he was quite domesticated and contented, since he got his board for nothing, and thought that he was well treated.

3 He occupied one window, and I the other; and I saw, that, if one stayed there long, his principal business would be to look out the window. I had soon read all the tracts that were left there, and examined where former prisoners had broken out, and where a grate had been sawed off, and heard the history of the various occupants of that room; for I found that even there was a history and a gossip which never circulated beyond the walls of the jail. Probably this is the only house in the town where verses are composed, which are afterward printed in a circular form, but not published. I was shown quite a long list of young men who had been detected in an attempt to escape, who avenged themselves by singing them.

4 I pumped my fellow-prisoner as dry as I could, for fear I should never see him again; but at length he showed me which was my bed, and left me to blow out the lamp.

5 It was like travelling into a far country, such as I had never expected to behold, to lie there for one night. It seemed to me that I never had heard the town-clock strike before, nor the evening sounds of the village; for we slept with the windows open, which were inside the grating. It was to see my native village in the light of the middle ages, and our Concord was turned into a Rhine stream, and visions of knights and castles passed before me. They were the voices of old burghers that I heard in the streets. I was an involuntary spectator and auditor of whatever was done and said in the kitchen of the adjacent village inn—a wholly new and rare experience to me. It was a closer view of my native town. I was fairly inside of it . . . .

6 In the morning, our breakfasts were put through the hole in the door, in small oblong-square tin pans, made to fit, and holding a pint of chocolate, with brown bread, and an iron spoon. When they called for the vessels again, I was green enough to return what bread I had left; but my comrade seized it, and said that I should lay that up for lunch or dinner. Soon after, he was let out to work at haying in a neighboring field, whither he went every day, and would not be back till noon; so he bade me good day, saying that he doubted if he should see me again.

7 When I came out of prison—for some one interfered, and paid that tax—I did not perceive that great changes had taken place on the common, such as he observed who went in a youth, and emerged a tottering and gray-headed man; and yet a change had come to my eyes come over the scene—the town, and State, and country—greater than any that mere time could effect. I saw yet more distinctly the State in which I lived. I saw to what extent the people among whom I lived could be trusted as good neighbors and friends; that their friendship was for summer weather only; that they did not greatly propose to do right; that they were a distinct race from me by their prejudices and superstitions . . . , that, after all, they were not so noble but they treated the thief as he had treated them, and hoped, by a certain outward observance and a few prayers, and by walking in a particular straight though useless path from time to time, to save their souls. This may be to judge my neighbors harshly; for I believe that many of them are not aware that they have such an institution as the jail in their village.

8 It was formerly the custom in our village, when a poor debtor came out of jail, for his acquaintances to salute him, looking

through their fingers, which were crossed to represent the grating of the jail window, "How do ye do?" My neighbors did not thus salute me, but first looked at me, and then at one another, as if I had returned from a long journey. I was put into jail as I was going to the shoemaker's to get a shoe which was mended. When I was let out the next morning, I proceeded to finish my errand, and, having put on my mended shoe, joined a huckleberry party, who were impatient to put themselves under my conduct; and in half an hour—for the horse was soon tackled—was in the midst of a huckleberry field, on one of our highest hills, two miles off; and then the State was nowhere to be seen.

This is the whole history of "My Prisons."

> Use "Day One" (pp. 149–152) to answer questions 1–13

1. During the first few moments of the protest, Kelsey felt—
   A bored
   B confused
   C angry
   D conflicted

2. The word *lark* in paragraph 31 means—
   F a song bird
   G a trick
   H a bit of fun
   J a practical joke

3. What is paragraph 4 primarily about?
   A Kelsey's boredom with the assignments
   B Mrs. Delaney's tedious routine
   C the change in Mrs. Delaney's teaching style
   D Kelsey's dislike of answering question after question

4. Which words from paragraph 32 help the reader understand the meaning of the word *derailed*?
   F Sat erect with eyes straight ahead
   G Ignored him the way she did everyone
   H Wanted to make a difference
   J planned to major in education

5. In paragraphs 22–24, Kelsey's thoughts indicate that she is—
   A saddened by the loss of her father
   B feeling too old to have a guardian
   C anxious about the outcome of the protest
   D angry that her father's will made Russ her guardian

6. The author develops this chapter primarily through—
   F chronologic narration
   G description
   H flashbacks
   J internal dialogue

7. In paragraph 6, Cobb introduces the fact that Mrs. Delaney has prepared assignments to show how—
   A boring the work Mrs. Delaney presented was
   B quickly she got back behind her desk
   C on at least some level she was doing her job
   D closely the assignments represented SAT exercises

8. In paragraph 28, Cobb uses a simile to convey that—
   F Kelsey's personality was far from calm
   G In actuality, Kelsey was usually calm and collected
   H JJ liked making fun of people
   J JJ often lied

9. Which of the following lines in the selection best express the theme of the story?
   A *She hated it when he fussed at her, just hated it. But if the protest continued, she'd have to stick.*
   B *To be joined with others in a collective stand felt exciting. . . .*
   C *She hated being accountable to anyone, let alone a thirty-year-old sibling. . . .*
   D *Then why don't you get up and leave?*

10. Which line from the passage serves as an example of sarcasm?
    F *If he gets to go to college.*
    G *How I teach is my business.*
    H *Five minutes down; fifty to go.*
    J *And she had no doubt that her law-abiding brother would expect her to maintain a standard of conduct that did not include taking part in a sit-in.*

11. What can the reader conclude about Kelsey from her reaction to her classmates actions expressed in paragraphs 44–47?
    A That she was angry with them for starting the protest
    B That she was concerned that the protest might escalate
    C That Russ was an understanding brother
    D That she felt the protest was wrong

12 The author ends paragraph 33 by saying, "Had Drew considered that?" in order to—
- **F** indicate Drew's lack of planning
- **G** hint that Drew had assumed control
- **H** show that sitting still for so long was difficult
- **J** point out that Drew needs to consider the consequences of his actions

13 In paragraph 38, what does Cobb imply about the protest?
- **A** It has been a huge success.
- **B** It isn't over.
- **C** It has grown beyond initial expectations.
- **D** It seems to have taken on its own, separate, identity.

Use "Civil Disobedience" (pp. 153–155) to answer questions 14–22

---

14 Read the following dictionary entries.

novel\näv-el\ *adjective* **1.** new, but in a pleasant way **2.** strange and unusual
novel, *noun* **1.** a fictitious prose narrative that tells a story through a complex series of events **2.** a literary genre

Which definition best matches the use of the word *novel* in paragraph 2?
- **F** Noun 1
- **G** Noun 2
- **H** Adjective 1
- **J** Adjective 2

15 Paragraph 1 is mainly about—
- **A** why Thoreau was jailed
- **B** the physical description of the prison
- **C** the reaction of the townsmen to Thoreau's plight
- **D** Thoreau's realization that his mind could never be imprisoned

16 How do the other prisoners react to Thoreau's imprisonment?
- **F** Congenially
- **G** Threateningly
- **H** Aloofly
- **J** Despairingly

17 Which statement best summarizes the essay?
- **A** While spending a night in jail for refusal to pay his poll tax, Thoreau met several prisoners. This gave him a greater insight as to the futility of incarceration, which he saw an unsuccessful attempt at confinement.
- **B** Spending a night in jail to protest being required to pay a poll tax, Thoreau gained a better understanding of the procedures and routine of prison life. This aided his awareness of the scope of incarceration.
- **C** Thoreau was put into jail for failure to pay his poll tax. While there he realized that even though his body was imprisoned, his spirit was free. The State's attempt to confine him had only been a futile effort, and most of his fellow townsmen had little concern with Thoreau's stand.
- **D** After spending a night in jail for failure to pay his poll tax, Thoreau resumed his daily routine, going to the cobbler to pick up a mended shoe and joining a huckleberry party. Little affected by the incident, he is eager to once again join in the normal activity of life.

18 Thoreau uses a simile in paragraph 5 to describe—
- **F** the sound of the town clock
- **G** the sensation of adventure that he is feeling
- **H** his feeling that he is a knight in the Middle Ages
- **J** his new view of his village

19 Knowing the historical context of this piece is important because it establishes the fact that—
  A prisoners in Thoreau's day were required to work
  B in Thoreau's day prisoners were not sufficiently fed
  C the experience of being taken to jail was less daunting in Thoreau's day than in modern times
  D huckleberry parties were a common thing

20 One of Thoreau's realizations from his night spent in jail is that—
  F many people do not seem to concern themselves with issues outside those that immediately affect their own lives
  G in the future it would be better to pay his poll tax
  H prisoners are in general a likeable group
  J being in jail is miserable

21 The reader can conclude that Thoreau—
  A is not regretful of having been jailed
  B wishes his neighbors understood him better
  C is glad to be released from jail
  D is grateful for the friend who paid the neglected tax

22 Which statement reflects the theme of this essay?
  F "This is the whole history of 'My Prisons.'"
  G My neighbors did not thus salute me. But first looked at me, and then at one another, as if I had returned from a long journey.
  H I saw yet more distinctly the State in which I lived.
  J I could not help being struck with the foolishness of that institution which treated me as if I were mere flesh and blood and bones, to be locked up.

Use "Day One" and "Civil Disobedience" (pp. 149–155) to answer questions 23 and 24

23 Unlike Kelsey in "Day One," Thoreau—
  A finds his situation was not solitary
  B was more concerned with what others would think of his actions
  C had more friends
  D had little doubt that his protest was a necessary event

24 Both Thoreau and Kelsey share in their—
  F concern for the overall good of others
  G determination to take action to call attention to a problem
  H careful planning of their protest
  J love of activity

Use the visual representation on page 155 to answer questions 25–27

25 The primary purpose of the ad is to—
  A evoke a negative response in connection to driving while drunk
  B show what can happen if you drive drunk
  C illustrate the loneliness of death
  D protest against those who drive drunk

26 Why is there only one wreath in the picture?
  F To simplify the message
  G To focus on the flowers
  H To personalize one individual death
  J To allow room for the caption

27 The message in small print is to—
  A fill up space on the page
  B educate the viewer on alcohol tolerance
  C clarify that the wreath represents someone killed by a drunk driver
  D explain how driving drunk kills

Answer the following questions in the boxes provided.

28 What is one conflict that Kelsey faces in "Day One?" Support your answer with evidence from the selection.

29 Explain how one of Thoreau's observations enhances his theme.

30 How is the concept of peaceful protest important to the theme of both "Day One" and "Civil Disobedience?"

Written Composition

> **Write an essay telling how making a stand for your beliefs has affected your life.**

The information below will help remind you of what you need to think about as you write your essay.

> MAKE SURE THAT YOU
> - address the topic
> - write in a way that is appealing and thoughtful
> - carefully construct each sentence
> - write clearly and distinctively using good transitions
> - express your ideas in a personal and authentic way
> - proofread carefully, correcting any errors you see

Prewriting/Planning Space

Prewriting/Planning Space

Revising and Editing

DIRECTIONS: Read the following selections, then answer the questions that follow each. For this section of the practice test, you are not permitted to use reference materials.

Thomas's English teacher has asked the class to write about someone who has worked hard to achieve a goal, and he has chosen to write about Michael Johnson, five-time Olympic gold medalist. During a peer editing session you have been assigned to read the report and make appropriate positive suggestions. After you have read the report, answer the questions below.

A Man with a Dream

(1) Anyone can have a dream, but making it come true takes hard work and determination. (2) Michael Johnson has lived his dream. (3) Becoming the first man to be ranked number one in the world at both the 200-m race and the 400-m race. (4) He did it by never giving up.

(5) Born in Dallas, Texas, in 1967, Michael is the youngest of five children. (6) His father is a trucker and his mother an elementary school teacher, and he was expected to take class seriously. (7) Not only did he participate in track and football, he took advanced classes as well. (8) He quit football his junior year, he found he enjoyed the individualized competition of track more than the aggression of a contact sport. (9) After high school he went to Baylor, where he was recruited for relays.

(10) Initially, his Baylor coach had no idea that Michael was going to be special. (11) But his trademark erect running style fooled everyone. (12) He started with the 200-m race, concentrating on that race while he learned the nuances of the 400-m race. (13) By the time he graduated in 1990 with a degree in business, he had earned five NCAA championships, but his ultimate goal was the Olympics.

(14) He prepared hard for the 1992 games, but two weeks before the events he came down with a severe case of food poisoning. (15) Their simply wasn't enough time for him to recover fully, and while he did win a gold medal with the 4 × 400-m relay team, he wanted to prove to the world that that he was the best.

(16) He turned his focus toward the Atlanta games. (17) He is an organized, meticulous man, carefully considering each decision. (18) He thinks of himself as a realist, and he trains hard. (19) In 1996 it paid off. (20) Not only did he win the 400-m final, three nights later he was winning the 200-m final with a spectacular time of 19.32. (21) Four years later in Sydney he became the first man to win the 400-m gold medal twice. (22) When he anchored the 4 × 400-m relay team, bringing it to victory, he secure the fifth Olympic gold medal of his career.

(23) In 1990, Johnson's first international competition was at the Goodwill Games in Seattle. (24) Eleven years later he ended his career in Brisbane, Australia, at the same event. (25) Anchoring the 4 × 1600-m relay, he crossed the finish line for a final time to a standing ovation. (26) In addition to his Olympic medals, he has won nine world championships and holds the world records at the 200-m and 400-m distances.

(27) Michael is a realistic man who has risen above disappointment and maintained his focus. (28) Through dedication and hard work he has set the mark for other's to strive. (29) No one thought a runner could be successful at both the 200 and 400 distances. (30) But Michael proved them wrong. (31) He has consistently proven that he was the best, challenging others to follow his lead. (32) He is a man who has chased his dream into the record books, because he never gave up.

31 What is the best way to rewrite sentences 2 and 3?
  F Michael Johnson has lived his dream, becoming the first man to be ranked number one in the world at both the 200-m and the 400-m race.
  G Michael Johnson has lived his dream. He is the first man to be ranked number one in the world at both the 200-m and the 400-m race.
  H Michael Johnson has lived his dream, which was to become the first man to be ranked number one in the world at both the 200-m race and the 400-m race.
  J Michael Johnson has lived his dream. He has become the first man to be ranked number one in the world. He runs both the 200-m and the 400-m race.

32 What correction, if any, would improve sentence 6?
  A Change *elementary* to **elimentary**
  B Put a semicolon in place of the comma
  C Change *he* to **Michael**
  D No change necessary

33 What correction, if any, would improve sentence 8?
  F Add a comma after *track*
  G Add the word **because** after the comma and delete the comma
  H Change *enjoyed* to **was enjoying**
  J No change necessary

34 What is the best way to combine sentences 10 and 11?
  A Initially, his Baylor coach had no idea that Michael was going to be special, but his trademark erect running style fooled everyone.
  B Initially, his Baylor coach had no idea that Michael was going to be special; but his trademark erect running style fooled everyone.
  C Initially, his Baylor coach had no idea that Michael was going to be special because his trademark erect running style fooled everyone.
  D Initially, his Baylor coach had no idea that Michael was going to be special, his trademark erect running style fooled everyone.

35 What correction, if any, would improve sentence 13?
  F Delete *with a degree*
  G Do not capitalize *Olympic*
  H Change *has* to **had**
  G No change necessary

36 What correction, if any, would improve sentence 15?
  A Change *team* to **teams**
  B eliminate the comma after *fully*
  C Change *their* to **there**
  D No change necessary

37 Which sentence, if any, should be eliminated in paragraph 5 (sentences 16–22)?
  F Sentence 16
  G Sentence 17
  H Sentence 18
  J No change necessary

38 What correction, if any, would improve sentence 20?
  A Delete the comma after *final*
  B Change *spectacular* to **specatculiar**
  C Change *was winning* to **won**
  D No change necessary

39 What correction, if any, would improve sentence 22?
  F Change *victory* to **victories**
  G Change *when* to **while**
  H Change *secure* to **secured**
  J No change necessary

40 What correction, if any, would improve sentence 23?
  A Omit the comma after **1990**
  B Change *internationial* to **international**
  C Put *Olympic Games* in lowercase letters
  D No change necessary

41 What correction, if any, would improve sentence 28?
  F Change *has* to **had**
  G Change *through* to **thorough**
  H Change *other's* to **others**
  J No change necessary

Kristen's teacher has asked for a personal narrative about a time when she learned something new. She has completed the assignment and is presenting it for evaluation in peer editing. You have been assigned to read the report and offer helpful suggestions. After reading her paper, answer the questions below.

Hitting the Road

(1) Having my own car and the ability to go places without my parents was something I started thinking about when I was around ten. (2) I mean, man was I ready. (3) When my Dad came home and said, "Want to go for a drive?" I didn't have to be asked twice. (4) I just headed out the door. (5) It was a long wait until I turned 16, but when the day came and I got my learner's permit, I was ready. (6) There I stood, knowing the road was mine, when he emerged with the keys.

(7) "Surely you don't think you're going to drive Mom's Lexus?" he asked. (8) Of course, that's exactly what I'd assumed.

(9) "Why not?" I asked.

(10) "Because it's just not going to happen," Dad said. (11) It was only then that I realised he was heading for the Ford, the old Ford, older even than I am. (12) But hey, a ride is a ride, so I needed to be careful because so far my folks had been real supportive of my dreams, and I didn't want to botch things up.

(13) Dad was already in the passenger seat with a grim look on his face when I got in.

(14) "Okay," I said, buckling up. (15) "Where are the keys?"

(16) He held them out and pointed toward the ignition. (17) "You either have to hold in the clutch or put the gear into neutral, which also means you have to hold in the clutch."

(18) "What's a clutch?" I asked, and I heard Dad sigh. (19) He pointed to the floor.

(20) "Why were there two brakes?" I asked again, and this time Dad groaned.

(21) After he'd regained his composure he began a calm explanation of the purpose of a clutch, and how you have to push it in to shift gears, and gently feed the car gas at the same time.

(22) I did exactly what he said, but the car jumped, spurted, and stalled, I tried again, and it stalled again.

(23) "Easy," Dad said, looking at the Lexus. (24) I raised my eyebrows in hope, but he shook his head no.

(25) At this point I wasn't sure that walking wouldn't be the best option.

(26) "Lets give it one more try," Dad said.

(27) I did, and this time the car inched smoothly forward. (28) I even managed to shift gears twice before it stalled.

(29) "Hey, I think I could get the hang of this," I told Dad, depressing the clutch as I turned the ignition. (30) Something about hearing the engine come alive made my heart beat faster. (31) "What other kinds of cars have clutches?"

(32) Dad went on to tell me about BMWs, VWs, and Mini Coopers. (33) As he talked, I carefully eased the car into gear, and soon we were moving down the street. (34) I really liked this driving thing. (35) Shifting wasn't so bad, not if it meant I'd be ready for a fine car someday. (36) Then the car stalled.

(37) "You just need some more practice," Dad said. (38) "You are doing great."

(39) I was, too, because now I knew why a car had two brakes, and the road was mine.

42 What is the best way to reorganize paragraph 1?
  A Move sentence 2 after sentence 5.
  B Delete sentence 4.
  C Move sentence 5 after sentence 1.
  D Delete sentence 2.

43 What correction, if any, would improve sentence 3?
  F Change *Dad* to **dad**
  G Change *"Want to go for a drive?"* to **"Want to go for a drive"?**
  H Add *he* before **said**
  J No change necessary

44 What correction, if any, would improve sentence 11?
  A Change *older than I am* to **older than me**
  B Change *realised* to **realized**
  C Change *Ford* to **ford**
  D No change necessary

45 What is the best way to reword sentence 12?
  F But hey, a ride is a ride. I needed to be careful because so far my folks had been real supportive of my dreams. I didn't want to botch things up.
  G But hey, a ride is a ride, and I needed to be careful. So far my folks had been real supportive of my dreams, and I didn't want to botch things up.
  H A ride is a ride, and I needed to be careful. My folks had always been supportive of my dreams.
  J I needed to be careful because so far my folks had been supportive of my dreams. I didn't want to botch things up.

46 What correction, if any, would improve sentence 20?
  A Change *were* to **are**
  B Change *brakes* to **breaks**
  C Put the question mark outside the quotation marks
  D No change necessary

47 What is the most effective way to reword sentence 21?
  F After he'd regained his composure, he began a calm explanation of the purpose of a clutch, and how you have to push it in to shift gears and gently feed the car gas at the same time.
  G After he'd regained his composure, he began a calm explanation of the purpose of a clutch. He said you have to push it in to shift gears and gently fed the car gas at the same time.
  H After he'd regained his composure he began a calm explanation of the purpose of a clutch, how you have to push it in to shift gears, and then gently feed the car gas at the same time.
  J After he'd regained his composure he began a calm explanation of the purpose of a clutch. He said you had to push it in to shift gears, and gently fed the car gas at the same time.

48 What is the best way to reword sentence 22?
  A I did exactly what he said. The car jumped, spurted, and stalled. I tried again. It stalled again.
  B I did exactly what he said, but the car jumped, spurted, and stalled. I tried again, and it stalled again.
  C I did exactly what he said, but the car jumped, spurted, and stalled, so I tried again, and it stalled again.
  D I did exactly what he said, but the car jumped, then spurted, then stalled. I tried again, It stalled again.

49 What correction, if any, would improve sentence 26?
  F Change *it* to **driving**
  G Change *Lets* to **Let's**
  H Put the quotation mark after *said*.
  J No change necessary

50 What correction, if any, would improve sentence 30?
  A Change *come* to **came**
  B Change *engine* to **motor**
  C Change *hearing* to **having heard**
  D No change necessary

Answer Explanations to Practice Test A

Question 1: Here is where your dictionary will come in handy. Kelsey definitely wasn't bored, so you can rule out **A**, and *angry* is an extremely intense word, far beyond Kelsey's feelings at this point of the story. So your choice is between **B** and **D**. Looking these two words up in a dictionary you should find that *confused* means mistaking one thing for another, whereas *conflicted* describes inner tension resulting from opposite, incompatible forces. Because Kelsey is struggling inwardly with the feelings of whether the protest is the right thing to do, **D** is the best answer.

Question 2: All definitions given for *lark* can be found in a dictionary or a thesaurus. So what you need to do here is substitute each possible answer in place of *lark* and see which one makes sense in this paragraph. Answer **F** is easy to rule out, and neither **G** nor **J** makes sense when substituted back into the sentence. The author has clearly stated that JJ's financial circumstances indicate a need for him to test out of freshman English. Therefore, he is taking the AP class to seriously enhance his collegiate experience, not as a *bit of fun*. Answer **J** is your best choice.

Question 3: This question can quickly be recognized as a main idea question, so think about the 5Ws exercise. Who? (Mrs. Delaney) What? (changed her teaching methods) Where? (not relevant) When? (this semester) Why? (Kelsey didn't know). If you put these ideas into a sentence you have that Kelsey wondered why Mrs. Delaney was teaching differently this semester. The only possible answer is **C**. Although the paragraph mentions that Kelsey was tired of Mrs. Delaney's tedious routine, that she didn't like the boring assignments, and that answering so many questions was becoming an aggravation, these are details, not what the paragraph is primarily about.

Question 4: Start by looking up the word in the dictionary. The literal definition of *derailed* means something that comes off the track, but a secondary meaning is to throw off course. In paragraph 32, Ratasha is shown to be someone who doesn't want to be thrown off course because she has a plan and purpose for her life. This is a cause-and-effect context clue. In other words, she doesn't want to lose sight of her goals (effect), because she wants to make something of herself (cause). She doesn't want to become derailed (effect), because she has a plan (cause). She wants to make a difference. The best answer, therefore, is **H**. The other choices do not shed sufficient light on her determination not to be distracted.

Question 5: To answer this question you have to really think about what is worrying Kelsey. She does comment on her frustration that her brother is her guardian, but this only comes up as a result of her worrying about his reaction to the protest. She is feeling isolated and alone, and questions whether she should just leave. Paragraph 25 ends with concern that Russ will not understand. All of this speaks to her anxiety, and therefore **C** is the best answer. You can discover this by thinking about the details offered. Her hands were *jittery* and her heart *racing*. She *frowns deeply*. She is worried about Russ's reaction. All of this fits with choice **C**.

Question 6: The word to notice in this question is *primarily*. A dictionary would confirm that it means "in the first place" or "fundamentally." Actually, the writing in this section includes all of the above, but the story is told *primarily* though Kelsey's internal musings. Mentally she talks to herself, sometimes even answering her own questions. Therefore, the best answer is **J**, because her internal dialogue is the glue that holds the chapter together.

Question 7: This is a cause and effect question, so ask yourself why Cobb included the scene in paragraph 6. Then, answer your own question before you look at the possible answers. Although the quick distribution time is brought up, the lessons are detailed and varied. And although they certainly don't look fun, they don't look boring either. So the process of elimination rules out answers **A** and **B**. Answer **D** might seem inviting, especially considering paragraph 6 ends with a comment on SAT exercises, and this would seem particularly tempting if you were unfamiliar with the SAT. But overall the assignments cover a variety of grounds and seem to indicate that some thought has gone into their preparation. So the best answer is **C**.

Question 8: A simile is a comparison linked by *like* or *as*. So ask yourself, what is being compared? The comparison is that calling Kelsey calm is like calling a lioness a lamb. Therefore, Kelsey must be like a lioness, which rules out **G**. Answer **J** is not indicated in the paragraph, and although JJ does *laugh uproariously*, his intent seems to be teasing rather than hurting, which eliminates **H**. Therefore, the best answer is **F**.

Question 9: In thinking about theme, you must look at the whole picture. What overall message is the author trying to convey? What is the one thing that lies beneath all that was written? In this passage, the protest is the focus point of the chapter, and, although Kelsey does mentally resist her brother's interest in her life, it isn't the core of the passage. The passage is about Kelsey's worries. Why has Mrs. Delaney changed teaching styles? What will happen to JJ if he doesn't test out of freshman English? What will Russ do if he finds out about the protest? She feels she is being torn in two different directions, so the best answer, the one that covers the whole passage, is **A**.

Question 10: You can probably rule out answer **F** and **H** immediately. Kelsey is genuinely concerned about JJ's situation, so she wouldn't be thinking sarcastically about it, and **H** is simply a stated fact. If you have trouble deciding between **G** and **J** go to your dictionary. There you will learn that *sarcasm* means a cutting, biting, or hostile remark, with harsh, caustic language. Thus, the best answer clearly is **G**.

Question 11: When you are dealing with questions about a character's motivation, you must notice the details and nuances of the action. In this case, Kelsey is dumbfounded, surprised by the way the students have acted following the protest. Beware of strong, defining words such as *anger*. There is no indication that her feelings are this clear, so you can rule out **A**. And she is too numb at this point to make a decision as to the validity of their actions. So you can rule out **D**. Answer **C** has yet to be determined, although Kelsey seems to think that Russ is a difficult presence in her life. This leaves **B**, which seems to fit, because if the protest continues, Kelsey will have to determine what to do, and this is causing her concern. So the best answer is **B**.

Question 12: Obviously it is harder to sit still for a long time than one might imagine, but answer **H** is not in line with the implied meaning of the statement. When Kelsey questions what Drew was thinking, the conclusion is that he wasn't. He just acted. Although Drew does seem to be a leader in the protest, to say he has *assumed control* is too strong, and there is no indication that he is greatly admired. Rather, the author seems to be using the question as a transition into Kelsey's observations about Drew. So the best answer is **F**.

Question 13: This question is asking you to predict what will happen next, but remember a prediction must come directly from information given in the text. Answer **A** may be true, but it is too early in the scheme of events to determine if Mrs. Delaney will react in a positive way. And paragraph 39 addresses only how the students exited the room, not whether the protest will continue. So **B** can be eliminated. The same is true of **C** because in this paragraph there is no indication that the protest has grown. This leaves **D**. If you reread the paragraph it seems as if the students are acting without plan or thought, simply reacting to the moment, and in some ways to Drew's lead. The actions are not premeditated; they just evolve from the moment. Therefore answer **D** is acceptable.

Question 14: The grammatical structure in paragraph 2 indicates that *novel* is being used as a predicate adjective, and the reader knows that this is Thoreau's first night in jail. Also, he is finding the experience *interesting*, which indicated that it has sense of excitement about it, rather than strangeness. Therefore, your best answer is **H**.

Question 15: This is a long paragraph, so it is important not to be sidetracked by the smaller details. If you do the 5Ws, you come up with the idea that Thoreau (who) greatly contemplates (what) his situation (why) during the night (when) he spent in jail (where). The result of this inner search is that he realizes his spirit can never be imprisoned. Your best answer, therefore, is **D**. Answer **A** is mentioned, but it only introduces the situation. The whole paragraph is not about not paying poll tax. And the jail is described in detail, but only to set up the contrast between Thoreau's physical incarceration and his mental freedom. The confusion of the townspeople is also mentioned, but it is only a supporting detail.

Question 16: First, in your own mind define how you think the other prisoners behaved. Basically they were cordial, friendly, and for the most part helpful. Then, look up any word you do not know in your dictionary. If you do this, then the only possible answer is **F**, which means being agreeable and pleasant.

Question 17: Think to yourself, what was this passage about? It was about how Thoreau (who), while spending a night in jail (where), gained insight into the futility of imprisonment (what). He also learned that the State could not really control his spirit, that he was as free as he allowed his mind to be. During the night (when) he saw his village differently, and this viewing caused sadness in him because of his fellow townsmen's lack of concern with political issue (why). If you think through the essay in this manner, the best possible answer is **C**. All answers sound reasonable. But he says nothing about the futility of imprisonment in general. His remarks are all specific to his own experience, which would rule out **A**, and the essay is not about the routines of the jail. So **B** is incorrect. Answer **D** covers only the last section of the essay and does not take into account Thoreau's musings. Thus the only possible choice remains **C**.

Question 18: Knowing that a simile is a comparison, you need to know what is being compared. The sentence opens with the word *it*, and you have to ask yourself to what is *it* referring? A quick review reveals that Thoreau is talking about the whole prison experience, and he likens this to travel to a distant country. Therefore, **G** appears to be the best answer. Although **F**, **H**, and **J** are all mentioned, they are not offered as a comparison to the whole prison experience.

Question 19: To answer this question you are being asked to draw a conclusion based on the historical tone of the piece. All answers are evident, and all are uniquely a part of Thoreau's age, but which one is important to an overall understanding of the piece? Answer **B** is based on a detail, but just because Thoreau's cell mate kept the brown bread does not mean he was underfed. Likewise, although the cell mate did work at haying, that is a small detail, not something that adds to the overall theme of the piece. So you can rule out **A**. Answer **D** takes the message of the text too far. Just because Thoreau joined a huckleberry party doesn't mean it was a common thing. On the other hand, Thoreau's experience in jail certainly seems less severe than modern incarceration—his fellow prisoners are friendly, and the jailer is a gentleman. Looking in the dictionary you would see that *daunting* means "intimidating," and certainly modern jails tend to be a bit more severe. So **C** is your best choice.

Question 20: This is an inference question, asking you to make a judgment about what Thoreau learned. He clearly isn't in agreement with paying his poll taxes, and is aggravated that someone else did so for him ("for someone interfered, and paid that tax"). Thus you can rule out **G**. And although the prisoners are a likeable group, that is not the core of Thoreau's learning. However, what did impress him was his townsmen's indifference, their lack of notice about the issues of life. So the best answer is **F**.

Question 21: When you draw a conclusion you must base your answer directly on evidence found in the text. Answers **D** and **C** might seem logical, but the text indicated that neither is correct. Thoreau found his night in jail to be most tolerable, and never mentioned that he was anxious to be released. And, as mentioned above, he was not pleased that someone "interfered" by paying his tax. He may wish that his neighbors understood him better, but in his musings he makes observations, not wishes. We do know, however, that he felt his protest to have been a valuable experience. So you best answer is **A**.

Question 22: Say to yourself, "What is the main point that Thoreau wants to reader to understand?" Then answer your own question before you look at the choices. Thoreau felt that on the night he spent in prison he gained a better understanding of people and their motives. He does mention in paragraph 1 that his spirit could not be confined, but that is not the complete message of the essay. In fact the word *institution* indicated that even when realizing that his mind could not be imprisoned, he is still thinking about the impact of the government on individual lives. Therefore, the best answer seems to be **H**.

Question 23: Kelsey and Thoreau are engaged in different types of protest. Thoreau's actions seem to be well defined, based on political concerns. His refusal to pay the poll tax is a conscious and considered decision. On the other hand, Kelsey's sit-in seems to have more or less just happened, and she worries whether the actions are correct. Kelsey is more concerned with what others will think, and there is nothing in the second passage that comments on the number of Thoreau's friends. Remember to be careful of qualifying words, like *more*. Thoreau's situation was definitely a solitary one, at least he was the only one imprisoned on that day for not paying his tax. So the best answer is **D**. Thoreau definitely had confidence that refusing to pay his taxes was correct, no matter what the consequences.

Question 24: In this question you must compare the similarities between Kelsey and Thoreau. The most obvious is that both were willing to take a stand for what they believed to be right. Kelsey hadn't planned to be involved in a sit-in, which rules out answer **H**, and while both may love activity, answer **J** is outside the scope of the writing. At first glance, answers **F** and **G** both appear attractive, but **G** has stronger wording. There is no doubt that both Kelsey and Thoreau were determined, that they wanted their actions to call attention to a particular problem. Therefore, your best answer is **G**.

Question 25: All answers to this question are partially right, but remember that the main purpose of advertising is to evoke an emotional response of some sort that connects to a desired action. Although the ad does imply what can happen if you drive drunk and it does comment on the loneliness of death, only answer **A** takes into account the emotional component of the ad. It is a protest against those who drive drunk, but the purpose of the ad is to make you feel that driving drunk is wrong. So **A** is your best answer.

Question 26: In a print ad, everything points to the message—the color, the design, everything. The purpose of the ad is not to focus on the flowers or to simplify the message. The hope would be that the message would make a strong impact on the viewer, and if more room were needed for the caption, the artist would simply redesign the ad. The more personal the message seems, the stronger the emotional response. Therefore, the best answer is **H**.

Question 27: The design of an ad isn't random. Messages are not put onto the page merely to fill up space, so you can immediately rule out **A**. Overall, the message has nothing to do with the wreath, nor does it explain how driving drunk kills. What it does clarify is how much alcohol, when consumed, is too much. Therefore, answer **B** is the best choice.

Question 28: A good answer would be something like this:

> Kelsey is conflicted by her feelings of compassion for Mrs. Delaney and her agreement with her classmates' frustrations. She says, "Mrs. Delaney seemed sensitive. Had anyone considered that she might get hurt?" But Kelsey also realizes that for some, like JJ, passing the AP test is important. She sees both sides of the issue and worries about which is right.

ELA TAKS-like analysis: This answer is highly effective in that the relevant quote and brief synopsis illustrate Kelsey's conflicting feelings. The writer has made meaningful connections between the text and his or her own thoughtful conclusion. This would score a 3.

Question 29: A good answer would be something like this:

> Thoreau's observations of the prison structure highlights the absurdity of trying to imprison the spirit. Although the jail is clearly stoutly built ("walls of solid stone, two or three feet thick"), Thoreau's meditations exit with the jailer. His only danger was his rebelliousness, and that could not be confined.

ELA TAKS-like analysis: This is an in-depth analysis, connecting textural evidence to an insightful conclusion. The quote solidly supports the writer's ability to make meaningful associations. This would score a 3.

Question 30: A good answer would be something like this:

> Both Kelsey and Thoreau are dealing with moral issues they feel strongly about. Thoreau is struggling with giving monetary support to a government involved in a questionable war, and Kelsey is frustrated with her teacher's lack of commitment. Both strive to make their ideas known. Without peaceful protest neither piece would have substance, because it is through the protests that each makes his or her voice heard.

ELA TAKS-like analysis: In this answer the student offers an insightful interpretation that is fully supported by relevant quotations. It shows the writer's depth of understanding as well as his or her ability to make meaningful connections across selections. This would score a 3.

Written Composition

A possible composition might be:

In his poem "The Road Not Taken," Robert Frost said that when he chose a path not commonly traveled by others, that for him, in his life, "it has made all the difference." While Frost may have been alluding to his decision to become a poet, the same idea can be applied to any stand made for right, no matter how small. Doing good always makes a difference. Like a small stone thrown into the ocean, it ripples, perhaps hardly noticed, but still, it ripples.

Never has this been more evident than in the summer before my junior year, when the current of my own life changed. It wasn't something planned. Rather, it was just one of those things that touches life with its own flow. Mother and I were bringing my brother back from college for the summer. We had two cars full of precious junk, and we were in the lead. How it happened, why it happened, I was never sure. A car came out of nowhere. Mom swerved, hitting the medium and our SUV rolled, over and over and over it rolled. I survived. Mom did not.

The events of the next few months were a blur. The funeral, which Mom in her ever-organized way had planned, was one of the largest the city had ever seen. Mom was loved by many, not just my father, brother and I, and for awhile we shared our grief, our memories, our love. And then life went on, with no Mom. School was still there, but no one was home when I burst through the door to share. My brother, dad and I tried, but our family was broken, and no Superglue could give it an easy fix.

    We needed help, and it came, in the package of our priest, who sensing our need, paid us a call. My brother had returned to school, so it was only Dad and me. We listened politely, as Mom would have wanted us to, expecting nothing. But one thing penetrated the dull numbness. Father John said that one way to honor Mother's memory was to let go of her weakness and imitate her strengths. In that way, he said, the impact of her life would go on and on.

    So that's what I did. I tried to emulate the qualities in my mother that I had admired, and I began to heal. But more importantly, I realized that as I carry with me the values and ideals mom's embraced, others will be influenced by her, too—my friends, my teachers, and someday my children. In this way mother's life will continue to inspire for generations to come. The stands she made for principle over the years may have happened a long time ago, but they mattered. Her influence will ripple out into the future, in perhaps small ways.

    But it will be there.

ELA TAKS-like analysis: This is a highly effective composition in which the writer makes a meaningful connection between a personal event and the prompt. The smooth progression of thought moves effortlessly from point to point, with transitions enhancing forward progress. Details create depth of development, showcasing the writer's authentic voice, and the theme is well supported by personal reflections. The writer is willing to take a compositional risk by surrounding a personal tragedy with personal reflection. This answer would rate a 4.

Question 31: Sentence 3 is a fragment, so it must be linked either to the sentence that comes before it or the sentence that follows it. To chop up the two sentences into small simple sentences, as is done in answer **J**, is not an improvement. Neither is answer **G**, which just adds a subject to sentence 3. Your best answer is **F**, because the word *becoming* forms a natural link to Johnson's dream. The construction in answer **H** is much more awkward.

Question 32: In this sentence the word *he* would refer to its immediate male antecedent, which is the word *father*. Therefore, for clarity, you must say *Michael*. Answer **C** is correct. The word *elementary* is not misspelled, and a semicolon in place of the comma would be incorrect.

Question 33: As it stands, sentence 8 is a run-on sentence, or two ideas incorrectly joined. You need to add a comma and conjunction or a semicolon, or you need to break the sentence into two complete sentences. You best answer is **G**, which would make the sentence read, "He quit football his junior year because he found he enjoyed the individualized competition of track more than the aggression of a contact sport."

Question 34: With sentences 10 and 11 you have two short, choppy remarks. Although they are not wrong, they aren't particularly exciting either. Answer **D** is a run-on sentence, so it should be immediately eliminated. The other possible choices all have some appeal, but this is a cause and effect type of sentence. Baylor's coach misinterpreted Michael's abilities because his running style was uniquely different. The best answer, therefore, is **C**.

Question 35: This entire composition has been written in the past tense. The word *has* is present tense, and not congruous with the rest of the writing. Your best answer is **H**.

Question 36: In this sentence *there* is misspelled. The correct answer is **C**.

Question 37: Paragraph 5 is mostly about how Johnson's determination was rewarded. Sentence 16 is a good transition, but the fact that he is an organized and meticulous man is irrelevant to his training. It may be an interesting detail, but it either needs to be expanded through elaboration or taken out. The best answer is **F**.

Question 38: Again, the words *was winning* shift the established tense of the writing. The word *was* continues with the simple past tense, which the author has used throughout, so your best answer is **C**.

Question 39: *Victory* is correctly spelled, and *when* represents time, which is the needed link for this sentence. The word *secure*, however, is present tense, so, as above, to be consistent with the writing, the best answer for this question is **H**.

Question 40: The word *international* is incorrectly spelled in the sentence, so the best answer is **B**.

Question 41: At this point in the essay, the shift in tense is okay. The author has chronologically brought Johnson's career up to the present day, so **F** is correct. However, *others* should be plural, not possessive, so the best answer is **H**.

Question 42: The natural order of this paragraph is to move chronologically from when the narrator was younger, waiting for the chance to drive, to the time she received her learner's permit. Thus, the age of ten would be followed by age sixteen. Sentence 5 should be placed adjacent to the first sentence, and then followed by the second exclamation of readiness. Your best answer is **C**.

Question 43: The word *dad* is capitalized only when it is used in place of a proper noun (e.g., when you are using it in place of your father's birth name). In this sentence, if you substituted the birth name for your father in place of *dad*, it would not sound right. So it would not be capitalized. Your best answer is **J**.

Question 44: The word *Ford* should be capitalized because it is the name of a company, and *than* is a conjunction linking *older* to its descriptor, which is correctly *I*. The word *realise*, however, is spelled according to British custom, not American. Here the correct spelling is *realize*, so the answer is **B**.

Question 45: This is way too much information for one sentence. It needs to be broken up into two or more sentences, but it shouldn't sound choppy as in answer **F**. You want to retain the author's voice, which rings so clear in the first phrase ("a ride is a ride"), so answer **G** is the best choice.

Question 46: The word *brakes* is correctly spelled here, and quotation marks go outside a question mark. On the other hand, we tend to speak in the present tense, and the word *were* is spoken in dialogue. Therefore, it is better to use *are,* making **A** the correct answer choice.

Question 47: Although this sentence is punctuated correctly, it is awkward. Adding a time sequence to the overall sentence pattern and taking out unnecessary words would add clarity. By removing the first *and,* and adding the word *then,* as in choice **H**, the meaning becomes plain.

Question 48: As is, sentence 22 is a run-on sentence. It needs to be broken into smaller sentences, but not too many. Your best answer is **B**.

Question 49: People tend to talk in shortcuts, so Dad would probably not say *driving,* and the quotations are correct. However, the word *let's* is a contraction for *let us*. Therefore, **G** is your best answer.

Question 50: In sentence 30, the narrator is making a comparison between what she is hearing and how it makes her feel. Together this comparison forms the object of the preposition *about*. If you substitute the word *it* for the phrase *hearing the engine come alive,* then the words agree. So the correct answer for this question is **D**.

Chapter 17

Practice Test B

Reading and Written Composition

DIRECTIONS: Read the two passages and the visual piece. Then answer the questions that follow.

Mary Freeman wrote this in 1891 about the ordinary life of rural New England at that time.

excerpts from "A New England Nun"
by Mary E. Wilkins Freeman

Notes

1 Louisa Ellis had been peacefully sewing at her sitting-room window all the afternoon. Now she quilted her needle carefully into her work, which she folded precisely, and laid in a basket with her thimble and thread and scissors. . . .

2 Louisa was slow and still in her movements; it took her a long time to prepare her tea; but when ready it was set forth with as much grace as if she had been a veritable guest to her own self. . . . Louisa used china every day. . . . She had for her supper a glass dish full of sugared currants, a plate of little cakes, and one of little white biscuits. Also a leaf or two of lettuce, which she cut up daintily. Louisa was very fond of lettuce, which she raised to perfection in her little garden. She ate quite heartily, though, in a delicate, pecking, way; it seemed almost surprising that any considerable bulk of the food should vanish. . . .

3 In about half an hour Joe Dagget came. She heard his heavy step on the walk, and rose and took off her pink-and-white apron. Under that was still another-white linen with a little cambric edging on the bottom; that was Louisa's company apron. . . . The door opened and Joe Dagget entered.

4 He seemed to fill up the whole room. A little yellow canary that had been asleep in his green cage at the south window woke up and fluttered wildly, beating his little yellow wings against the wires. He always did so when Joe Dagget came into the room.

5 "Good-evening," said Louisa. She extended her hand with a kind of solemn cordiality.

6 "Good-evening, Louisa," returned the man, in a loud voice.

7 She placed a chair for him, and they sat facing each other, with the table between them. He sat bolt-upright, toeing out his heavy feet squarely, glancing with a good-humored uneasiness around the room. She sat gently erect, folding her slender hands in her white-linen lap.

8 "Been a pleasant day," remarked Dagget.

9 "Real pleasant," Louisa assented, softly.

10 "Have you been haying?" she asked, after a little while.

11 "Yes, I've been haying all day, down in the ten-acre lot. Pretty hot work."

12 "It must be."

13 "Yes, it's pretty hot work in the sun."

14 "Is your mother well to-day?"

15 "Yes, mother's pretty well."
16 "I suppose Lily Dyer's with her now?"
17 Dagget colored. "Yes, she's with her," he answered, slowly.
18 He was not very young, but there was a boyish look about his large face. Louisa was not quite as old as he, her face was fairer and smoother, but she gave people the impression of being older.
19 "I suppose she's a good deal of help to your mother," she said, further.
20 "I guess she is; I don't know how mother'd get along without her," said Dagget, with a sort of embarrassed warmth.
21 "She looks like a real capable girl. She's pretty-looking too," remarked Louisa.
22 "Yes, she is pretty fair looking."
23 Presently Dagget began fingering the books on the table. There was a square red autograph album, and a Young Lady's Gift-Book which had belonged to Louisa's mother. He took them up one after the other and opened them then laid them down again, the album on the gift-book.
24 Louisa kept eyeing them with mild uneasiness. Finally she rose and changed the position of the books, putting the album underneath. That was the way they had been arranged in the first place.
25 Dagget gave an awkward little laugh. "Now what difference did it make which book was on top?" said he.
26 Louisa looked at him with a deprecating smile. "I always keep them that way," murmured she.
27 "You do beat everything," said Dagget, trying to laugh again. His large face was flushed.
28 He remained about an hour longer, then rose to take leave.... When Joe Dagget was outside he drew in the sweet evening air with a sigh, and felt much as an innocent and perfectly well-intentioned bear might after his exit from a china shop.
29 Louisa, on her part, felt much as the kind-hearted, long-suffering owner of the china shop might have done after the exit of the bear.
30 ... He came twice a week to see Louisa Ellis, and every time, sitting there in her delicately sweet room, he felt as if surrounded by a hedge of lace. He was afraid to stir lest he should put a clumsy foot or hand through the fairy web, and he had always the consciousness that Louisa was watching fearfully lest he should.
31 Still the lace and Louisa commanded perforce his perfect respect and patience and loyalty. They were to be married in a month, after a singular courtship which had lasted for a matter of fifteen years. For fourteen out of the fifteen years the two had not once seen each other, and they had seldom exchanged letters. Joe had been all those years in Australia, where he had gone to make his fortune, and where he had stayed until he made it....
32 But the fortune had been made in the fourteen years, and he had come home now to marry the woman who had been patiently and unquestioningly waiting for him all that time.
33 Shortly after they were engaged he had announced to Louisa his determination to strike out into new fields, and secure a competency before they should be married. She had listened and assented with the sweet serenity which never failed her, not even when her lover set forth on that long and uncertain journey. Joe, buoyed up as he was by his sturdy determination, broke down a little at the last, but Louisa kissed him with a mild blush, and said good-by.

Notes

34. "It won't be for long," poor Joe had said, huskily; but it was for fourteen years.
35. In that length of time much had happened. . . . Louisa's feet had turned into a path, smooth maybe under a calm, serene sky, but so straight and unswerving that it could only meet a check at her grave, and so narrow that there was no room for any one at her side.
36. Louisa's first emotion when Joe Dagget came home (he had not apprised her of his coming) was consternation, although she would not admit it to herself, and he never dreamed of it. Fifteen years ago she had been in love with him—at least she considered herself to be. . . .
37. She had been faithful to him all these years. She had never dreamed of the possibility of marrying any one else. Her life, especially for the last seven years, had been full of a pleasant peace, she had never felt discontented nor impatient over her lover's absence; still she had always looked forward to his return and their marriage as the inevitable conclusion of things. However she had fallen into a way of placing it so far in the future that it was almost equal to placing it over the boundaries of another life.
38. When Joe came she had been expecting him, and expecting to be married for fourteen years, but she was as much surprised and taken aback as if she had never thought of it.
39. Joe's consternation came later. He eyed Louisa with an instant confirmation of his old admiration. She had changed but little. She still kept her pretty manner and soft grace, and was, he considered, every whit as attractive as ever. As for himself, his stent was done; he had turned his face away from fortune-seeking, and the old winds of romance whistled as loud and sweet as ever through his ears. All the song which he had been wont to hear in them was Louisa; he had for a long time a loyal belief that he heard it still, but finally it seemed to him that although the winds sang always that one song, it had another name. But for Louisa the wind had never more than murmured; now it had gone down, and everything was still. She listened for a little while with half-wistful attention then she turned quietly away and went to work on her wedding clothes. . . .
40. . . . There were some peculiar features of her happy solitary life which she would probably be obliged to relinquish altogether. . . . There would be a large house to care for; there would be company to entertain; there would be Joe's rigorous and feeble old mother to wait upon; and it would be contrary to all thrifty village traditions for her to keep more than one servant. . . . Joe's mother, domineering, shrewd old matron that she was even in her old age, and very likely even Joe himself, with his honest masculine rudeness, would laugh and frown down all these pretty but senseless old maiden ways. . . .
41. . . .[Her dog] Caesar at large might have seemed a very ordinary dog, and excited no comment whatever—chained, his reputation overshadowed him, so that he lost his own proper outlines and looked darkly vague and enormous. Joe Dagget, however, with his good-humored sense and shrewdness, saw him as he was. He strode valiantly up to him and patted him on the head, in spite of Louisa's soft clamor of warning, and even attempted to set him loose. Louisa grew so alarmed that he desisted, but kept announcing his opinion in the matter quite forcibly at intervals. "There ain't a better-natured dog in town," he would say, "and it's down-right cruel to keep him tied up there. Some day I'm going to take him out."

Notes

42 Louisa had very little hope that he would not, one of these days, when their interests and possessions should be more completely fused in one . . .Louisa looked at the old dog munching his simple fare, and thought of her approaching marriage and trembled. Still no anticipation of disorder and confusion in lieu of sweet peace and harmony, no forebodings of Caesar on the rampage, no wild fluttering of her little yellow canary, were sufficient to turn her a hairsbreadth. Joe Dagget had been fond of her and working for her all these years. It was not for her, whatever came to pass, to prove untrue and break his heart. . . . .and the time went on until it was only a week before her wedding-day. It was a Tuesday evening, and the wedding was to be a week from Wednesday.

43 There was a full moon that night. About nine o'clock Louisa strolled down the road a little way. . . . Presently Louisa sat down on the wall and looked about her with mildly sorrowful reflectiveness. . . . She sat there some time. She was just thinking of rising, when she heard footsteps and low voices, and remained quiet. It was a lonely place, and she felt a little timid. She thought she would keep still in the shadow and let the persons, whoever they might be, pass her.

44 But just before they reached her the voices ceased, and the footsteps. She understood that. Their owners had also found seats upon the stone wall. She was wondering if she could not steal away unobserved, when the voice broke the stillness. It was Joe Dagget's. She sat still and listened.

45 The voice was announced by a loud sigh, which was as familiar as itself. "Well," said Dagget, "you've made up your mind, then, I suppose?"

46 "Yes," returned another voice; "I'm going, day after tomorrow."

47 "That's Lily Dyer," thought Louisa to herself. The voice embodied itself in her mind. She saw a girl tall and full-figured, with a firm, fair face, looking fairer and firmer in the moonlight, her strong yellow hair braided in a close knot, a girl full of a calm rustic strength and bloom, with a masterful way which might have beseemed a princess. Lily Dyer was a favorite with the village folk; she had just the qualities to arouse the admiration. She was good and handsome and smart. Louisa had often heard her praises sounded.

48 "Well," said Joe Dagget, " I ain't got a word to say."

49 "I don't know what you could say," returned Lily Dyer.

50 "Not a word to say," repeated Joe, drawing out the words heavily. Then there was a silence. " I ain't sorry," he began at last, "that that happened yesterday—that we kind of let on how we felt to each other. I guess it's just as well we knew. Of course I can't do anything any different. I'm going right on an' get married next week. I ain't going back on a woman that's waited for me fourteen years, an' break her heart."

51 "If you should jilt her to-morrow, I wouldn't have you," spoke up the girl, with sudden vehemence.

52 "Well, I ain't going to give you the chance," said he; "but I don't believe you would, either."

53 "You'd see I wouldn't. Honor's honor, an' right's right. An' I'd never think anything of any man that went against 'em for me or any other girl—you'd find that out, Joe Dagget."

54 "Well, you'll find out fast enough that I ain't going against 'em for you or any other girl," returned he. Their voices sounded almost as if they were angry with each other. Louisa was listening eagerly.

Notes

55 "I'm sorry you feel as if you must go away," said Joe, "but I don't know but it's best."

56 "Of course it's best. I hope you and I have got common-sense."

57 "Well, I suppose you're right." Suddenly Joe's voice got an undertone of tenderness. " Say, Lily," said he, " I'll get along well enough myself, but I can't bear to think—You don't suppose you're going to fret much over it?"

58 "I guess you'll find out I shan't fret much over a married man."

59 "Well, I hope you won't—I hope you won't, Lily. God knows I do. And—I hope—one of these days—you'll—come across somebody else—"

60 "I don't see any reason why I shouldn't." Suddenly her tone changed. She spoke in a sweet, clear voice, so loud that she could have been heard across the street. "No, Joe Dagget," said she, "I'll never marry any other man as long as I live. I've got good sense, an' I ain't going to break my heart nor make a fool of myself; but I'm never going to be married, you can be sure of that. I ain't that sort of a girl to feel this way twice."

61 Louisa heard an exclamation and a soft commotion behind the bushes; then Lily spoke again—the voice sounded as if she had risen. "This must be put a stop to," said she. "We've stayed here long enough. I'm going home."

62 Louisa sat there in a daze, listening to their retreating steps. After a while she got up and slunk softly home herself. The next day she did her housework methodically; that was as much a matter of course as breathing; but she did not sew on her wedding-clothes. She sat at her window and meditated. In the evening Joe came . . . .

63 She never mentioned Lily Dyer. She simply said that while she had no cause of complaint against him, she had lived so long in one way that she shrank from making a change.

64 "Well, I never shrank, Louisa," said Dagget. "I'm going to be honest enough to say that I think maybe it's better this way; but if you'd wanted to keep on, I'd have stuck to you till my dying day. I hope you know that."

65 "Yes, I do," said she.

66 That night she and Joe parted more tenderly than they had done for a long time. Standing in the door, holding each other's hands, a last great wave of regretful memory swept over them.

67 "Well, this ain't the way we've thought it was all going to end, is it, Louisa?" said Joe.

68 She shook her head. There was a little quiver on her placid face.

69 "You let me know if there's ever anything I can do for you," said he. "I ain't ever going to forget you, Louisa." Then he kissed her, and went down the path.

70 Louisa, all alone by herself that night, wept a little, she hardly knew why, but the next morning, on waking, she felt like a queen who, after fearing lest her domain be wrested away from her, sees it firmly insured in her possession. Now the tall weeds and grasses might cluster around Caesar's little hermit hut, the snow might fall on its roof year in and year out, but he never would go on a rampage through the unguarded village. Now the little canary might turn itself into a peaceful yellow ball night after night, and have no need to wake and flutter with wild terror against its bars. . . .That afternoon she sat with her needle-work at the window,

Notes

and felt fairly steeped in peace. Lily Dyer, tall and erect and blooming, went past; but she felt no qualm. If Louisa Ellis had sold her birthright she did not know it, the taste of the pottage was so delicious, and had been her sole satisfaction for so long. Serenity and placid narrowness had become to her as the birthright itself. She gazed ahead through a long reach of future days strung together like pearls in a rosary, every one like the others, and all smooth and flawless and innocent, and her heart went up in thankfulness. Outside was the fervid sunnier afternoon; the air was filled with the sounds of the busy harvest of men and birds and bees; there were halloos, metallic clattering, sweet calls, and long hummings. Louisa sat, prayerfully numbering her days, like an uncloistered nun.

This speech was delivered to the Massachusetts Anti-Slavery Society in Boston in 1865, shortly before the end of the Civil War and President Lincoln's assassination.

From "What the Black Man Wants"
by Frederick Douglass

1   I have had but one idea for the last three years to present to the American people, and the phraseology in which I clothe it is the old abolition phraseology. I am for the "immediate, unconditional, and universal" enfranchisement of the black man, in every State in the Union. Without this, his liberty is a mockery; without this, you might as well almost retain the old name of slavery for his condition; for in fact, if he is not the slave of the individual master, he is the slave of society, and holds his liberty as a privilege, not as a right. He is at the mercy of the mob, and has no means of protecting himself.

2   It may be objected, however, that this pressing of the Negro's right to suffrage is premature. Let us have slavery abolished, it may be said, let us have labor organized, and then, in the natural course of events, the right of suffrage will be extended to the Negro. I do not agree with this. . . . I fear that if we fail to do it now, if abolitionists fail to press it now, we may not see, for centuries to come, the same disposition that exists at this moment. Hence, I say, now is the time to press this right.

3   It may be asked, "Why do you want it? Some men have got along very well without it. Women have not this right." Shall we justify one wrong by another? This is the sufficient answer. Shall we at this moment justify the deprivation of the Negro of the right to vote, because some one else is deprived of that privilege? I hold that women, as well as men, have the right to vote, and my heart and voice go with the movement to extend suffrage to woman; but that question rests upon another basis than which our right rests. We may be asked, I say, why we want it. I will tell you why we want it. We want it because it is our right, first of all. . . . Again, I want the elective franchise, for one, as a colored man, because ours is a peculiar government, based upon a peculiar idea, and that idea is universal suffrage . . . here where universal suffrage is the rule, where that is the

fundamental idea of the Government, to rule us out is to make us an exception, to brand us with the stigma of inferiority, and to invite to our heads the missiles of those about us; therefore, I want the franchise for the black man....

4   ... It may be said, What doth it profit a nation if it gain the whole world, but lose its honor? I hold that the American government has taken upon itself a solemn obligation of honor, to see that this war—let it be long or short, let it cost much or let it cost little—that this war shall not cease until every freedman at the South has the right to vote. It has bound itself to it. What have you asked the black men of the South, the black men of the whole country to do? Why, you have asked them to incur the enmity of their masters, in order to befriend you and to befriend this Government. You have asked us to call down, not only upon ourselves, but upon our children's children, the deadly hate of the entire Southern people. You have called upon us to turn our backs upon our masters, to abandon their cause and espouse yours; to turn against the South and in favor of the North; to shoot down the Confederacy and uphold the flag—the American flag. You have called upon us to expose ourselves to all the subtle machinations of their malignity for all time. And now, what do you propose to do when you come to make peace? To reward your enemies, and trample in the dust your friends? Do you intend to sacrifice the very men who have come to the rescue of your banner in the South, and incurred the lasting displeasure of their masters thereby? Do you intend to sacrifice them and reward your enemies? Do you mean to give your enemies the right to vote, and take it away from your friends? Is that wise policy? Is that honorable? Could American honor withstand such a blow? I do not believe you will do it. I think you will see to it that we have the right to vote. There is something too mean in looking upon the Negro, when you are in trouble, as a citizen, and when you are free from trouble, as an alien. When this nation was in trouble, in its early struggles, it looked upon the Negro as a citizen. In 1776 he was a citizen. At the time of the formation of the Consitution the Negro had the right to vote in eleven States out of the old thirteen. In your trouble you have made us citizens. In 1812 Gen. Jackson addressed us as citizens—"fellow-citizens." He wanted us to fight. We were citizens then! And now, when you come to frame a conscription bill, the Negro is a citizen again. He has been a citizen just three times in the history of this government, and it has always been in time of trouble. In time of trouble we are citizens. Shall we be citizens in war, and aliens in peace? Would that be just?

5   I ask my friends who are apologizing for not insisting upon this right, where can the black man look, in this country, for the assertion of his right, if he may not look to the Massachusetts Anti-Slavery Society? Where under the whole heavens can he look for sympathy, in asserting this right, if he may not look to this platform? Have you lifted us up to a certain height to see that we are men, and then are any disposed to leave us there, without seeing that we are put in possession of all our rights? We look naturally to this platform for the assertion of all our rights, and for this one especially. I understand the anti-slavery societies of this country to be based on two principles,—first, the freedom of the blacks of this country; and, second, the elevation of them. Let me not be misunderstood here. I am not asking for sympathy at the hands of abolitionists, sympathy at the hands of any. I think the American people are disposed often to be generous rather than just. I look over this country at the present time, and I see Educational Societies, Sanitary Commissions, Freedmen's Associations, and the like,—all very good: but in regard to the colored people there is always more that is benevolent, I perceive, than just, manifested towards us. What I ask for the Negro is not benevolence, not pity, not sympathy, but simply justice. The American people have always been anxious to know what they shall do with us. Everybody has asked the question, and they learned to ask it early of the abolitionists, "What shall we do with the Negro?" I have had but one answer from the beginning. Do nothing with us! Your doing with us has already played the mischief with us. Do nothing with us! If the apples will not remain on the

tree of their own strength, if they are worm eaten at the core, if they are early ripe and disposed to fall, let them fall! I am not for tying or fastening them on the tree in any way, except by nature's plan, and if they will not stay there, let them fall. And if the Negro cannot stand on his own legs, let him fall also. All I ask is, give him a chance to stand on his own legs! Let him alone! If you see him on his way to school, let him alone, don't disturb him! If you see him going to the dinner table at a hotel, let him go! If you see him going to the ballot-box, let him alone, don't disturb him! If you see him going into a work-shop, just let him alone,—your interference is doing him a positive injury. Let him fall if he cannot stand alone! If the Negro cannot live by the line of eternal justice, the fault will not be yours, it will be his who made the Negro, and established that line for his government. Let him live or die by that. If you will only untie his hands, and give him a chance, I think he will live.

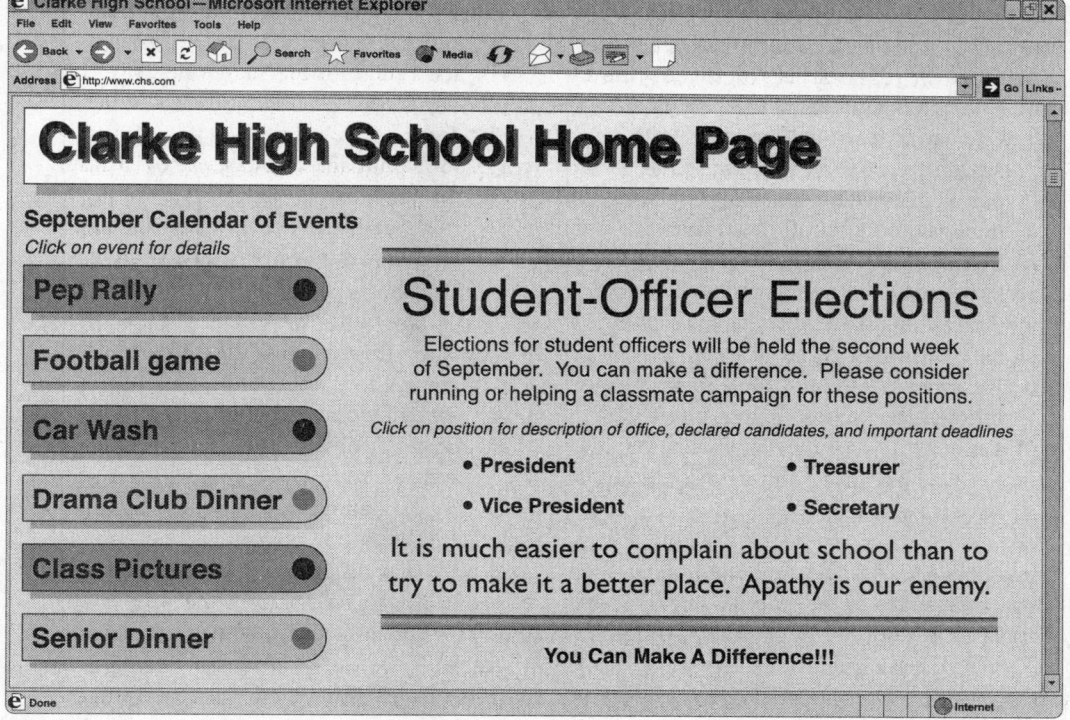

Use "A New England Nun" (pp. 178–183) to answer questions 1–12

1. The author uses the canary and the dog to symbolize—
   A the importance of pets in a home
   B the narrowness of Louisa's lifestyle
   C Louisa's unhappiness with her life
   D Joe's intolerance of animals

2. How is Lily Dyer a foil to Louisa?
   F She threatens to leave her job.
   G She doesn't care for Louisa.
   H Her strengths point out Louisa's weaknesses.
   J She doesn't care for Joe.

3. What is the climax of this story?
   A Joe leaves to go to Australia.
   B Daggett disrupts her orderly household.
   C Louisa overhears Joe and Lily talking.
   D Lily quits her job.

4. How does Louisa's reaction to Joe's departure fourteen years earlier foreshadow the end of the story?
   F She had listened and assented with sweet serenity, foreshadowing the peace with which she accepted being uncloistered after all those years.
   G She had been upset when he announced his plans, just as she was at the end of the story when she would still be unmarried, as is a nun.
   H He had not told her of his plans, so she felt deserted and without a mate, as is a nun.
   J She had felt like a nun who could not have male friends.

5. How does the character of Louisa determine the ending of the story?
   A She does not mix with others, and this makes her a nun.
   B She values her house and pets more than she does people, making her choose them over a husband.
   C She lacks self-confidence, making her spy on one she loves.
   D Her sense of morals dictate she give up her life's plans.

6. Why does the author include paragraphs 23–27?
   F To stress the incompatibility between the two
   G To show Joe's carelessness
   H To show Louisa's inflexibility
   J To create suspense

7. Why does the author use the simile in paragraph 28?
   A To share the scents of evening air
   B To further explore the discontent Joe felt in Louisa's presence and in her home
   C To show he was innocent of any wrongdoing against Louisa
   D To introduce the idea of a china shop in that New England village

8. What does the "fairy web" in paragraph 30 symbolize?
   F Joe's sense of fear in her home
   G The materials and untidiness in her home
   H Joe's clumsiness and sense of distaste for her lifestyle
   J Joe's realization of how delicate and private Louisa's life has been the past 14 years

9. How does the author set the tone in the paragraph 1?
   A By using only two sentences
   B By using adverbs *peacefully, carefully,* and *precisely*
   C By explaining how busy she had been all afternoon
   D By sharing the tiring details of sewing

10. What is the effect of the imagery in paragraph 40?
    F It explains in detail what each was seeing.
    G It shows how their activities were different.
    H It symbolizes nature.
    J It shows the change in both of their feelings.

11 Read the following dictionary entry.

deprecating \'de-pri-ˌkāt-ing\ *verb* **1.** expressing disapproval of **2.** belittling **3.** disparaging **4.** warding off by prayer.

Which definition best matches the use of the word *deprecating* in paragraph 26?
- **A** Definition 1
- **B** Definition 2
- **C** Definition 3
- **D** Definition 4

12 Paragraph 41 is mainly about—
- **F** Louisa's affections for Caesar
- **G** Joe's affections for Caesar
- **H** Joe's and Louisa's differing opinions of Caesar
- **J** The mistreatment of Caesar

Use "What the Black Man Wants" (pp. 183–185) to answer questions 13–23

---

13 Which quotation from the selection best summarizes the author's view of what the black man wants?
- **A** "Let us have slavery abolished."
- **B** "What I ask for the Negro is not benevolence, not pity, not sympathy, but simple justice."
- **C** "I am for the 'immediate, unconditional, and universal' enfranchisement of the black man, in every state in the Union."
- **D** "We want it because it is our right, first of all."

14 How does the author support the idea that "now is the time to press this right" in paragraph 2?
- **F** By stating that people think it is premature at this time to make his demands
- **G** By saying that once labor is organized, it will happen anyway, so why push for it now
- **H** By saying there is a disposition to learn righteousness and it will happen in its own time
- **J** By reminding them that they are almost at the point of conceding the right of suffrage, and if they don't insist on it now, they might not get another chance for years

15 In paragraph 4 of this passage, Douglass refers to the wars of 1776 and 1812 and the passing of the conscription (military draft) in order to:
- **A** prove he is well educated
- **B** support the historical precedence for recognizing the citizenship of the black man
- **C** confuse his listeners with too many details
- **D** to lengthen his speech by making a bandwagon appeal

16 What is the effect of his talking about apples falling from the tree in paragraph 5?
- **F** To add humor to his speech
- **G** To show the importance of nature and the laws of gravity
- **H** To provide the listeners with a concrete comparison they can understand
- **J** To offer an example of a metaphor

17 Which words from paragraph 3 help the listener understand the meaning of the word *suffrage*?
- **A** *Elective franchise*
- **B** *Undervalue ourselves*
- **C** *Particular deprivation*
- **D** *Fundamental idea*

18 What is the effect of the rhetorical technique of anticipating and stating the arguments that one's opponent is likely to give?
  F   His use of glittering generalities effectively rebuts his opponents argument.
  G   He effectively answers the arguments before his opponents have a chance to voice them.
  H   It confuses the reader with which side of the question he is arguing.
  J   He convinces the audience why he should not have voting privileges.

19 Which of these is the best summary of the selection?
  A   Frederick Douglass explains why not giving the black man the right to vote is making a mockery of his freedom from slavery. He supports this by saying that the time is correct for this to take place, and it is the right of the black man. He asserts that he is not asking for sympathy but for simple justice. He assures his listeners that the black man is capable of living by the line of eternal justice.
  B   Frederick Douglass talks about his three years of work. He reviews some of the scenes of the bloodiest battles of the Civil War and says these are difficult times. In agreeing that it is a shame that women cannot vote, he compares the black man to apples on a tree.
  C   Frederick Douglass addresses the problems facing black men in America in 1865. He rejoices that slavery has been abolished and wants the hands of black men to be untied so the black man can live.
  D   Frederick Douglass presents his list of desires to the Massachusetts Anti-Slavery Society. He wants the black man not to be disturbed on his way to school or to a workshop. He wants the black man to be able to go to a dinner table at a hotel. He wants him to be let alone if he is going to a ballot box.

20 Who is Douglass's intended audience?
  F   The senate
  G   The House of Representatives
  H   All people of the United States
  J   The voting citizens

21 What rhetorical device does he use in paragraph 4 when he repeats, "You have asked them to . . ." and "You have asked us to. . ." and then "you have called upon us. . ." and again "you have called upon us. . ."?
  A   Parallel construction
  B   Allusion
  C   Redundancy
  D   Confusion

22 In paragraph 4, how does Douglass create the support for the Negro man as necessary to the country?
  F   By asking questions
  G   By showing specific examples of support
  H   By making accusations
  J   By quoting from military officers

23 Why does Douglass contrast justice with benevolence in paragraph 5?
  A   He wants to begin dialogue.
  B   He hopes to confuse the listener.
  C   He believes benevolence should prevail.
  D   He believes justice should prevail.

Use "A New England Nun" and "What the Black Man Wants" to answer questions 24 and 25

24. What do both Louisa Ellis in "A New England Nun" and Frederick Douglass in "What the Black Man Wants" have in common?
    F Both act according to their beliefs.
    G Both are unhappy with their lives.
    H Neither is married.
    J Neither has respect in the community.

25. The historical setting in both these pieces is important because—
    A it adds suspense
    B it makes the reader think
    C it helps to teach history
    D it helps the reader to understand the conflict

Use the visual representation on page 185 to answer questions 26–28

26. One underlying message of this Web page is that—
    F elections are important
    G many students are running for office
    H they can easily find out the list of the candidates
    J students can have a voice in their campuses

27. What is this campaign's slogan?
    A Elections are soon.
    B See the list of candidates.
    C You can make a difference.
    D Hurry!

28. The purpose of this content page is probably to—
    F encourage student involvement in student government
    G publish a list of popular students
    H persuade students to vote
    J publicize upcoming events

Answer the following questions in the boxes provided.

29. In "A New England Nun," how does Joe's visit to Louisa foreshadow the outcome of the story? Support your answer with evidence from the story.

30 In "What a Black Man Wants," does Frederick Douglass refute his opponents' arguments? Support your answer with evidence from the story.

31 How do Louisa Ellis and Frederick Douglass remain true to their convictions? Support your answer with evidence from both selections.

Written Composition

> **Write an essay explaining the importance of doing what you believe in.**

The information below will help remind you of what you need to think about as you write your essay.

> MAKE SURE THAT YOU
> - address the topic
> - write in a way that is appealing and thoughtful
> - carefully construct each sentence
> - write clearly and distinctively using good transitions
> - express your ideas in a personal and authentic way
> - proofread carefully, correcting any errors you see

Prewriting/Planning Space

Prewriting/Planning Space

Revising and Editing

DIRECTIONS: Read the following selections, then answer the questions that follow each. For this section of the practice test, you are not permitted to use reference materials.

Pablo has written this essay for an English assignment about an important tradition. He has asked you to read the report and think about the corrections and improvements that he needs to make. Read the story, then answer the questions that follow.

(1) If I was in Mexico today on Cinco de Mayo, I would be very happy. (2) My mother would be up early preparing the food like the mole, enchiladas, and menudo, and we would be getting ready for a special day in our school. (3) On this day the students come to school in the colors of the flag red, white, and green. (4) We practice in our school classrooms the singing of the national anthem. (5) When it is the right time we will all go to the plaza to join with the other schools.

(6) We would sing the national anthem together we would then join a parade through the important streets of our town to celebrate the Battle of Puebla. (7) Our soldiers won this against the French and that is why we are a Mexican nation. (8) After the parade we would go back to our school and enjoy food and decorations.

(9) In the evening we would all come together and have dancing like la Negra. (10) We would watch fireworks and be happy that Mexico is a free country.

(11) I am not in Mexico this Cinco de Mayo. (12) I am in Texas and our school wants to celebrate this day with us. (13) I need to explain this celebration to my new school.

(14) I want my new school to hear the music that is so important to my people. (15) This is the music that makes us happy and makes us proud. (16) We dance to this music and wear the special clothes that make this music look pretty. (17) We all follow the steps and movements we have been taught.

(18) I want my new school to understand our flag. (19) Its colors represent our people. (20) Green is for hope and victory. (21) White is for the purity of our ideas. (22) Red is for the blood our national heroes shed. (23) Our flag also has an emblem, based on a legend. (24) This legend tells how the Mexicans traveled in search of the sign that we had been told we would find in the place where we should establish our empire. (25) The sign was an eagle on top of a Nopal cactus devouring a serpent. (26) We found this on a small island in the middle of a lake. (27) We settled here and founded the city that is now Mexico City. (28) We honor our flag on February 24. (29) Our flag is the soul of our country.

(30) I want my new school to see our decorations and why our flag's colors are so important to us. (31) I want to make serapes, flowers, posters, and designs that show the happy spirit of our country. (32) I want to share the home of my ancestors with my new home countrymen.

32 What change, if any, should be made in sentence 1?
  A Delete the comma after *Mayo*
  B Change *was* to **were**
  C Change *Mexico* to **mexico**
  D No change necessary

33 What is the most effective way to rewrite the ideas in sentence 3?
  F Today the students would come to school wearing red, white, and green, the colors of the flag.
  G On this day the flag colors would be worn. They are red, white, and green.
  H The flag colors come to school on this day of red, white, and green.
  J No change necessary

34 What is the most effective way to combine the ideas in sentences 4 and 5?
  A We practice in our classrooms the singing of the national anthem and when it is the right time we will all go to the plaza to join with the other schools.
  B In our classrooms we practice the singing of the national anthem and we will all go to the plaza to join with the other schools when it is the right time.
  C After practicing singing the national anthem in our own schools, we will join the other schools in the plaza.
  D No change necessary

35 What transition should be added to the beginning of sentence 6?
  F Because we would be singing the national anthem together,
  G After singing the national anthem together,
  H However, singing the national anthem together,
  J No change necessary

36 Which sentence could be added to the fifth paragraph (sentences 14–17) to support the ideas in that paragraph?
  A Therefore we have worked really hard on our dances to perform for our school.
  B all really enjoy these dances.
  C I want my new school to enjoy our celebration.
  D The steps and movements are important.

37 What is the best way to combine sentences 11–13?
  F I am not in Mexico this Cinco de Mayo; I am in Texas, and our school wants to celebrate this day with us, so I need to explain our celebration.
  G I am not in Mexico this Cinco de Mayo, and I am in Texas, and our school wants to celebrate this day, and I need to explain our celebration.
  H Although I am not in Mexico this Cinco de Mayo I am in Texas, and therefore I need to explain this celebration.
  J However, I am not in Mexico this Cinco de Mayo and I am in Texas and I need to explain this celebration because our school wants to celebrate this day with us.

38 What change, if any, should be made to sentence 19?
  A Change *Its* to **It's**
  B Change *colors* to **colours**
  C Change *people* to **People**
  D No change necessary

39 What is the best way to combine sentences 20–22?
  F Green is for hope and victory and white is for the purity of our ideas and red is for the blood our national heroes shed.
  G Green is for hope and victory; white is for the purity of our ideas; red is for the blood our national heroes shed.
  H Green is for hope and victory, white is for the purity of our ideas, and red is for the blood of our national heroes.
  J Even though green is for hope and victory, white is for the purity of our ideas, but red is for the blood our national heroes shed.

40 What change, if any, should be made to sentence 23?
  A Remove the comma after *emblem*.
  B Change *legend* to **Legend**.
  C Change *flag* to **Flag**.
  D No change necessary

41 The meaning of sentence 26 can be clarified by changing *this* to—
  F the cactus
  G the eagle
  H the scene
  I the serpent

Roderick has written this essay for his English class about a quality or a tradition he admires. As part of a peer-editing assignment, you have been asked to make suggestions for improvement. Read the story, then answer the questions that follow.

(1) A tradition that I admire, is playing basketball at the local church park. (2) We built the park there three years ago and from the very first moment the basketball goal went up, we've been playing there. (3) All our neighborhood admires it.

(4) The significance of basketball in my neighborhood lies in the heart of the players. (5) People of all ages and colors come to the court for a clean game of hoops. (6) One can leave his problems far behind with a single flick of the wrist. (7) An angry dad can releive some pressure with a free throw; a stressed out high school student can forget about the big test tomorrow with a game of 25, and a person who just wants to get away from it all can shoot all their problems away with the swishing of the net.

(8) Some of the older people in our neighborhood enjoy the traditional game of horse. (9) Any number can play, and no referees are needed. (10) What happens is that the first player attempts any kind of shot. (11) If he or she makes the shot, the other players must make the exact same shot. (12) If the following player misses, the first player gets the letter H and the next player is the new "leader." (13) I forgot to say that if the first player misses, then the second player becomes the new leader. (14) The game continues until one player has accumulated all the letters of HORSE. (15) That player is the winner. (16) Horse gets pretty funny when some of our grandfathers try to compete. (17) The real excitement comes when our moms or grandmothers come out and see the old guys play—they start stroking big time!

(18) Some of my homies and I kick back with 3 on 3. (19) That is the afternoon tradition in our 'hood. (20) The first three take on the next three, and it is good clean fun on half the court.

(21) Sure, every now and then our perfect little spot is overrun with the neighborhood thugs and gangs, but not too often and when they do decide to leave, the court belongs to the guys who love to play.

(22) Basketball is a tradition that is cherished by the people in my neighborhood. (23) We love the atmosphere of nice people having a good time and just being themselves. (24) Situations like this just makes life worth living.

42 What change, if any, should be made in sentence 1?
 A Insert a comma after *basketball*
 B Delete the comma after *admire*
 C Capitalize *Church Park*
 D No change necessary

43 What change, if any, should be made in sentence 2?
 F Change *there* to *their*
 G Change *three* to *3*
 H Add a comma after *ago*
 J No change necessary

44 What is the most effective way to improve the organization of paragraph 1?
 A Delete sentence 1
 B Insert *The church park is important* after sentence 1
 C Move sentence 2 after sentence 3
 D No change necessary

45 What change, if any, should be made in sentence 3?
 F Change *it* to **basketball**
 G Capitalize *it*
 I Change *neighborhood* to **neighbourhood**
 J No change necessary

46 What change, if any, can be made to sentence 18?
   A Some of my homeys relax with 3 on 3.
   B Some of us relax with three-on-three.
   C I relax with some others with 3 on 3.
   D No change necessary

47 What change, if any, should be made to sentence 7?
   F Change *dad* to **Dad**
   G Add the transition *But* to the beginning of the sentence
   H Change *releive* to **relieve**
   J No change necessary

48 How should sentence 7 be corrected?
   A Replace *their problems* with **his or her problems**
   B Add *however,* after **throw**
   C Replace *25* with **twenty-five**
   D No change necessary

49 How can paragraph 3 be better organized?
   F Put **13** after **10**
   G Place **13** after **11**
   H Have **8** follow **12**
   J No change necessary

50 What change, if any, should be made to sentence 21?
   A Add a comma after *often*
   B Change *too* to **to**
   C Capitalize *Court*
   E No change necessary

51 What change, if any, should be made to sentence 24?
   F Add a comma after *this*
   G Change *makes* to **make**
   H Change *life* to **lives**
   J No change necessary

Answer Explanations to Practice Test B

Question 1: The correct answer is **B**. Letters **C** and **D** are incorrect because Louisa is perfectly content with her life, and Joe understands Caesar and wants to befriend him. Answer **A** does show that Louisa's pets are important to her home and lifestyle, but they function in an even more important role in the story. By suggesting the upheaval in their lives if this marriage takes place, they represent the rigid, inflexible life Louisa has created, thus becoming the symbols of the narrowness of her lifestyle.

Question 2: The correct answer is **H**. On this section of the test, you can look *foil* up in your dictionary. One definition is a character who underscores the character of another by contrasts. You can see why Joe has fallen in love with Lily. His mother couldn't get along without her, and Joe agrees that she is pretty fair looking. Because Louisa thinks of his mother as being a feeble old mother to wait upon and as a "domineering, shrewd old matron," the contrast between Louisa and Lily is obvious, with Lily winning the competition for Joe. Answers **G** and **J** are untrue. Although answer **F** is true, her threat to leave her job doesn't have anything to do with Louisa's character, only her position in the household.

Question 3: The climax of the story is answer **C**. You could have looked up *climax* in the dictionary and found that it is the point of greatest intensity. You will remember that your English teacher talks of the climax in plot development of stories as being the point when things change direction and falling action begins. It was when Louisa overheard the private conversation between Lily and Joe that she decided to call off the marriage. Answers **A**, **B**, and **D** all occur in the plot, but they are not significant enough to change what is going on.

Question 4: The correct answer is **F**. Letters **G** and **H** are not true. She wasn't upset at all. Letter **J** is not supported in the story because human friends are never discussed.

Question 5: The correct answer is **D**. When she overheard Joe and Lily's conversation, she realized they valued loyalty over their desires. Her own sense of morals ruled that she make the sacrifice they could not. She was putting the desires of others before her own. While **B** might seem like a likely choice, the character portrayal of Louisa is more extensive. Even while showing concern for her house and pets, she remains loyal to her commitment until she realizes the sacrifices two others were making on her behalf.

Question 6: The correct answer is **F**. Although he is careless, she is inflexible, and the conflict is apparent, it is this incompatibility that is stressed and the reason for including this detail here.

Question 7: The correct answer is **B**. This is a comparison to the proverbial bull in a china shop and shows how the two will never be compatible and will never be able to live together.

Question 8: The fairy web metaphor symbolizes Joe's realization of the life Louisa has constructed for herself. The material in her home and his clumsiness are important contributors here, but the symbolism is of the delicate life Louisa has woven for herself that doesn't seem to be flexible or accommodate a man. Answer **J** is the correct answer.

Question 9: The tone is created by the choice of the adverbs that describe the activities in which she was involved. Answer **B** is the correct answer.

Question 10: Because imagery allows the reader imagine through the senses, the answer would have to be one involving the five senses. This question goes beyond naming which sense is involved and asks for an evaluation of the effect of that imagery. The correct answer is **J**, since showing a difference in the songs and sounds each had heard through their courtship gave the effect of showing their cooling affections for each other.

Question 11: Answer **A** is correct; she clearly disapproves of the way he rearranged her books. She had been eyeing this new arrangement with uneasiness, finally rising and changing their position to the way she has always kept them.

Question 12: Answer **H** correctly points out that the different attitudes are important in the story.

Question 13: Answer **C** is correct. It best summarizes the full extent of his desires. Answers **A**, **B**, and **D** are all accurate statements, but they state only one part of his thesis, whereas **C** is broader and more all-inclusive.

Question 14: Answer **J** is correct. The others are all stated in that paragraph, but the key word here is *support*. Reminding the listener of where they are at this time stresses the timeliness of this action.

Question 15: Answer **B** is correct. He wants to remind them of the history of the country and what the Black Man has already accomplished for this country. Answer **A** is true, but not his primary cause for the information. Perhaps **C** and **D** occur, but they would not be intentional on his part.

Question 16: Answer **H** is correct. Answers **F**, **G**, and **J** might occur, but they do not indicate the main effect of this comparison. Remember, he wants to convince them, not impress or entertain them.

Question 17: The correct answer is **A**. Again, use your dictionary here. He is talking about extending suffrage to women. Your dictionary would have told you that suffrage is the right to vote. It might also have listed the synonym *franchise*, so *elective franchise* is what helps the reader understand *suffrage*. The other words are used, but they do not indicate the meaning. Remember that a thesaurus may be used. In these kinds of questions, its use might help you in your answer selection.

Question 18: The correct answer is **G**. Answers **H** and **J** are clearly incorrect. Answer **F** refers to *glittering generalities*, but Douglass was not using vague words to produce a pleasant effect. He effectively states his opponents' arguments before they can be voiced, as is given in **G**.

Question 19: The correct answer is **A**. It covers all of his main points. The other answers are all mentioned in the speech, but they are not complete summaries. Remember the strategies for creating a summary? Did you form a statement of the 5Ws from his speech? Remember: Who (Frederick Douglass), what (insists that the black man be extended the right to vote), where (in a speech), when (before the end of the Civil War), when (now is the time), and why (it is justice and a right).

Question 20: From the introductory material, one can exclude **F** and **G**. Through careful reading one will find that not all citizens have the right to vote. By process of elimination, the answer is correctly deduced to be **J**. He wants to convince those with voting power to extend that privilege, because they are the only ones who can make that happen.

Question 21: The rhetorical device, because it is productive, must also be positive. Answers **C** and **D** can be ruled out as being negative. You will recognize that repetition is a characteristic of the rhetorical device of parallel construction when you consult your dictionary. **A** is the correct answer—parallel construction.

Question 22: The correct answer is **G**. The speech lists the specific examples the black man has been asked to do to support the government. He does ask questions, he does suggest accusations, and he does quote from General Jackson, but these are all details or examples to support why the black man should be given the right to vote.

Question 23: Douglass intentionally contrasts justice with benevolence, choosing justice over the two; the correct answer is **D**. He says that he does not ask for benevolence, and he clearly does not want to confuse the listener. He does desire dialogue—but not the beginning of it—the result of it.

Question 24: The correct answer is **F**. Louisa believes it is morally right to let Joe out of his commitment, and Douglass believes it is morally right that the black man should have a vote. **H** is irrelevant. Neither **G** nor **J** is supported in either text.

Question 25: Answer **D** is correct. These conflicts are understandable as true in this historical setting.

Question 26: Answer **J** is correct. It is not clearly stated; it is the underlying message.

Question 27: The slogan is **C**. The other answers are other pieces of information about the product.

Question 28: The correct answer is **F**. All the information and the links are provided to show the students how easy it is to get involved and uses the bandwagon approach of joining everyone else who wants to run for office.

Question 29: A good answer would be something like this:

> Every detail of Joe's initial visit foreshadowed that the marriage will never work, from his "heavy step on the walk" to when "he seemed to fill up the whole room," leaving no space for Louisa. His departure, leaving Louisa feeling "like the owner of a china shop after the exit of a bear," suggests the relief she will experience when the marriage is called off.

ELA TAKS-like analysis: This open-ended response would have likely earned a 3, or exemplary. The writer indicates what is foreshadowed and supports that assertion with a solid combination of relevant quotes and a synopsis of the passage. It provides strong evidence of depth of understanding.

Question 30: A good answer would be something like this:

> Frederick Douglass cleverly cuts off his opponents' arguments. First, against the argument of granting suffrage now being premature, he says it may be a long time before there is another chance. Then, against the argument that women don't have the right, he asks if one wrong justifies another.

ELA TAKS-like analysis: This highly effective response includes two specific examples with a strong connection to the text. The writer offers specific paraphrasing of the opposition and Douglass's responses showing an ability to draw evidence from the text to support an answer. The response would have likely earned a 3, or exemplary.

Question 31: A good answer would be something like this:

> When Louisa broke her commitment to Joe by telling him that change would be too difficult at this point in her life, she was faithful to the lifestyle she had established for herself in being "so narrow that there was no room for any one at her side," making her like a nun. Likewise, Douglass successfully presents his convictions concerning his thesis of "immediate, unconditional, and universal" suffrage for the black man. Both characters' actions exhibit their beliefs.

ELA TAKS-like analysis: The insightful interpretation is solidly supported with relevant quotations showing a strong connection between both pieces of the triplet. This evidences the writer's depth of understanding and would earn a score of 3, or exemplary.

Written Composition

A possible composition might be:

  My grandfather has taught me the Vietnamese proverb, "When eating a fruit, think of the person who planted the tree." He tells me this when I beg to do something different. He tries to explain to me my cultural heritage, even though I am a new American and want to do things the American way.

  The lecture always begins the same way, in 111 B.C. when Vietnam was under Chinese Rule. In 939 A.D., we drove the Chinese out and ruled ourselves for 900 years. He tells me we were independent until the Age of Imperialism when Europe found us in the 1500s. We can all recite his account of how Ho Chi Minh formed the Vietminh and revolted against the French. When the French surrendered, we were split at the 17th parallel by the Geneva Peace Accords. After World War II, Americans were in a Cold War against Communism. The U.S. government seemed to believe that they should fight in South Vietnam to stop North Vietnam and the communists. When Saigon fell in April 1975, my mother's baby was evacuated in Operation Baby Lift. My mother and grandfather, fearing for their lives because he was a South Vietnamese soldier, finally managed to escape in a crowded, unseaworthy boat. Many on the boat died. The rest of our family was killed. In the United States, he believed, they would be safe.

  My grandfather continues the story telling us how he started at the refugee camp in Pendleton, California, then was moved to the Texas coast by the U.S. government to avoid "ghettoism" and to earn a living as a shrimper, just as his father had done. He couldn't speak English, and he didn't understand the rules and regulations. He didn't understand the customs of this new country, large and spacious with wide open skies and room for everyone.

He tells us of how some of the Americans didn't accept him or the other Asian fishermen or their ways. He tells us of the Americans' distrust when they would gather in the evenings on the docks, talking in Vietnamese.

He says we must all be allowed to live the way we choose, and for me it is important to carry on my culture and heritage and not to get lost among so many different ideas. He reminds me of my name, Chau, and that it means pearls, or precious stones. When he says my name, it is soft and gentle and delicate, and he gently touches my hair, letting me know that to him I am fragile like the frail photograph of my grandmother. I look like her, he says, and her spirit remains in me. I must honor her.

My grandfather tells me that if he hadn't continued to support me and my mother in the only way he knew, using the skills that his father taught him and his father before that, that today I would not be an honor student preparing to graduate from high school in Texas. I can see that if my grandfather did not do what he believed in, my life would be very different. I owe my grandfather my thanks for the privileges I have in my life. When I eat of this fruit, it is my grandfather and his fathers I remember.

ELA TAKS-like analysis: This would likely earn a 4, or highly effective. This writer uses a personal narrative to reflect on the importance of doing what one believes in. The introduction and conclusion tie satisfactorily together, referencing the Vietnamese proverb, which then becomes a metaphor for the student's plans to honor her family and traditions. The composition has a sense of completeness, and the writing is fluent and demonstrates good control of the English conventions.

Question 32: Answer **B** is correct; change *was* to **were** because the subjunctive tense of the verb is needed to state what is not true (here you just have to know the answer, not the explanation).

Question 33: Answer **F** is the correct answer, combining all of the information in a concise manner.

Question 34: Sentences 4 and 5 can best be combined in sentence **C**. Both **A** and **B** contain run-on sentences—or those with comma splices.

Question 35: Answer **G** is correct because it shows the chronologic order being used in this composition.

Question 36: Answer **C** best summarizes the information, providing a nice conclusion to the paragraph.

Question 37: Answer **F** is the only response without fragments or run-ons.

Question 38: Sentence 19 is correctly written. Answer **D** is correct.

Question 39: Answer **G** is correct. The other answers all have run-ons.

Question 40: Answer **A** is correct because **it** could apply to flag or emblem.

Question 41: Answer **H** is correct. It correctly identifies the entire picture in the emblem, not just one part.

Question 42: Answer **B** is the correct answer because the subject should not be separated from the verb.

Question 43: Answer **H** is correct because a comma is needed when two independent clauses are joined by a coordinating conjunction.

Question 44: Answer **C** is correct. This continues the organizational pattern of the paragraph.

Question 45: Answer **F** correctly names the admired tradition of basketball.

Question 46: Answer **B** is correct. It uses appropriate register of language for a school paper.

Question 47: From the choices given for this question, letter **H** correctly spells the word.

Question 48: Answer **A** makes his or her problems agree with the singular antecedent.

Question 49: Answer **F** is correct because sentence 13 directly following sentence 10 follows the chronological order of the piece.

Question 50: Answer **A** is correct. The two independent clauses are joined with and following the word *often*.

Question 51: Answer **G** is correct. The verb *make* must agree with the subject *situations*.

Chapter 18

Final Review

Below are questions that quickly touch on the most important aspects of the book. See how many you can answer.

Chapter 1: Examining the Structure of the Test

1. Approximately how long is the ELA TAKS?
2. Name and describe the two parts of the test.
3. What three types of testing strategies will you find on the test?
4. What is the most significant difference between Part I and Part II?
5. What are three techniques you can use on testing day to help yourself succeed?
6. What are three things you could do today to help prepare for the ELA TAKS?

Chapter 2: Surveying the ELA TAKS Objectives

7. Objective I of the ELA TAKS assesses what type of skills?
8. Objective II of the ELA TAKS examines what aspect of language?
9. What does Objective III measure?
10. What is required for Objective IV?
11. Objective V is designed to measure what part of your literary training?
12. What does Objective VI assess?

Chapter 3: Answering Objective Questions

13. Name the two parts of an objective question.
14. Describe five strategies to use when answering objective questions.

Chapter 4: Responding to Open-Ended Questions

15. What part of the triplet do open-ended questions address?
16. What two key words must you remember when composing your responses?
17. What must be in an open-ended response answer for you to receive credit?
18. Name the ways to reference the triplet when answering an open-ended question.
19. Describe the difference between a grade of 2, or sufficient, and a grade of 3, or exemplary, when responding to an open-ended question.

Chapter 5: Writing the Composition

20. Describe what should occur during the prewriting stage of crafting your composition.
21. Describe what should occur during the drafting stage of crafting your composition.
22. Describe what should occur during the editing stage of crafting your composition.
23. Describe what should occur during the revision stage of crafting your composition.
24. What can you do today to help prepare for the writing portion of the ELA TAKS test?
25. What is the difference between a score of 3 and a score of 4 on the composition?

Chapter 6: Identifying Literary Elements

26. What are literary elements?
27. The ELA TAKS will ask you not only to recognize various literary terms but also to do what with them?

Chapter 7: Utilizing Reading Strategies

28. How can you best prepare for the reading portion of the ELA TAKS?
29. Describe three types of reading questions that might be presented on the test?
30. Describe the strategy you would use if you were asked to determine a main idea or a summary.
31. What is the main difference between a fact and opinion on a reading test?
32. Describe two strategies to use when determining time sequence in a passage.
33. When questions ask *what* or *why*, what reading skill is being assessed?
34. What is the difference between *connotation* and *denotation*?
35. What are the two best things to remember when answering reading questions?

Chapter 8: Detecting Historical Impact on Literary Texts

36. Describe how to detect historical influences when reading the passages on the ELA TAKS test.

Chapter 9: Determining an Author's Purpose

37. What must you remember about everything that you read?
38. What is the underlying intent of a fictional piece?
39. What are the three basic categories of nonfiction writing?
40. What type of words offer the strongest clues about the author's intent?

Chapter 10: Comprehending Visual Representatives

41. What is the first question you should ask yourself when you see the visual?
42. Specifically describe things that are important to notice when studying the viewing and representing piece.
43. What is the difference between the persuasive methods called *celebrity endorsement* and *plain folk*?
44. What is meant by the term *transfer*?
45. If a visual encourages you to act quickly to avoid missing out on a great opportunity, what persuasive technique is being employed?
46. What is meant by the term *glittering generalities*?
47. When a group of students is having a great time at a party, and the implication is that if you use a certain product you will too, what persuasive method is being used?

Chapter 11: Distinguishing Voice and Style

48. What is an author's voice?
49. Describe one effective strategy to encourage yourself to write in an authentic voice.

Chapter 12: Investigating Organizational Patterns in Writing

50. At what stage in the writing process should you determine the organizational pattern of your composition?
51. Name and describe three different types of organizational patterns.
52. Why are transitions a necessary part of the organization of your composition?

Chapter 13: Studying the Development of Ideas

53. What is meant by the term *sensory imagery*?
54. At what part of the writing process should expansion and elaboration of ideas take place?

Chapter 14: Reviewing Mechanics and Usage

55. On which part of the test will mechanics and usage be evaluated?
56. Name two types of spelling mistakes that the ELA TAKS might include.
57. What word offers you a clue as to whether or not words are directly spoken by a person?
58. What are two functions of apostrophes?
59. What is meant by parallel construction?
60. What is meant by subject-verb agreement?
61. What is a quick way to check for active and passive voice?

Chapter 15: Analyzing Proofreading Skills

62. What is a good strategy for checking sentence boundaries, to be sure punctuation is correct?
63. What is a good technique for checking spelling?
64. How many indefinite pronouns can you remember?
65. Are indefinite pronouns singular or plural?

Each of these questions is answered in this book. If you found yourself faltering, go back and reread the chapter under which the question was placed.

Glossary

active voice: grammatical structure in which the subject of the sentence is performing the verb
allegory: a piece in which the people, events, or objects stand for abstract qualities; a symbolic narrative
alliteration: repetition of initial consonant sounds
allusion: reference to a well-known person, event, or place, either fictional or real, to enhance understanding
analogy: comparison of two ideas in order to create an image or clarify meaning
analysis: identification and separation of components of a literary work in order to carefully examine literary work to increase understanding
answer document: document upon which answers are recorded for the ELA TAKS; must be neat, clean, and free from all stray marks
antagonist: character or force in opposition to the main character (see protagonist)
antecedents: word, phrase, or clause to which the pronoun refers or replaces
assonance: repetition of vowel sounds in two or more stressed syllables
authentic: genuine, worthy of trust, reliance, or belief
authentic voice: writing in a voice or style that is distinctively unique
author's purpose: expected intent of any written piece, as in to entertain, inform, or persuade

bandwagon: propaganda technique wherein you are encouraged to do something because it is the fad
brainstorming: thinking and planning creatively; coming up with ideas to include in writing

cause: something that makes something else happen
celebrity endorsement: method of persuasion that uses well-liked celebrities telling you they use a certain product, implying that you should, too
character: participants in the action of a story
character trait: quality exhibited through the style, actions, or words of a character that reveals motive and personality
chronological order: literary pattern that flows from the beginning to the end in a successive time sequence, presenting events in the order in which they occur
coherence: linking ideas logically together in a consistent pattern
comma fault/comma splice: when two independent clauses are separated only by a comma, causing a run-on sentence
comparing: showing the similarities between two or more things
compositional risk: ELA TAKS term that implies writing in a unique and individual manner, either through subject choice, grammatical pattern, or compositional form
conclusion: stating the outcome or the result in a piece of writing; a judgment or decision
conflict: struggle between two opposing forces within a story; basic conflicts that appear in fiction:
- external conflict
  - man against nature
  - man against man
  - man against society
- internal conflict
  - man against himself

connotation: indirect, suggested meaning of a word
consonance: repetition of consonance sounds within or at the end of a word
context clues: hints in a text that reveal the meaning of surrounding words
contrasting: showing the differences between two or more things
conventions: usage or custom; components of correct English; part of standards used in evaluating open-ended responses and response to writing prompt

coordinating conjunctions: words joining words or word groups that are used in the same way
critical evaluation: judgment of the merits, faults, and values of a piece of writing
crossover items: open-ended questions that require open-ended responses referring to both pieces (literary/fiction and expository/nonfiction); must have quotes, paraphrases, or summaries from both pieces, as well as a conclusion or an explanation
culture: beliefs, behaviors, traditions, goals, customs, or values of a group of people

denotation: direct, specific meaning of a word
dependent clauses: word groups with both subject and verb that do not complete a thought; sentence fragments
detail: fact stated directly in the passage
development of ideas: connection made between ideas suggested in the triplet to the writer's own experiences or ideas; ideas fully developed or explained
dialect: form of speech characteristic of a geographic area or particular group of people
direct quote: exact words that are spoken
distracter: answer choices that sound reasonable but are incorrect
drafting: composing a piece

editing: reexamining and correcting writing to make it better
effect: what happens as the consequence of a cause
elaboration: adding specific details to a piece of writing to enhance and clarify meaning
engaging the reader: writing that captures the reader's attention
essential information: ideas or facts necessary to the meaning of the sentence and not set off by commas
evaluation: examination and judgment of a literary work
exigency: method of propaganda wherein pressure is put on you to do something, suggesting that if you don't, you will forever lose an opportunity
expository selection: one piece in the triplet; nonfiction and informational, such as a biography, autobiography, essay or news report
extension: adding a second or third point of description in support of an idea

fact: something that can be verified or proven by an outside source
fiction: writing that originates in the writer's imagination
figurative expression: expression that communicates meaning beyond the literal interpretation
flashback: action in a story that goes back to a former time
focus and coherence: ELA TAKS term implying that one general theme or thesis drives the complete essay, including a clear introduction and conclusion
foil: a character or thing that makes another seem better by contrast
foreshadowing: presenting suggestions beforehand

generalization: principle, statement, or idea with general applications
genre: form or type of a piece of a literary work
glittering generalities: advertising technique wherein general words, which are vague and lack specific meaning, are strung together to produce a pleasant association with a product

historical context: time period in which a piece is set, or the era in which it was written
hyperbole: figure of speech using great exaggeration for emphasis or humor

imagery: words and phrases using sensory detail to create a vivid mental picture
indefinite pronoun: word that stands for a person, place, or thing that is not definitely named
independent clauses: word groups containing both subject and verb and completing a thought; same as simple sentences
inference: making an informed guess about what will happen next in a story, based on the information presented in the reading
insightful: perceptive; discerning the true nature of a situation

interpretation: to explain the meaning of a literary work
ironic/irony: contrast between what appears to be true and what really is true

literary elements: essential items that make up a piece of literature (e.g., plot, setting, character, mood, tone, theme)
literary selection: ELA TAKS term for the fiction piece using literary terms and elements, such as a short story
literary skills: abilities that enable the reading, understanding, and interpreting of a piece of literature to be successful
literary techniques: term describing the methods that an author uses to convey his or her thoughts

main idea: fundamental or core idea of a passage
margin notes: notes a reader makes in the blank area outside the printed text
meaningful connections: ELA TAKS term meaning to link specific references from the triplet to support your ideas
mechanics of writing: spelling, punctuation, and capitalization; rules of good writing
media: mass communication through which ideas are shared; on ELA TAKS found in the viewing and representing section of the triplet; may be forms such as as Web pages, cartoons, posters, pictures, or advertisements
metaphors: figure of speech in which a comparison is made between ideas or objects, without the use of *like* or *as*
modifiers: words that describe other words to make their meanings more clear
mood: overall feeling or atmosphere a writer creates
multiple-choice responses: answer choices given in response to a stem question or an incomplete sentence; only one answer is correct

name-calling: propaganda technique using negative words to imply that you will be part of an unacceptable group if you do not use a certain product or think a certain way
nonessential information: ideas or facts not necessary to the meaning of the sentence and set off by commas
nonfiction: writing based on truth

objective: a broad statement, serving as a heading, that details student expectations tested on the ELA TAKS
onomatopoeia: using words to imitate the sound
open-ended response: answer to a question about the texts to which the student provides the answer; answer must be reasonable, relevant, and supported from the text using direct quotes, paraphrasing, or synopsis for textual evidence
opinion: information that cannot be verified by a second source
organization: logical flow of ideas that are easy to follow, with transitions pulling the reader along
organizational pattern: logical structure of an essay that acts as a blueprint, cohesively bonding ideas together, thus illuminating theme and voice
- **chronological organizational pattern:** writing pattern in which events are recorded in the sequence in which they occurred
- **cause and effect (or causal) organizational pattern:** writing pattern that revolves around a reason (or cause) for an event and the subsequent result (or effect) of that cause
- **spatial organizational pattern:** writing pattern that moves the reader from one point to the next in an orderly fashion, describing the scene
- **climactic organizational pattern:** writing pattern that builds gradually, through examples or descriptions, to a final focus point
- **compare-and-contrast organizational pattern:** writing pattern that discusses both the similarities and the differences of an issue

original: fresh and unusual; your own ideas
overwrite: contrived, artificial style of writing, with description overdone, seemingly added just for the sake of having the description

parallel construction: using the same grammatical forms to balance related ideas
paraphrasing: restating the text in other words
passive voice: grammatical structure in which the subject of the sentence is being acted upon
peer editing: reviewing another's work to offer suggestions for improvement; a skill tested on the revising and editing section of ELA TAKS
personification: figure of speech giving human qualities to objects, animals, or ideas
persuasion: convincing others to do or believe a certain thing
plain folks: method of persuasion using ordinary people to endorse a product
plot: series of events that occur in a literary work
polished rough draft: ELA TAKS term for a student-produced essay that will be graded as a refined piece; should show careful planning, reflection, understanding, explanation, and correct use of the mechanics of the English language
predictions: educated guesses based on information directly presented in a reading passage
prompt: suggested idea to which the student must refer in a polished draft composition format
proofread: to read over the text to cite all faults or make corrections
protagonist: main character in a literary work
punctuation: act of inserting standard marks in written manner in order to enhance communication
purpose: reason for writing

quotation: exact words of speaker, set off with quotation marks; one way to provide textual evidence for your ideas

reading and written composition: name given to the first section of the TAKS ELA exam; involves reading two pieces and evaluating a visual representative, and answering multiple-choice questions, open-ended questions, and a writing prompt
reasonable: sound judgment; sensible; rational
reference materials: dictionaries, thesauruses, etc., which state guidelines require will be made available for student use during Part I of the ELA TAKS
reflective piece: written piece based on personal reflections
related to the matter at hand; obviously applicable
relevant: pertinent; logically connected; related to the matter at hand; obviously applicable
repetition: technique in which words, sounds, or phrases are repeated at regular intervals
revising and editing: second section of the ELA TAKS where students are given examples of student compositions to edit and revise by selecting correct multiple-choice answers
rubric: explanatory tool, often in chart form, offering a comparative scale of evaluation
run-on sentence: several independent clauses written together without correct punctuation

satire: making fun of customs, ideas, or behavior to inspire reform
sensory description: imagery that refers to the five senses
sentence boundaries: ending the sentence appropriately, avoiding sentence fragments and run-on sentences
sentence fragment: when the subject or the verb is missing or the idea expressed is incomplete
sentence structure/syntax: classifying a sentence as simple, compound, complex, or compound-complex depending on the number of independent and dependent clauses
sequencing: determining the order of events in a reading passage
setting: time and place in which the action of a story occurs
similes: figure of speech in which a comparison is made between ideas or objects using *like* or *as*
sound devices: use of language that appeals to the ear
stem: question or unfinished statement forming the core of a multiple-choice question
stereotyping: conventional or stock character with little or no development or individuality
style: features that identify one writing from another; choice of words, sentence construction, and details that make writing distinct and individual
subordinate clause: a clause that does not express a complete thought and therefore cannot stand alone

subordinating conjunctions: words that introduce a subordinate clause to the main part of the sentence; commonly used to express the relationship between the two parts, such as comparison, time, condition, purpose, and cause
summary: condensation of the major points of an article
supportable details: specific details that support an idea
sustained reading: reading for at least 15 minutes or longer
symbol: object or event that stands for or represents something else
synopsis: brief statement or outline

textual evidence: using direct quotations, paraphrasing, or synopsis from the text to support your idea
theme: underlying meaning in a literary work that the author wishes to share with the reader
thesis: main point writer is trying to make
tone: quality, effect, atmosphere, or attitude in a piece of literature
transfer: form of persuasion wherein advertisers use someone just like you, a teenager, whose life is together, to sell their products
transitions: links between sentences or paragraphs that pull your reader along; also, words that create connections among ideas and build coherence
triplet: three passages with similar themes upon which the test is based; one fiction piece (literary selection), one nonfiction piece, and one visual

unity: relating all ideas cohesively to a single theme or event
usage: using the language correctly

viewing and representing piece: one-page graphic piece with minimal text, which the student analyzes and interprets
voice: distinctive way an author uses words, phrases, sentences, and paragraphs to uniquely express ideas through writing; writing that reflects the personality of the author

word choice: choosing appropriate words for the idea to be conveyed
writing prompt: essay question suggested by the triplet that acts as a springboard for ideas
written composition: ELA TAKS term for a polished draft wherein the writer has responded in a reasonable and relevant manner to a writing prompt; must be prose, not poetry; must employ standard conventions of written English

Index

A
Active voice, 136
Advertising, 106
Apostrophes, 133
Author's purpose:
   description of, 96
   fiction vs. nonfiction passages, 97
   practice exercises, 98–104
   word choice, 96–97

B
Bandwagon propaganda technique, 107

C
Capitalization, 134
Cause and effect pattern, 120–121
Cause and effect questions, 74–75
Celebrity endorsement propaganda technique, 107
Character traits, 27, 80
Characterization, 64
Chronological pattern, 120
Chronological sequencing, 76
Clauses, 131–132
Climactic pattern, 121–122
Colons, 134
Commas:
   definition of, 130
   for joining of clauses, 132
   for nonessential information, 132
Compare and contrast pattern, 122
Compare and contrast questions, 80
Comparisons, 126
Conflicts, 27
Connotation, 79
Critical evaluation, 10
Crossover questions, 28, 38–39

D
Denotation, 79
Descriptive details:
   description of, 63
   historical influences identified by, 91
Details:
   description of, 9
   descriptive, 63, 91
   focus on, 128
   specificity of, 125
Direct quote:
   definition of, 28
   example of, 31

E
Editing, 48, 140, 142–143
Essay:
   beginning of, 45–46
   cause and effect pattern of, 120–121
   chronological pattern of, 120
   climactic pattern of, 121–122
   compare and contrast pattern of, 122
   comparisons used in, 126
   description of, 42
   details in, 125
   development of, 47
   drafting of, 45
   editing of, 48, 140, 142–143
   ending of, 48
   example of, 44–49
   objectives of, 10–11
   opening paragraph of, 45–46
   order pattern of, 122
   organization of, 45
   organizational patterns in, 119–120
   practice exercises, 50–59
   prewriting, 44–45
   proofreading of, 49
   reader's connection with, 124
   revising of, 48, 140, 142–143
   scoring of, 60
   sensory description in, 126
   spatial pattern of, 121
   topics for, 43
   transitions in, 47–48, 122
   word choices in, 125
Exigency propaganda technique, 107

F
Fact questions, 79
Fictional passages:
   author's purpose, 97
   character traits, 27, 80
   conflicts, 27
   literary themes in, 26
   open-ended questions about, 25–27
   practice exercises, 32–35

G
Gerunds, 142
Glittering generalities propaganda technique, 107
Glue words, 131

H
Highlighting, 16–17
Historical influences, 90–95
Hyphens, 134

I
Independent clauses, 131–132
Inference, 81
Infinitives, 142

L
Literary elements:
   characterization, 64
   descriptive details, 63
   open-ended responses to, 69–73
   practice exercises, 66–69
   setting, 64–65
   story structure, 63
Literary techniques, 65
Literary terms, 27, 65
Literary themes, 26

M
Main ideas:
   description of, 9
   questions about, 78
Mechanics of writing:

215

description of, 129
practice exercises, 137–139
punctuation. *See*
    Punctuation
spelling, 129–130
Media influences:
    description of, 106
    practice exercises, 108–110
    propaganda techniques, 106–107
Mental images, 17
Modifiers, 135

N
Name-calling propaganda technique, 107
Nonfiction passages:
    author's purpose, 97
    open-ended questions, 27, 35–38

O
Objectives section:
    answering questions in, 15–24
    preparatory work for, 15–17
    reading, 8–10
    writing, 10
Open-ended questions:
    crossover questions, 28, 38–39
    description of, 25
    fictional passages, 25–27, 32–35
    length of answers to, 31
    literary elements, 69–73
    nonfiction passages, 27, 35–38
    scoring of, 41
    triplet connecting of, 28
Opinion questions, 79
Order pattern, 122
Organizational patterns in writing:
    cause and effect, 120–121
    chronological, 120
    climactic, 121–122
    compare and contrast, 122
    description of, 119–120
    order, 122
    spatial, 121

P
Parallel construction, 135–136
Paraphrase:
    definition of, 28
    example of, 31
Participles, 142
Persuasion:
    description of, 106
    techniques for, 106–107
Plain folks propaganda technique, 107
Practice tests, 149–205
Predicting, 81
Preparatory work, 15–17
Prewriting, 44–45
Pronouns:
    checking for errors in, 142
    description of, 135
Proofreading:
    description of, 49, 140
    gerunds, 142
    importance of, 140
    infinitives, 142
    participles, 142
    pronouns, 142
    sentence structure, 141
    spelling errors, 141
    subject-verb agreement, 141
    symbols used in, 146
Propaganda techniques, 106–107
Punctuation:
    apostrophes, 133
    capitalization, 134
    colons, 134
    commas, 130, 132
    hyphens, 134
    for joining clauses, 131–132
    quotation marks, 133
    semicolons, 130–131

Q
Questions:
    cause and effect, 74–75
    compare and contrast, 80
    crossover, 28, 38–39
    fact, 79
    inference, 81
    main idea, 78
    open-ended. *See* Open-ended questions
    opinion, 79
    predicting-related, 81
    sequencing, 76–78
Quotation marks, 133

R
Reading:
    critical evaluation of, 10
    description of, 8
    details in, 9
    main ideas, 9
    for meaning, 75
    objectives of, 8–10
    practice exercises, 82–89
    strategies for improving, 74
    sustained, 74
    vocabulary, 8–9, 79–80
Revising, 48, 140, 142–143
Run-on sentences, 131

S
Semicolons, 130–131
Sensory description, 126
Sentences:
    checking for errors in, 141
    structure of, 136–137
Sequencing, 76–78
Setting, 64–65
Spatial pattern, 121
Spelling:
    checking for errors in, 141
    description of, 129–130
Story structure, 63
Style, 113
Subject-verb agreement, 134–135, 141
Subordinate clauses, 131–132
Summary, 30–31, 78
Sustained reading, 74
Synopsis, 28

T
Test:
    academic strategies for, 5
    parts of, 3–4
    questions on, 4
    scoring of, 5
    strategies for, 5–6
    structure of, 3
Themes, 26
Transfer propaganda technique, 107
Transitions, 47–48, 122
Triplet:
    definition of, 3–4
    open-ended questions connected to, 28

U
Usage:
    active voice, 136
    description of, 134
    parallel construction, 135–136
    practice exercises, 137–139

pronouns, 135
sentence structure, 136–137
subject-verb agreement, 134–135

V

Venn diagram, 80
Vocabulary, 8–9, 79–80
Voice:
  active, 136
  writer's, 114–116

W

Words:
  choice of, 96–97, 125
  sensory description in, 126
Writer's voice, 114–116
Writing. *See also* Essay
  description of, 42
  example of, 44–49
  good, 43
  mechanics of. *See* Mechanics of writing
  objectives of, 10–11
  organization of, 45
  organizational patterns in, 119–120
  practice exercises, 50–59
  prewriting, 44–45
  scoring of, 60
  style of, 113
  topics for, 43
  usage. *See* Usage